W9-AES-896

REFLECTIONS ON BECKETT

THEATER: THEORY/TEXT/PERFORMANCE

Series Editors: David Krasner and Rebecca Schneider
Founding Editor: Enoch Brater

Recent Titles:

Reflections on Beckett

A CENTENARY CELEBRATION

Edited by Anna McMullan and S. E. Wilmer

The University of Michigan Press | Ann Arbor

Copyright © by the University of Michigan 2009
All rights reserved
Published in the United States of America by
The University of Michigan Press
Manufactured in the United States of America
⊗ Printed on acid-free paper

2012   2011   2010   2009   4   3   2   1

A CIP catalog record for this book is available from the British Library.

Library of Congress Cataloging-in-Publication Data

Reflections on Beckett : a centenary celebration / edited by Anna
    McMullan and S. E. Wilmer.
        p.   cm. — (Theater—theory/text/performance)
    Includes bibliographical references and index.
    ISBN-13: 978-0-472-11664-5 (cloth : acid-free paper)
    ISBN-10: 0-472-11664-9 (cloth : acid-free paper)   1. Beckett,
    Samuel, 1906-1989—Criticism and interpretation.
    I. McMullan, Anna,1957–   II. Wilmer, S. E.
    PR6003.E282Z7896   2009
    848'.91409—dc22   2008038939

Dennis Kennedy

Foreword: Beckett and Trinity
College Dublin

This book, a collection of essays first delivered at Trinity College Dublin in conferences and in the annual Samuel Beckett Lecture Series, provides the opportunity to reflect for a moment on Beckett's conflicted relationship with his alma mater. When he walked through Front Gate of Trinity College as a junior freshman in October 1923, "a shy, retiring 17-year-old," he told his tutor, the philosopher A. A. Luce, that his likely careers were law or chartered accountancy. A skinny lad more enraptured by sport than letters—he remains the only Nobel laureate to be mentioned in *Wisden's Cricket Almanac*—he was nonetheless formed in Trinity. Within a few years he had become a hardworking student in modern languages. Unfortunately the work, together with an uncertain constitution, led to insomnia, night sweats, panic attacks, and what he called "the old internal combustion heart."[1] His biographers imply he might have felt paralyzed by the level of scholarship his college demanded. His escape was sport, including cricket, motorcycle racing, and as many as thirty-six holes of golf a day in term time and seventy-two in the vacations. The golf course was a hermit's cell for him, according to Anthony Cronin, but perhaps it was more of a mountaintop refuge. All this might suggest a serious reservation about academic work, but despite his later rejection of the European rationalism then promoted at Trinity, he never lost his affection for the institution that formed him as an intellectual.

After gaining a First Class degree and a gold medal in modern languages in 1927, and teaching for a time (very unsatisfactorily) at Campbell College in Belfast, he took up a post as Trinity exchange lecturer at the École Normale Supérieure in Paris, an elite institution of the highest reputation. There was little teaching to do, so he slept late and joined the Irish expatriate crowd centered around Joyce. Paris in the 1920s, that dream place for international artists, affected his life and work much more than Trinity had, and after the year's sojourn the necessary return to Dublin was not a welcome prospect. "In the Irish lexicon," Cronin says, "there ought to be a word for the despair of returning, particularly in youth . . . between the 1920s and the 1950s a return to the old, obsessive, dull, puritanical, provincial Ireland often created a special sickness in the returning heart."[2]

In Beckett's case the special sickness was compounded with a massive uncertainty of purpose. From the time he succeeded in the Trinity Scholarship exam in 1926, which provided rooms and meals in college, Beckett's course had been set fair for an academic career. The professor of Romance languages, Thomas Rudmose-Brown, who had encouraged him in a number of ways, now offered Beckett a three-year lectureship in French at a salary of two hundred pounds, rising in increments of fifty pounds. This was a generous circumstance for anyone interested in the university profession, clearly designed to set his star pupil on his way. Even late in life Beckett recalled "Ruddy" with great affection, but it soon became obvious that the new lecturer was extremely ill-suited for the academy; Trinity only added to the unhappiness of returning. Paris had given him a life that was "reasonable," while the Senior Common Room in the Ruddy circle was a combination of "cheap quip and semi-obscene entirely contemptible potin."[3]

As to teaching, "he delivered his lectures with his back to the window beside the rostrum and with his eyes apparently fixed on a point on the ceiling above the door, speaking slowly and deliberately but with little expression."[4] One former student remembered him as "a tall thin streak of misery—standing in front of the fireplace, leaning against the mantelpiece, a large lock of hair falling down on his forehead. He hardly ever looked up at us. The term he was missing, I asked 'Where's our Sam?' Someone replied: 'Gone to Paris to commit suicide.'" Another reported that "the only thing which roused us from our somnolent lethargy was when he set himself on fire by letting the sleeve of his gown drop down into the open fire when he was leaning his fevered brow on the marble mantelpiece."[5] He usually dressed in what became the Beckettian uniform: a gray shirt, gray Aran sweater, and gray flannel trousers, usually soiled by food and drink. The unsolvable problem was that standing up to speak in public was sheer torture for him. In March 1931 he admitted to his friend Tom MacGreevy, "I don't want to be a professor."[6]

If his ailments were psychosomatic, as the biographers propose, it is no wonder that they grew in severity. To MacGreevy he described how he spent six or seven hours over the fire each evening, "mooching about between the bed and the dark." On weekends he shut himself in his room, lying in bed in hopeless despair over another bout of lecturing waiting to ambush him on Monday. He hated "this terrible Dublin," could not read much or write at all. Dealings with students were now very poor, lecturing a daily torture, neglect of elementary hygiene severe, heart palpitations a constant worry. He planned to decamp for Germany after Christmas, realizing he was incapable of continuing.

He knew that leaving his post would cause practical problems for Ruddy and disappointment for his parents, and he spoke to no one about his impending flight. At last, on December 20, 1931, when the boat to Ostend was already booked, he wrote MacGreevy: "If I have let them down, tant pis. Some charming little cunt of a gold medallist will be nominated [my] deputy for a term."[7] It was what Hugh Leonard has called an Irishman's resignation. Eventually he sent a telegram to Ruddy that excused his sudden departure on the grounds of ill health. Beckett regarded himself as a coward and traitor, but the Trinity authorities were less concerned about the disappearance of a lecturer than the disappearance of a college master key he neglected to return, and decided a number of locks had to be changed.

If his years as a lecturer in Trinity were a disaster, a great positive nonetheless ensued. "When I first met Joyce," Beckett said in 1989, "I didn't intend to be a writer. That only came later when I found out that I was no good at all at teaching. When I found I simply couldn't teach."[8] The common vector, the clichéd literary professor's progress, is to move to teaching after failing at writing. It is quite rare to go the other way, as Beckett did. His rise to fame was not quick, but by the time he returned to Trinity in an official capacity in 1959, he was internationally respected as the creator of some of the most innovative fiction and drama of the century in French and English. Though he hated fame, he was put in an awkward spot by H. O. White, Trinity emeritus professor of English, who asked if he would accept an honorary doctorate. Since this was precisely the kind of attention Beckett congenitally ran from, his reply to White is intriguing:

> I am knocked all of a heap by the news that the Board contemplate giving me a D.Litt. to which I honestly feel I have no title . . . But there is no question of my declining such an honour from my own university. I shall accept it . . . with emotion and gratitude.[9]

He was more explanatory to Con Leventhal:

The first movement is to decline as usual, but I finally realize this is hardly possible . . . I don't underestimate it, nor pretend I am not greatly moved, but I have a holy horror of such things and it is not easy for me. If I were a scholar or man of letters it might be different. But what in God's name have doctoracy and literature to do with work like mine?[10]

He did indeed hate public events, and the Trinity honorary degree is the only one he ever accepted. James Knowlson proposes that he "regarded it as a gesture of forgiveness for having walked out of his lectureship over 25 years before." Whatever the explanation he was quietly delighted by the honor. He forced himself to put up with the ceremony because to refuse the tribute from the institution that made him an intellectual would have appeared truculent and discourteous. He dreaded the "Commencements farce," fretted at the public nature of the event and the thought of dressing up: "I have no clothes but an old brown suit," he continued to Leventhal, "if that's not good enough they can stick their *Litt. D.* up among their piles." (In the end he wore his brother's dinner jacket, far too large for his thin frame.) The ceremony and the Commencements dinner were much more pleasant than he expected, and he was grateful. Among his many subsequent generosities was a substantial gift for the building of the Berkeley Library in Trinity. Later when the college athletic club asked him to contribute to the construction of the new tennis courts, offering a club tie as a token, he sent a note from Paris with a generous check: "Delighted to help with the tennis court appeal. Don't bother to send me a tie. I never wear one."[11]

The honors rolled on, including the one he most dreaded, the Nobel Prize in 1969. But the final scene in Beckett's relation to Trinity occurred in 1986, when Provost William Watts paid him a visit in Paris. As Watts has it, "I was driven by curiosity more than anything else . . . I decided to ask him if we might have his permission to name our new theatre, then under construction, in his honour." They met in the usual bar, Beckett dressed in the usual Aran sweater, and Beckett "began by saying that he owed Trinity an apology for his sudden departure." Otherwise "he talked about cricket and rowing. I asked for permission to use his name which he gave without hesitation."[12]

When Anna McMullan and I started the Samuel Beckett Lectures in Trinity as an annual series in 1996, at the time of the ninetieth anniversary of Beckett's birth, we sought to establish an intellectual and theatrical context for remembering him in his city and university. It is gratifying to see that this volume prints most of those lectures, delivered by distinguished scholars and artists, including some from the international centenary symposium we hosted in 2006. In that celebratory year Trinity had good reason to claim a role in the formation of its most famous graduate of the twentieth century, even if it was in part a negative formation. The Samuel Beckett Centre building, its theater, a studentship, the chair I was privileged to occupy for a dozen years, are all named for him, and together with a substantial number of Beckett manuscripts in the library add up to quite a lot of memorializing for someone who, three-quarters of a century ago, walked off with the college master key.

NOTES

1. James Knowlson, *Damned to Fame: The Life of Samuel Beckett* (London: Bloomsbury, 1996), 53, 55.

2. Anthony Cronin, *Samuel Beckett: The Last Modernist* (London: Flamingo, 1997), 124.

3. Knowlson, *Damned to Fame,* 123.

4. Cronin, *Samuel Beckett,* 127.

5. James Knowlson and Elizabeth Knowlson, eds., *Beckett Remembering, Remembering Beckett: Uncollected Interviews with Samuel Beckett and Memories of Those Who Knew Him* (London: Bloomsbury, 2006), 53–54.

6. Knowlson, *Damned to Fame,* 126.

7. Knowlson, *Damned to Fame,* 142.

8. Knowlson, *Damned to Fame,* 105.

9. Letter to H. O. White, February 3rd 1959, Trinity College Dublin Library, Department of Archives and Manuscripts, MS 3771.

10. Knowlson, *Damned to Fame,* 465.

11. Trevor West, *The Bold Collegians* (Dublin: Lilliput Press, 1991), 101.

12. William Watts, *A Memoir* (Dublin: Lilliput Press, 2008), 138.

Acknowledgments

Earlier versions of this material have appeared in the publications below. The editors and publisher gratefully acknowledge the permission to reproduce the copyright material in this book.

Linda Ben-Zvi, "Biographical, Textual, and Historical Origins," in *Palgrave Advances in Samuel Beckett Studies,* ed. Lois Oppenheim (London: Palgrave, 2004). Reproduced with permission of Palgrave Macmillan.

Herbert Blau, "Among the Deepening Shades: The Beckettian Moment(um) and the Brechtian Arrest," *The Brecht Yearbook,* 27 (2002): 65–82. Reproduced with permission from *The Brecht Yearbook.*

S. E. Gontarski, "Revising Himself: Performance as Text in Samuel Beckett's Theatre," *Journal of Modern Literature* 22, no. 1: 131–146. Reproduced with permission from Indiana University Press.

Joseph Roach, "'The Great Hole of History': Liturgical Silence in Beckett, Osofisan and Parks," *The South Atlantic Quarterly,* 100 (2001): 307–317. Reproduced with permission from Duke University Press.

Antony Tatlow, "Saying Yes and Saying No: Schopenhauer and Nietzsche as Educators," *The Brecht Yearbook,* 27 (2002): 9–42. Reproduced with permission from *The Brecht Yearbook.*

The editors would like to thank Trish McTighe and Aoife Lucey for their help with editorial research. They also are grateful to the Long Room Hub at Trinity College Dublin for financial assistance.

Contents

Section B | Beckett in Practice

Anna McMullan and S. E. Wilmer

Introduction

In 2006, on the centenary of Samuel Beckett's birth, Ireland celebrated one of its most illustrious writers in a festival lasting several months. Throughout the world, academic conferences and performances of his work demonstrated the enormity of his impact on international literature and theater. This book brings together the reflections of leading Beckett scholars, practitioners, and cultural critics on Beckett's connections with writers from Samuel Johnson to Suzan-Lori Parks and on his creative practice as writer and director. Originating as lectures given at Trinity College Dublin, his alma mater,[1] these essays place Beckett in a network of genealogies and legacies that reflect the complexity and variety of his oeuvre.

An abiding characteristic of Beckett's work is its contrariness or contradictory features. Beckett always resisted explicating the meaning of his works, as when he famously replied to Alan Schneider that if he knew who Godot was, "he would have said so in the play."[2] He avoided publicity wherever possible. However, he was very conscious of his place in literature and was meticulous in the crafting of each work, whatever the medium. His later plays are a testament to the art of economy. Yet this strategy of "shrinking from the nullity of extracircumferential phenomena, drawn in to the core of the eddy,"[3] does not specify meaning. On the contrary, Beckett created multiple layers and nuances of signification and poetic or musical resonance. Refusing specific locations and contexts, his works are nonetheless striated with historical fragments embedded in the work as myriad shards and layers. Like a stone being thrown in a pool, his words and images create ripples of meaning and memory that extend far beyond the original source.

In this interplay of perspectives and reflections, the status of Beckett's characters and fictions are never certain. They often undergo strange transformations and metamorphoses: what is the relationship between Watt and Sam, between Godot and Pozzo (whom the tramps at first mistake for Godot), between Vladimir and Estragon, between Listener and Reader in *Ohio Impromptu?* The borders between self and other, liveness and spectrality, sound and silence are breached. Beckett resolutely resisted realism: his worlds and subjects are self-consciously created, imagined, however ill, and yet they reflect back on our own ways of constructing world, self, and other, offering us new ways of seeing, or of perceiving what lies beyond the limits of habitual perception.[4]

In the later plays, the characters become progressively more and more like ghosts, occupying a space between being and nonbeing. In *Play,* the characters are apparently dead, inhabiting urns, and regurgitating past events and memories in a never ending cycle of purgatorial recrimination. In *Footfalls,* we are never sure if the mother is alive or dead, there or not there, since she is a disembodied voice. And the character of the daughter, May, who creates a fictional alter ego, Amy, disappears toward the end of the play.[5] And in his other short plays, Beckett continued to experiment with being and nonbeing, embodiment and disembodiment, presence and absence, first and third person, actual voice versus recorded voice, such as in *Rockaby, Not I,* and *Ohio Impromptu.*[6]

In addition to the opposition between language and meaninglessness, and between character and noncharacter, Beckett also opposed time and timelessness, and space and nonspace. In his plays there is rarely a clear sense of when or where the action is happening. Perhaps the stage plays that are most time and space specific are *Krapp's Last Tape, Happy Days,* and *Catastrophe,* for example, Krapp's sixty-ninth birthday in his den and Winnie's desert and *Catastrophe*'s setting in a theater. However, even these plays confound the specificity of any time and space. Krapp's room could be anywhere, and the age of the tape recorder that is used on stage may give us more of a sense of a specific time period than any dialogue in the play. Moreover, Beckett is playing with time and space, with the tape recorder in *Krapp's Last Tape* as a kind of time machine that can whisk the character far into the past with the flick of a switch, contrasting his youthful vigorous voice on the tape with his current old age. Equally Winnie could be in any desert(ed) space in a not very specific time.

Beckett's other plays are even less definite with regard to time and space. *Endgame* could be happening in a postholocaust universe or in a fantasy space and time. It could be a metaphorical environment suggesting a psychological time and space, or it could be a kind of posthuman purgatory, a step into the void between existence and nonexistence.

Waiting for Godot could be happening on any road at any time, with the characters unsure where they are and whether one day is any different from the last or the next. Again it could be a kind of psychological space where fantasy characters come and go and one waits for something or nothing to happen. And so, in many of these works, there is a sense of a floating time and space, a purgatorial existence between being and non-being, existence and nonexistence.

In addition to these formal contradictions between language and meaninglessness (or sense and nonsense), characters and noncharacters (or being and nonbeing), time and timelessness, and space and the void, Beckett plays with a number of other binary contradictions that create plural meanings: such as between humor and tragedy, birth and death, the real and the imagined, sound and silence, shadow and light, self and other, iteration and reiteration, power and impotence, order and chaos, knowledge and the unknown (or unknowable), sight and blindness, memory and forgetfulness, mobility and immobility, hope and despair, speech and silence, freedom and compulsion, the able-bodied and the disabled, health and sickness, familiarity and strangeness, poverty and plenitude, image and reflection, the perceiver and the perceived. His work is full of contradictions, multiple meanings, and embedded historical references that puzzle us and create enormous scope for scholarly and philosophical enquiry.

This book reflects some of the multiple contexts of Beckett scholarship as well as a range of concrete issues that emerge in theater production. In the first section, several of the essays juxtapose Beckett with other authors and historical genealogies, reading him through them and vice versa. Linda Ben-Zvi analyzes corporeality in Beckett's work through an analysis of his obsession with Samuel Johnson, the English author and lexicographer known for his wit and his morbidity. Johnson and his household were the subject of Beckett's early, abandoned dramatic fragment, "Human Wishes." Ben-Zvi forges links between this early dramatic draft and the corpus of Beckett's writing.

Terry Eagleton traces a line of Irish philosophical and theological thought from medieval times through Berkeley, Swift, and Edmund Burke to Beckett, around the theme of nothingness. Terence Brown continues Beckett's dialogues with the dead. In an essay that plays on spiritualist and technological meanings of the "medium," Brown discusses the technological mediations of subjectivity in the drama of Yeats and Beckett in the context of the diverse technological and recording devices developed during the twentieth century. These have paradoxically produced a sense of the fragmentation and dispersal of the self, so that selfhood "has come to seem a fragile thing, phantasmal, lost amid a set of performative acts and texts made possible by technology."

Marina Warner opens up the landscape of the French language. She compares Beckett's creative and multifaceted use of language and translation with that of Mallarmé, reading Beckett's French through Mallarmé's English. She connects language and body, sound and sense or nonsense. Antony Tatlow and Herbert Blau use Brecht as a point of comparison for investigating both differences and similarities in aesthetic practice and ideology. Finally, Joseph Roach places Beckett in a framework that is both Irish (he discusses the Irish Famine, for example) and global. He connects *Waiting for Godot* with Suzan-Lori Parks's *The America Play* (1994) and with *The Oriki of a Grasshopper,* written in the 1980s by Nigerian postcolonial playwright, Femi Osofisan, through the concept of liturgical silence. Translated into theatrical terms, such resonant silences allow "the enormity of the consequences of certain unspeakable catastrophes" to be vividly enacted.

The second section of the book is geared more to Beckett's theater practice. Stan Gontarski argues forcefully that Beckett's impact on twentieth- and twenty-first-century theater is due to his directorial practice as well as to his play texts, which were frequently altered following the rehearsal process. Gontarski provides a detailed account of Beckett's self-collaboration as he worked on his own texts, arguing that Beckett developed into a major theoretician of the theater in the process of staging and rewriting his plays. Barry McGovern's interpretations of Beckett, whether readings of the prose and poetry or performances for stage and radio, are renowned for their precision, intelligence, and musicality, and for their ability to convey both the dark humor and the emotional depth of Beckett's vision. McGovern offers insights into how he prepares for a Beckett role, instances particular performance choices, and underlines his view of the centrality of music and rhythmic pattern to performing Beckett. Though Beckett once declared that if he had his way he would empty the theater, McGovern redefines entertainment as "to hold together . . . to keep up and maintain a process. In other words, to keep going, going on." Enoch Brater returns to a motif that several authors mention, and considers Beckett's preoccupation with silence throughout his work. We end the book however, not with silence, but with the vivid memory of a dialogue.

Professor Ruby Cohn's essay offers a unique glimpse, from the scholar often credited with founding the discipline of Beckett studies, of her long-standing friendship with Samuel Beckett. For half a century, Ruby Cohn has been writing on Beckett and sharing her scholarship and insights with rigor and generosity. Hers was the first Ph.D. entirely on Beckett, and she edited the first journal edition, of *Perspective* in 1959, devoted to Beckett. Professor Cohn re-creates a series of nine scenes, playing on Beckett's love of trinities, in which she remembers particular moments of composition or erasure that she observed or participated in. These scenes span the era between *En Attendant Godot* to Beckett's last piece of writing, the poem "What is the Word." Ruby Cohn's scenes place Beckett not at all as the solitary creator, but as a generous friend and lively conversationalist, deeply engaged in the life of theater and rehearsal processes.

These essays look both backward and forward: they acknowledge Beckett's own immersion in multiple historical genealogies, whether philosophical, literary, or dramatic, and the global legacies of his work, which are set to multiply as new directions and discourses in Beckett studies emerge in the twenty-first century.

NOTES

1. The series was launched by Professor James Knowlson, whose lecture "Beckett and Painting" was incorporated into *Images of Beckett* (New York: Cambridge University Press, 2003).

2. Alan Schneider, "Waiting for Beckett," in *Beckett at 60: A Festschrift,* ed. John Calder (London: Calder and Boyers, 1967), 38. See also S. E. Gontarski, *The Intent of Undoing in Samuel Beckett's Dramatic Texts* (Bloomington: Indiana University Press, 1985).

3. Samuel Beckett, *Proust and Three Dialogues with Georges Duthuit* (London: Calder and Boyers, 1965), 65–66.

4. See Peggy Phelan, "Lessons in Blindness from Samuel Beckett," *PMLA* 119 (2004): 1279–88.

5. When Billie Whitelaw, who was playing the daughter, asked Beckett if her character was alive or dead, he replied, "Let's just say you're not quite there." Billie Whitelaw, *Billie Whitelaw . . . Who He?* (New York: St. Martin's Press, 1995), 143.

6. For a discussion of ghostlike characters in Beckett's work, see Katherine Worth, "Beckett's Ghosts," in *Beckett in Dublin,* ed. S. E. Wilmer (Dublin: Lilliput, 1992), 62–74; and Terence Brown, "Yeats and Beckett: The Ghosts in the Machines," in this volume, for a discussion of the use of technology to achieve the fragmentation of character.

Section A | Interconnections

Linda Ben-Zvi

Beckett's Bodies, or Dr. Johnson's "Anatomy Lesson"

"Body Worlds" is the title of one of the most shocking, controversial, and financially successful traveling exhibits ever mounted, drawing, since its inception in 1995, more than sixteen million viewers in Asia, Europe, and—most recently—the United States.[1] What has attracted the crowds, notoriety, and attempts at litigation to close it (in the United Kingdom and Germany) are the "objects" on display: preserved human male and female corpses in various poses, as well as over 150 torsos, heads, and organs, all treated by a process called plastination, which replaces bodily fluids with a variety of hardening plastic substances, the invention of the exhibit's creator, German physician Dr. Gunther von Hagens. In the case of one of the earliest and most graphic displays, entitled "Suit of Skin," a flayed male, his bones and blood vessels delineated in white and red plastic, stands upright, looking at his raised left hand which holds the actual skin that covered his body, still indicating the contours of the skeleton it protected. There is a slight smile on the corpse's upturned face. He is the exhibit's logo, prominently displayed in color on its elaborate website and adorning the ever growing number of product spin-offs such as T-shirts, mouse pads, wristwatches, and backpacks. More recent displays feature bodies engaged in sports, such as a javelin thrower, skateboard rider, basketball player, and jumping goalkeeper, all great crowd pleasers. When "Body Worlds" opened in Los Angeles, in order to dissipate criticism, health awareness educational displays were also added: lungs showing the effects of smoking, a heart with arteries clogged by plaque, an obese figure illustrating the dangers of a fat-laden diet, and an entire section—blocked off by cloth to prevent underage entrance—featuring fetuses in different stages of development and a cross section of a woman still bearing an embryo.[2]

Answering charges that the exhibition is a desecration of the dead and a cynical attempt to provide a sated, contemporary society with yet

another grotesque thrill, von Hagens argues that he is, in fact, continuing the long tradition of "anatomical theater" practiced for centuries by
surgeons as a teaching tool. To strengthen his claim, on November 21,
2002, at London's East End Atlantis Gallery (where "Body Works" was
on view), he performed the first public autopsy in England in 185 years,
under a large reproduction of Rembrandt's famous painting *The
Anatomy Lesson of Dr. Nicholas Tulp,* attired in a white coat and trade-
mark black fedora that he claimed was patterned after the one worn by
Tulp.[3]

"Body Worlds" could serve as a contemporary coda to Francis
Barker's well-known study *The Tremulous Private Body: Essays on Subjection,* which traces the ways in which conceptions of the body shifted in
the seventeenth century, the body losing its place as a privileged site of
subjectivity, becoming progressively more disguised, veiled, hidden, and
subdued.[4] Only when neutralized, and no longer threatening, its "trou-
bling corporeality" erased, was it reinscribed, in the name of science and
progress, as an object of inquiry, a *thing* to be studied, dissected, manip-
ulated, and displayed, like the man in "Body Worlds" holding his "body
suit." To support his argument, Barker also turns to Rembrandt's
Anatomy Lesson. In the canvas, he points out, none of the seven black-
clad men who have come to observe the dissection of the executed
criminal Aris Kint, look at the corpse. Five concentrate their gazes on a
point at the lower right-hand corner of the painting, presumably focusing on a text describing the procedure that Dr. Tulp is beginning to perform. The body is present—in fact it occupies the center of the composition, practically touching the assembled observers—but it is no longer
a fleshly body but rather an object, "dead meat,"[5] "the anatomy of a
conception,"[6] explained and delineated on the pages of Tulp's medical
manual, according to accepted categories, rather than apprehended
where it lies before the assembled group, its left arm already stripped of
its flesh. For Barker the painting is a clear example of the way in which
the body in the seventeenth century underwent a disappearing act,
Hamlet's call for this "'too too sullied flesh' to 'melt / Thaw, and resolve
itself into a dew' [I.ii.129–30] . . . taken at his word."[7]

Barker contends that this dismissal and reinscription of the body,
shifting it from subject to object, follows the model set out by Descartes,
who writes in the *Meditations:*

> I have a body to which I am very closely united, nevertheless, be-
> cause, on the one hand, I have a clear and distinct idea of myself in

so far as I am only a thinking and unextended thing, and because, on the other hand I have a distinct idea of the body in so far as it is only an extended thing but which does not think, it is certain that I, that is to say my mind, by which I am what I am, is entirely and truly distinct from my body, and may exist without it.[8]

However, just as in *The Anatomy Lesson* (which Barker suggests that Descartes may have seen while in Amsterdam) the body is not totally banished in Cartesian analysis; it can be reinstated as an object of enquiry, a means by which knowledge of the body's workings can be gained, in an attempt to alleviate disease. However, this reinscribed "positive" body, like the bodies on display in the "Body Worlds" exhibit—claiming legitimacy as learning tools for laypeople who wish to know more about "bodily performance at a depth never before possible on such a comparative scale" (website)—is a body without flesh, its corporeality and pain, like its blood and bodily fluids, carefully drained.[9]

I.

Samuel Beckett is also an anatomist, yet his anatomy lessons are quite different from those performed by von Hagens or Tulp. For one thing, his bodies won't keep still; they slip off the operating table just as they slip off the pages and stages that attempt to display or confine them. The central given in Beckett's writing is the very recalcitrance of his bodies against dismissal and their gross insubordination, refusing to assume their places in the Cartesian hierarchy, where mind holds ultimately sway. Theirs are bodies that matter, that are matter, their desires and pain refusing the process that would transform them into abstractions. There are no positive, healthy reinscribed bodies in the Beckett canon. Anyone reading his texts or seeing performances of his plays is immediately struck by his infirm, decrepit figures, presented in all their fleshly imperfections, never beautified nor airbrushed for flaws. They are, as Beckett describes them, "falling to bits."[10] Few are young, most are incapacitated, and almost all are depicted in the process of physical decay, graphically played out and accelerated in the stories and theater works in which they appear, this decay a central theme Beckett returns to again and again.

In the early fiction, almost all are marked by some physical ailment. Watt suffers from poor healing skin; Camier has a cyst; Mercier a fistula;

Belacqua, Molloy, Moran, and assorted unnamed protagonists suffer from cramps, arthritis, corns, and lameness of legs and feet. Walking, a passion they commonly share, is, therefore, particularly arduous. In order to move at all, they often resort to complex series of movements to propel themselves forward, including splayed feet and bent or contorting trunks to bear the shock of stiff limbs. In the later novels and short works, bodies in closed spaces proliferate: still cramped, crabbed with age, not even sure of their physical contours or conditions, the borders of their bodies often impossible for them to distinguish from their environments. In the plays, through the agency of the live actor, the spectacle of illness, contortion, and fleshly indeterminacy and embodiment is visually repeated, the characters' infirmities, as actor-director Pierre Chabert puts it, becoming that "lack" or limitation "which gives the body its existence, its dramatic force and its reality as a working material for the stage," since "one's body exists all the more strongly when it begins to suffer."[11] And suffer they do: Vladimir endures prostate problems; Estragon a weak left lung and sore, smelly feet; Pozzo goes blind, Lucky mute; Hamm is also sightless and confined to a wheelchair, his infirmities divided between A and B in *Rough for Theatre I;* Clov is barely able to walk; and the "wearish" Krapp nearsighted and hard of hearing. Even the most basic human functions—breathing, urinating, and defecating—are sources of great pain. Dan Rooney's question in *All That Fall,* "Did you ever know me to be well?"[12] could be asked by most who inhabit Beckett's world.

Progressively in both fiction and drama, bodies in decay give way to bodies barely visible and gradually disappearing. While most are, in the words of Mrs. Rooney, "not half alive nor anything approaching it,"[13] some are no longer even that: the triad in *Play* interned in burial urns; Mouth in *Not I* just lips, tongue, and teeth "whole body like gone";[14] the solitary walker in *Footfalls* literally walking herself to oblivion on the stage, a shade to join the shade of her specter mother alive only in her head, or she in her absent mother's words, the very pronoun indeterminacy mirroring the indeterminacy of the body. Yet, even when it is barely possible for the speakers to discern their own forms, buried, hidden, or forgotten, they are not totally effaced or objectified. Mouth may be a tiny orifice hovering eight feet above a stage enshrouded in darkness, but her words continually refer, like a litany, to body parts, their positioning, and their functioning. Even beyond the grave, presumably beyond corporeality, M in *Play* can still hiccup, indicating either that

Beckett's people never entirely give up the ghost or that what passes for life is not that different from after life, "that rude awakening," as Beckett called his own death.[15] The very absences bespeak a body that was and still is struggling to be seen and experienced.

The same pull between corporeal presence and absence can be found in the late fiction as well as in the late plays. The speaker in *Company* may begin as a voice in the dark, but he is fully aware that he is on his back, feeling "the pressure on his hind parts,"[16] and he ends his chronicle of memory in the same way, in the dark, still in a body, in an encapsulated space, "that bonewhite flesh for company."[17] The narrated "she" in *Ill Seen Ill Said,* "This old so dying woman,"[18] also continues to leave "a tenacious trace,"[19] even when, presumably there is "Not another crumb of carrion left."[20] And in *Worstward Ho,* Beckett's last extended fiction, the struggle of the "nohow on" is still to "Say a body."[21] The threnody echoed twice in *Waiting for Godot* seems applicable to them all, seen or unseen, shade or ghost: "We have time to grow old. The air is full of our cries."[22] The air is also full of pants, wheezes, coughs, hiccups, farts, and screams as well as those smells "the living emit, [from] their feet, teeth, armpits, arses, sticky foreskins and frustrated ovules," as the narrator of "First Love" enumerates.[23] These bodily sounds and odors are used by Beckett as if to ensure that physical embodiment is not to be easily dismissed nor displaced entirely onto the metaphorical or metaphysical plane. It is difficult to think of another modern writer who has so consistently, thoroughly, and relentlessly focused on questions of the body. Repeatedly in his early fiction, Beckett's characters talk about their wish to rid themselves of corporeality. Murphy goes as far as to bind his naked body to a rocking chair, attempting to rock himself into a state in which he would be "free in the mind";[24] Belacqua tries to enter a similar gray umbra by pressing his body down on his mattress. Neither succeeds. Beckett characters may dream of somatic-free lives, alive only in the mind, but such a state eludes them.

Beckett's particular body work is central to his writing; it is also highly complex. On the one hand, he seems to accept, as Steven Connor puts it, "the impossibility of disembodied thought" refusing "the refusal of the body."[25] On the other hand, he faces the problems of how to invoke this body without resorting to the very methods of objectification that deny its presence; how to represent what is constantly in the process of decomposition; and how to convey pain, which is something that is ultimately unrepresentable. As Elaine Scarry has argued, the "it" of pain is "so incontestably and unnegotiably present" for the sufferer while "so elusive that 'hearing about pain' may exist as the primary model of what it is 'to have doubt.'"[26]

To further complicate his task, Beckett casts doubt not only on the possibility of fixing the body but on language with which to describe it. In his first published essay, the 1929 "Dante . . . Bruno. Vico.. Joyce," a defense of James Joyce's "Work in Progress" *(Finnegans Wake),* Beckett applauds Joyce's ability to bypass "abstraction" and "metaphysical generalization,"[27] to "snare the sense"[28] through words which are themselves alive and able to present "a statement of the particular."[29] By 1937, however, in his oft-quoted letter to his German acquaintance, Axel Kaun, Beckett indicates his reservations about "that terrible materiality of the word surface,"[30] and his determination to find an alternative solution to the one Joyce chose, by using "some form of Nominalist irony,"[31] an idea Beckett came across in 1929, when, at Joyce's behest, he read the *Beiträge zu einer Kritik der Sprache (Contributions toward a Critique of Language)*[32] by Austrian skeptical nominalist Fritz Mauthner.[33] In his three-volume critique of language, Mauthner argues that all knowledge comes through the body, but the body itself is a poor conductor of experience, given its physical limitations. What little it does know, it cannot say because of the vagaries of language, the only vehicle through which a sense of self and of the world can be ascertained or shared.[34] The solution Mauthner suggests is to find a means of using language to indict itself, to call attention to its own paucity through words. In "Three Dialogues with George Duthuit," written in 1949, in which Beckett describes the artist's impasse, "there is nothing to express, nothing with which to express, nothing from which to express, no power to express, no desire to express, together with the obligation to express,"[35] he seems to be practicing what Mauthner preached: using language to both critique itself and to point to the impossibility of all critiques, a verbal maneuver to elude the net of signification language imposes. At the same time Beckett faced the dilemma of how to make this writing live without going in the direction of Joyce, and without imposing extraneous forms and conditions that denied the very impotence that he recognized as inevitable. As John Pilling notes, no wonder at the end of "Three Dialogues" Beckett says "ironically, but wearily 'Yes, yes, I am mistaken, I am mistaken.'"[36] He knew the difficulty of the road he was following and what lay ahead.

Beckett's skepticism, like Mauthner's, goes beyond language, to deny the very possibility of certain knowledge of the self. Unlike

Descartes, who could claim that he had both "a clear and distinct idea of myself" and "a distinct idea of the body," Beckett recognizes that neither can be known with any certainty. Just as he explodes traditional notions of narrative in his fiction, and Aristotelian principles of order in his drama, Beckett explodes the concept of a unified self and a stable body. Instead he offers up a fleshly, decaying body, whose very contours are constantly shifting and indeterminate, on page and stage, not the positive, healthy body Descartes reinscribes as an object of inquiry, but, rather, a body marked by its own impotence.[37] The positive, healthy body in Beckett's writing becomes coterminous with the lucid narrative and ineluctable dramatic plot, something to be unveiled as fraudulent and disposed of as a given in fiction and drama. In its place Beckett introduces a body that can be brought to life, if at all, through its own infirmities. It is this decaying body that becomes one of the central marks of what is meant by the term *Beckettian*. As Connor notes, "It is especially in Beckett's attention to the defective or otherwise deviant body that his work runs parallel to some of the most important and influential rethinkings of the relation between rationality and physicality in our culture."[38]

That Beckett found a way of both presenting the body as seat of knowledge and then erasing its potency and even at times much of its corporeality is striking. What is even more striking is that he began turning out his "gallery of moribunds"[39] when he himself was just thirty. One of the questions that is often asked but not often explored is how did such a young man have such an affinity to illness and decrepitude, and how did he come to settle on this technique, and the notion of impotency, reflecting as it does bodily inability to act or perform in given circumstance, as a means of both invoking and problematizing bodies in his work? A starting point, of course, is in Beckett's own biography. In fact, although photographs indicate a tall, lean, athletic figure, James Knowlson, in *Damned to Fame,* lists under the heading "Beckett's illnesses" 109 entries in the 704 pages of the biography, and he organizes these illnesses under eight specific medical problems including poor eyesight, lung problems, panic attacks and racing heart, and a general category of "other illnesses." These do not include Beckett's near fatal stabbing on a Paris street in 1938, the wound just missing the heart and lung. To create people dealing with illnesses, Beckett did not have to use great leaps of imagination.

In addition to his own medical problems, Beckett could use illnesses he observed in his family. When, for example, Lady Beatrice Glenavy, a

Beckett family friend, first saw *Endgame,* she immediately associated the crippled Hamm with Beckett's Aunt Cissie (Beckett) Sinclair,[40] whose Parkinson's disease and severe arthritis so greatly incapacitated her that Beckett had to wheel her to the hospital when her husband, William "Boss" Sinclair, was dying there of tuberculosis, a disease that had claimed their daughter Peggy—Beckett's first love—four years earlier. Later in his life, on trips back to Dublin, Beckett would also witness his mother's gradual deterioration from Parkinson's disease and the dementia it precipitated.[41] There were also those physical sufferers he encountered in Dublin, London, and, later, in France: old men for whom Beckett had a particular fondness, "gerontophilia," he called it;[42] the patients in London's Bethlem Royal Hospital, which he visited in 1936, and those whose extreme suffering he witnessed in France under the Nazi regime, and later in the hospital at St.-Lô where he worked with the medical staff. He could also have found models for physical infirmity and suffering flesh in the works of writers and painters he admired: Dante, Shakespeare, the Bruegels and Bosch.[43] From all of these sources, Beckett had ample examples for what the Unnamable calls "the stench of decomposition,"[44] and a validation for Hamm's cry in *Endgame:* "Use your head, can't you, use your head, you're on earth, there's no cure for that!"[45]

Examples of Beckett's use of decrepitude can be found in his writing as early as *More Pricks Than Kicks:* the blind paralytic "all tucked up" in "Ding Dong"[46] and "A Wet Night"[47] and Belacqua's "grotesque exterior, spavined gait," and feet "in ruins" in "Ding Dong."[48] In *Pricks, Dream of Fair to Middling Women,* and *Murphy,* however, these references to the body are still filtered through a perceiving, third-person mind that comments on infirmity rather than living it, as Beckett illustrates in chapter 6 of *Murphy.* In general, the early fictions still held to formal markers of the genre. As John Pilling puts it, "As long as Beckett hoped to 'snare the sense' . . . the snare of arbitrary form claimed him as its victim."[49] So, to an extent, did the language of Joyce continue to hold him in thrall, those words that could body forth a world. By 1937, however, as Beckett explained to Kaun, he was already looking for a different way of writing. What is significant is that at exactly this time, July 1937, Beckett was in the throes of a project that he imagined could lead him to this new type of writing, one less confined by formal means. The theme was to be impotence in the face of desire; the genre was to be drama; and the subject was to be Dr. Samuel Johnson.

II.

Samuel Johnson holds a special place in Beckett studies. Of all the many writers, philosophers, and intellectuals to whom Beckett was drawn and from whom he gained inspiration, Johnson proved one of the most compelling, enduring, and intractable. While Beckett was able to distill elements of his study of Descartes in the 1930 poem "Whoroscope,"[50] and the next year turn his intensive reading of Proust into a seventy-one-page essay,[51] as revelatory of the author as it is of the subject, his extensive reading on the life and times of Dr. Samuel Johnson, the eighteenth-century classicist, lexicographer, critic, poet, and renowned figure in Augustan literary circles, produced only one eleven and a half page typed scene of an aborted play he entitled "Human Wishes," the title derived from Johnson's famous poem "The Vanity of Human Wishes." Beckett later admitted to Ruby Cohn that he could not remember what it was that first drew him to Johnson,[52] why he decided to write about him, or why he chose drama as his form, the first play Beckett ever attempted to write.[53] What was certain was the theme he clearly wished to pursue: Johnson in love.

Beckett's interest in Samuel Johnson and his writing dates back at least to the early 1930s. His "Whoroscope" notebook (in the Beckett archives of the University of Reading), covering the years 1932–38, includes notes on Johnson's *Rasselas,* a nihilistic fable that Beckett continued to admire, "a grand book" he would call it many years later,[54] not surprisingly given its theme, stated in chapter 11, that "life is everywhere a state in which much is to be endured and little to be enjoyed."[55] The notebook contains as well materials from Johnson's *The Lives of the English Poets* and from Boswell on Johnson. In 1935, continuing his habit of visiting the residence of writers that interested him, Beckett traveled to Lichfield, Johnson's birthplace.[56] In the fall of 1936, before setting out on an extended trip to Germany to visit museums and view the new art being done in the country, Beckett began thinking more seriously of writing about Johnson, and turned his attention to finding materials for what he soon was calling his "Johnson fantasy."[57] In a "private notebook," dating from 1936, he translated Johnson's famous "Letter to Lord Chesterfield" into German, probably as an exercise to test his language skills before his departure.[58] During the six months he traveled in Germany, from October 1936 to April 1937, he did not actively work on Johnson, but he did not leave him behind. In a December 13 letter to his friend Mary Manning, he wrote, "There are 50 plays in [Johnson's] life."[59] The one he fixed on was based on his hypothesis that Johnson had been in love with Mrs. Hester Thrale, the woman who had served as his closest confidant and support during the fifteen years that she and her husband had taken the widowed, lonely man into their family, and provided him with the comforts of wealth and the companionship and care of friends that the brooding Johnson, for all his wit and conviviality, seemed desperately to need.[60] When Henry Thrale died on April 4, 1781, Hester was forty-one, a mother of thirteen children, four living, a still attractive woman, who had been a partner in an arranged marriage to a husband ten years older, and who, free of "Thrale's bridle . . . off her neck," as Johnson described her situation,[61] could plot a new life for herself. This she soon did: she declared her love for her children's Italian music teacher, Gabriel Piozzi, married him in 1784, and moved to Italy.

Johnson at the time of Henry Thrale's death was seventy-two, a sick man who grew progressively more enfeebled in his last years. All his life he had been plagued by illnesses, starting with scrofula, a form of tuberculosis, which from his infancy marred his features and may have given rise to many of those compulsive tics, gesticulations, and odd bodily habits for which Johnson was infamous: eating in a grotesque fashion, his jaws working seemingly independent of the rest of his face; walking with legs stretched as far as they could go, heels pressed down, body hurtling forward as if from some internal volition.[62] In addition to physical maladies, including deafness and poor eyesight, he was also plagued by severe bouts of depression, fears of insanity, and preoccupations with death and mortality: symptoms alleviated, Mrs. Thrale notes, only by constant companionship late into the night (which she provided), large quantities of tea, injection of opium, or arithmetic.[63] Counting, Johnson explained, was "a way of steadying his mind generally, or steadying his resolve" by "breaking things down into smaller, more manageable units."[64] In his youth he had sought to overcome his physical infirmities by vigorous physical activity, such as swimming in rough seas and taking extensive walking tours; but by 1781, the year that Beckett fixed on to begin his play, Johnson's body overtook his resolve. He became increasingly afflicted by dropsy, circulatory problems, bronchitis, emphysema, congestive heart failure, and sarcocele of the testicle, illnesses too pervasive to slough off, even with his prodigious will. It is this Johnson, the towering intellect now in decay, who seems to have captured Beckett's imagination, or rather the thought that such a physical wreck could wish to be the next husband of Hester Thrale. "What interested me especially was the breakdown of Johnson as soon as [Mr.] Thrale disappeared," Beckett wrote to Manning from Germany, "the platonic gigolo or house friend, with not a testicle, auricle or ventricle to stand on when the bluff is called."[65]

In the diary he kept during his travels in Germany, Beckett makes no mention of Johnson; his entries are concerned almost entirely with two subjects: his impressions of the art, people, and places he was seeing and his own physical and psychological ailments, which uncannily resembled several from which Johnson suffered, particularly a cyst on the scrotum that made walking excruciating, and bouts of extreme lethargy, thrown into sharp relief by the "industriousness" of those Germans he saw around him.[66] Beckett during this period took in much art, but produced no writing nor seemed able to clarify for himself the direction he wished to take in his life.

However, on April 25, 1937, only three weeks after his return to Dublin, he could report to his friend Thomas MacGreevy that he was "working . . . on the Johnson thing to find my position . . . more strikingly confirmed than I had dared hope."[67] Beckett's supposition was that Johnson was impotent, a theory he admits for which "there is no text,"[68] and when finally free to woo Thrale, could not do so. There was, however, some text for the possibility of a match between these two seemingly mismatched people. Boswell, Johnson's faithful chronicler and hero worshipper, in fact wrote an anonymous "epithalamium" ("in appalling taste" Johnson's biographer W. Jackson Bate calls it)[69] in which an ardent Johnson expresses his joy that "I myself am Thrale's entire" (the pun on *entire* pointing to a stud not a gelding, as another modern Johnson biographer, John Wain, points out).[70]

For the next six months, except for an extended period in May 1937, after the death of Boss Sinclair, Beckett seems to have spent much of his time in the National Library in Dublin voraciously reading all available books and related material on the life of Johnson, Hester Thrale, and the wide circle of people who interacted with them. His primary sources were Birkbeck Hill's 1887 edition of Boswell's *Life of Johnson,* the six-volume work that Beckett would later misplace, repurchase in 1961, and have in his library at his death;[71] C. E. Vulliamy's *Mrs. Thrale of Streatham,* which had just been published in 1936, as well as Mrs. Piozzi's *Anecdotes,* entries from the *Dictionary of National Biography,* and related letters and secondary material, particularly John Hawkins's 1787 *Life of Samuel Johnson.* Relying on these and numerous other primary and secondary sources, Beckett filled three notebooks with over two hundred pages of notes on his readings.[72] While Beckett may have left academe several years before, he was still very much a scholar, recording every possible detail related to his subject, going so far as to list the birth dates of each of Thrale's thirteen children.

Beginning with notebook 2, however, it becomes apparent that Beckett was drawn more to details concerning Johnson's body and its physical decay than to the theme of marriage, the subject of impotence increasingly overshadowing that of love. In this notebook, for example, he writes down all of Johnson's illnesses during the four years preceding his death, even copying his autopsy or "neuopsy" and translating its medical terms from Latin. He also copies quotations and comments about Johnson's fear of death and annihilation, and preoccupations with the infirmity of his body. At one point, when Johnson describes his friend Sir John Flower, an asthma specialist who "panted on to 90 as was supposed," Beckett underlines the phrase in blue pencil, his way of indicating something of significance for his project, and he repeats the phrase twice, once on verso, a place reserved for his comments and for material which struck him as particularly important, noting that the line would be "spoken towards end of last act, when, with J panting in silence after 'sent to hell, Sir, etc.' curtain falls."[73]

In notebook 3, finally abandoning the Johnson-Thrale marriage theme entirely, Beckett takes up one of the alternative scenarios he had listed in notebook 1: the group Johnson called his "seraglio,"[74] those ill-assorted, constantly bickering companions for whom he had provided an income and a home in his private residence, Bolt Court. They included blind Mrs. Anna Williams, a friend of Johnson's late wife Tetty, who now functioned as his taciturn, official hostess; Mrs. Elizabeth Desmoulins, another friend inherited by Johnson; Dr. Robert Levett, a lay doctor, serving those who could not afford professional services; Francis Barber, a black Jamaican-born young man, who came and went in the household; a Miss Poll Carmichael, who seems to have been a prostitute Johnson found lying in the street one night and brought home to nurse and to "put her into a virtuous way of living,"[75] and Johnson's cat Hodge.

In Boswell's scurrilous wedding hymn, he had written, "'Desmullins [*sic*] may now go her ways,' cries the ecstatic Johnson, 'And poor blind Williams sing alone. . . . I with my arms encircle heaven.'"[76] When it became clear that the heavenly body of Mrs. Thrale had eluded him, Johnson was forced to rely for succor and companionship on that "wretched Household" who "shared his Bounty and increased his dirt," as Mrs. Thrale described the Bolt Court residents.[77] Among Johnson's friends it was well known that they were "anything but a happy family."[78] Johnson confided as much to Mrs. Thrale, and Beckett copied the lines in his notebook: "Williams hates everybody; Levett hates Desmoulins, and does not love Williams; Desmoulins hates them both; Poll loves none of them."[79] It was clearly a disgruntled group and, with the exception of Poll, elderly: in 1781 Mrs. Williams was seventy-five, Dr. Levett seventy-six, Mrs. Desmoulins sixty-five, and the cat Hodge, indeterminably aged. It was also, as Mrs. Thrale describes them, sickly: "the lame, the blind, the sick, and the sorrowful [who] found a sure retreat from all the evils whence his [Johnson's] little income could secure them."[80] In fact, during the time period Beckett investigated, both Levett and Williams died, and Desmoulins departed the residence. There is no mention of what became of Poll.

It was with this cast of characters that Beckett tried once more to synthesize his Johnson material into a four-act, four-year form: from Thrale's death to Johnson's. The result is the brief scene entitled "Human Wishes" set on April 4, the date of Henry Thrale's death, in which several of the Bolt Court inhabitants await the arrival of the unnamed "Dr." who "is late."[81] While waiting, Beckett specifies that Williams meditates, Desmoulins knits, Carmichael reads, and Hodge the cat sleeps, "if possible," the stage direction read.[82] Engaging more in mutual monologues than dialogue, the three women touch on a variety of subjects, including their dislike for each other, an extended inquiry on who in the household could be considered merry (the conclusion "nobody"), and a list of those who have "departed," that is, whose "debt to nature is discharged," or—as Mrs. Williams finally shouts—are "Dead. D-E-A-D."[83] The theme of death is extended and reinforced by a quotation from the book Poll is reading, *The Rules and Exercises of Holy Dying,* by Jeremy Taylor, a man Johnson admired, though he "found little more in the book than he brought himself," a comment Beckett noted.[84] However, more than death, it is "the peevishness of decay" that pervades the scene, illustrated by the petty bickering among the women and punctuated by the repeated silences that threaten to stop what little action there is. Blind Mrs. Williams, an early avatar of Hamm, aggressively seeks to control the action; Mrs. Desmoulins, an unwilling Clov, continually comes and goes (as she did in the Bolt Court household), and Levett performs the first of Beckett's silent pantomimes, entering midway through the scene "slightly, respectably, even reluctantly drunk"[85] (another one of Beckett's wonderful stage directions), and emits a powerful hiccup that almost knocks him off his feet. His otherwise silent appearance and disappearance precipitate a metatheatrical exchange, Mrs. Williams commenting, "Words fail us," a later Beckett refrain, and Mrs. Desmoulins replying, "Now this is where a writer for the stage would have us speak no doubt."[86] Speak they do for another five pages of the printed text about who has died and when, and who has written the treatise on the subject of death from which Poll quotes. Although Beckett was able to use a few of his research facts in these brief exchanges—some titles of plays, dates of deaths (one incorrect), and phraseology that caught his ear—for the most part the welter of material he had amassed proved unusable in his dramatic project.

III.

Beckett's work on the Johnson project was one of the most protracted in his career: he first conceived of it in 1936; worked on it steadily for the six months preceding his 1937 move to Paris; continued to think about it when settled in his new home, he told MacGreevy in August 1938;[87] and finally produced "half of a first act of Johnson," he indicated to George Reavey on May 21, 1941.[88] There are several theories about why Beckett finally abandoned the work. Deirdre Bair reports that Beckett told her the problems of putting the eighteenth-century phrasing into "the Irish accent" for a production scheduled for Ireland proved too daunting.[89] Cohn and Löwe question this reason, arguing that much of the phraseology of the play already comes from primary sources and is consistent with modern usage and understanding, Cohn suggesting that finally Beckett "could not resolve the conflict between the realistic biographical drama he had painstakingly prepared himself to write and the verbal ballet he actually found himself writing."[90]

Even while he was still struggling with the Johnson material, and had not yet "degraded it to paper,"[91] Beckett sensed its importance to his writing in general: "I have not written a word of the Johnson blasphemy," he informed Mary Manning. "I trust that acts of intellection are going on about it somewhere. Which will enable me eventually to see how it coincides with the Pricks, Bones and Murphy, fundamentally and fundamentally with all I shall ever write or want to write."[92] At first glance it is difficult to see how the "Human Wishes" fragment, which finally emerged, lives up to its author's expectations. It does offer indications of what Beckett would later do in *Godot* and beyond—the use of circuitous conversations, overlapping ideas and speeches, long silences, habitual activities, name calling, metatheatrical references, and sudden arrivals and departures to fill time while waiting for someone who never arrives—but that is far from fulfilling its intended promise, as Beckett imagined it.

If, however, critical attention focuses on Johnson the man rather than on "Human Wishes" the play, and on Beckett's battle with the material rather than his results, it becomes clearer just how prescient Beckett was about his debt to Johnson. In "Cascando," a poem that probably dates from the same period when he was struggling with Johnson,[93] Beckett writes, "is it not better abort than be barren."[94] He may well have had "Human Wishes" in mind. Although Beckett aborted the project, Samuel Johnson remained "a soul mate," someone who, as James Knowlson claims, "prefigures the concerns of his later writings."[95] Anne Atik, who, with her husband, the artist Avigdor Arikha, was a close friend of Beckett from the early 1960s until his death, confirms his abiding fascination with Johnson, a fascination that she shared. Mention of Johnson, she notes, could always animate Beckett, even when he fell into one of his despondent moods. He appreciated Johnson's conversational skills, "the paradigm of civilization and proportion," his "hospitality to the poor and helpless," and his "not liking 'to come down to vacuity.'"[96] In 1956 he would confide to the British actor Peter Woodthorpe that he still dreamed of writing a play about Johnson,[97] and the next year wrote to Alan Schneider: "Yes, I always had a passion for that crazy old ruffian."[98]

The passion, as Beckett intuited, can be seen in his future writing, as it "coincided" with what came before. For one thing, Johnson provides a model for one of Beckett's most oft-used characters: the old, decrepit man, who, as Johnson wrote of himself and Beckett copied in his notebook, was "born almost dead,"[99] and never got much better; and who claimed that he "did not enjoy a days ease"[100] because of endless physical problems, during "this long Disease, my Life." He also served as another case study of that lethargy Beckett had already delineated in his first fictional protagonist, Belacqua Shuah, in *Dream of Fair to Middling Women*. Despite Johnson's prodigious activity and accomplishments, he admitted to "an inclination to do nothing,"[101] believing that all activity was simply something "to fill up the time," a maxim to which early and later Beckett progeny ascribe. Yet, one activity could always rouse Johnson's interest: the scrutiny of his own mind, or inner world, as Mrs. Thrale called it. "Will *any* body's mind bear this eternal microscope that you place upon your own so?"[102] she queried her friend, and Beckett recorded. Johnson after a lifetime of probing came to the conclusion that the mind could finally not be controlled, try as one might, and he had Imlac say in *Rasselas,* "There is no man whose ideas will come and go at his command,"[103] an awareness that Beckett's characters also share. Imagination, which Johnson defined in his dictionary as "the power of forming ideal pictures, or the power of presenting things absent," could be called on to mitigate the pain of the present; so too memory and its ally forgetfulness, necessary to remembrance, but such recourses, Johnson held, only served to delude the thinker into a false sense of hope. "Life is a progress from want to want, not from enjoyment to enjoyment," Boswell quotes him as saying.[104] Yet as painful and arduous as life might be, Johnson feared death and annihilation above all else, clinging, Boswell wrote, "to life with an eagerness at which many have wondered."[105] Mrs. Thrale explains the apparent contradiction by pointing to a central Johnson tenet: "Where there is nothing to be done something must be endured."[106] The mind would finally be of little help in making sense of what the body experienced. *Rasselas* ends with "The Conclusion in which Nothing is Concluded."

If Johnson acted as a model for his future works, Beckett's failure at writing drama, at least the type of drama he wished to create, provided him with an important lesson that would also shape his later work. His approach to Johnson had been scholarly: he had made him the object of investigation, seeking him out in texts, attempting to abstract the subject and reinscribe him within a set structure, carefully worked out to accommodate his thesis: a Cartesian methodology. Beckett at this point in his career had little experience in the construction of drama; that certainly was an impediment to his work, but only part of the problem. Looming larger was his inability to capture what became the central focus of his research: Johnson's decaying body, which the great Cham himself could not finally subdue to mind. It was this body that finally pushed all else aside in Johnson's life and in Beckett's notebooks of his life.

The approach Beckett employed had failed; the impotence had been his. This awareness that "scholarly thoroughness is no guarantee of truth"[107] became a central theme in Beckett's next novel *Watt,* written in English during the war years. Sam, the narrator in the novel, describes his own inability to fit all the details concerning Watt into any coherent form, "though I was most careful to note down all at the time, in my little notebook,"[108] a possible reference to the Johnson project. Certainly,

Beckett's parody of the scholarly method in *Watt*—the eleven pages on the Lynch family, the elaborate system describing the disposal of Mr. Knott's food, the repeated question marks that punctuate the text—point to the bankruptcy of rational enquiry, as he had experienced it during his work on Johnson. Yet Watt still remains a figure glimpsed from the outside, just as Murphy and Belacqua had been, described but not embodied in the flesh.

In 1946, after the war years, a different kind of Beckett fiction appeared. Beginning with the short story "La Fin" ["The End"][109] he turned to writing in French and adopted the first-person pronoun for his speakers, protagonist-narrators who, as Ruby Cohn puts it, "spurn coherence, causality, and concatenation of events,"[110] and who are aware of the workings of their own bodies, particularly their physical afflictions. This shift from third to first person is usually described as a result of Beckett's "revelation" that "my own way was in impoverishment, in lack of knowledge, in subtracting rather than adding."[111] Instead of focusing on the world of ideas, apprehensible through logic and rational means, he began to focus on the body from the inside out, presenting only what the body itself is capable of knowing or remembering. "Impotence" and "ignorance"—the words Beckett employed to explain this new authorial position and aesthetics[112]—replace logic and rationality, and their correlatives become the decrepit, infirm bodies proliferating in his fiction and his plays.

Beckett's focus on the body can be traced to many causes, his direct experiences in the war probably contributing most directly to his awareness that logic, as well as words, are, as Arsene says in *Watt,* finally "doomed to fail, doomed, doomed to fail."[113] However, his work on Johnson certainly played a part in his shift to an aesthetics of impotence, the very word he tried to ascribe to Johnson. By presenting the unmediated, infirm body, Beckett could overthrow the Cartesian legacy, making the body the seat of knowledge, limited as it is.

In taking this position, Beckett was, in fact, a precursor of recent eighteenth-century scholarship that claims that Johnson, along with Swift, Defoe, and Fielding, began to rethink Cartesian theories of mind and body in their own lives and their writings, no longer submerging corporeality or veiling it, as the seventeenth-century thinkers had attempted to do, but becoming increasingly obsessed with the body, particularly the body in decay.[114] As Carol Flynn puts it: "After Hobbes, after Locke, and in spite of Descartes, the body, at least in eighteenth-century England, would not go away easily. It became instead matter difficult, perhaps impossible, to idealize—matter in the way."[115] It was this "matter in the way," present in the public and private writing of Samuel Johnson, that thwarted Beckett in "Human Wishes." In Beckett's later work, the very recalcitrance of the body to be fixed in art or in life becomes a dominant theme he returns to again and again, using new narrative and theatrical means to show it. On the stage, as Anna McMullan has shown, Beckett's plays repeatedly return to "the dilemma of investing and divesting corporeal images with subjectivity at the limits of representation,"[116] a locale in which few other artists have dared to set up camp.

However, Beckett's decrepits are not, as Leslie Hill warns, to be taken as "simply illustrative of ontological decay."[117] On the contrary, Beckett, after 1946, began an interrogation of what it means to have a body, how that body is constructed, how it struggles to emerge, and how it is thwarted by its own corporeal limitations, the vagaries of mind and memory, and the constraints imposed on it by social, cultural, and political forces that seek to control and define it. Many of the central issues about the body and selfhood raised over the past twenty years by feminist, Foucauldian, and poststructural studies can be found embedded in Beckett's fiction and drama. Beckett also experiments with new ways of creating embodiment, predicated on an aesthetics of impotence and indeterminacy. On the stage, through the body of the actor, "an agent of disclosure," he both displays and problematizes the body; showing its corporeality and its instability in time and memory, while providing it with subjectivity continually being undermined in performance. In short, the very issues that had thwarted him in "Human Wishes," that he had struggled to keep under, become the center of the theater that follows.

Richard Ellmann describes one way of distinguishing between the works of Joyce and Beckett: "Joyce claimed to have given a voice to the third of human life that is spent in sleep. Beckett could claim to have given a voice to the third of every existence likely to be spent in decay."[118] The two Samuels, Johnson and Beckett, both lovers of arithmetic, would probably have snickered at Ellmann's poor calculation. Both knew well that decay starts with the birth cry, accompanying the gravedigger's forceps, and it cannot be understood as a concept or a theory but only as felt experience on the body itself, little enough but all that they could. That is the anatomy lesson of Dr. Johnson, that helped shape the body in, and of, Beckett's works, and that he in turn passed on to those playwrights who followed. As George Tabori puts it: "What theatre could teach science is that true memory is only possible through sensual memory. . . . It is impossible to overcome the past without having re-experienced it through the skin, the nose, the tongue, the buttocks, the stomach."[119] As Johnson knew and Beckett came to understand, there is no getting away from or looking beyond the body. It demands that it be seen; it challenges the observer to confront its flesh directly, and not some simulacrum of plastaline or paper that purports to represent it. It illustrates "the irreducibility of the body, and reminds us that it remains an agent of disclosure."[120]

NOTES

A revised and shortened version of this essay was published as "Biographical, Textual, and Historical Origins," in *Palgrave Advances in Samuel Beckett Studies,* ed. Lois Oppenheim (London: Palgrave, 2004). A version of the sections on Beckett and Johnson was published as "Beckett and Johnson: Two Sams Abroad in Hamburg" in *Das Raubauge in der Stadt: Beckett liest Hamburg,* ed. Michaela Giesing, Gaby Hartel, Carola Veit (Gottingen: Wallstein Verlag, 2007), 48–59.

1. For updated information about "Body Worlds," see its website at http://www.bodyworlds.com/en/pages/gunther_von_hagens.asp. It includes summaries of attendance at all exhibitions, products, testimonials, and future plans.

2. Before openings in Los Angeles, Chicago, and Philadelphia, von Hagens organized panels of local clergy, physicians, ethicists, and educators whose endorsements served to limit demonstrations. In recent years exhibits have opened in U.S. cities including Miami and New York City without public preparation or demonstrations.

3. The autopsy was witnessed by approximately 450 people who paid nineteen dollars each, and by an estimated 1.2 million, who later that evening tuned into Channel 4, which ran a tape of the event. London authorities threatened to stop the performance and the television replay, but failed to do so.

4. Francis Barker, *The Tremulous Private Body: Essays on Subjection* (London: Methuen, 1984), 73–112.

5. The phrase appears in Barker's preface to the 1995 printing of *The Tremulous Private Body* (Ann Arbor: University of Michigan Press), xiv.

6. Barker, *Tremulous Private Body,* 96.

7. Barker, *Tremulous Private Body,* 12.

8. René Descartes, *Discourse on Method, and Meditations,* ed. F. E. Sutcliffe (Harmondsworth, Middlesex: Penguin, 1968), 156.

9. Barker in his careful dissection of the painting indicates that the very distortions in the composition, for example the elongation of the flayed arm and its faulty position, indicate Rembrandt's struggle to naturalize what is unnatural: the banishment of the body itself.

10. Israel Shenker, "An Interview with Samuel Beckett," in *Samuel Beckett: The Critical Heritage,* ed. Lawrence Graver and Raymond Federman (London: Routledge, 1979), 148.

11. Pierre Chabert, "The Body in Beckett's Theatre," *Journal of Beckett Studies* 8 (1982): 24.

12. Samuel Beckett, *The Collected Shorter Plays* (New York: Grove Weidenfeld, 1984), 31.

13. Beckett, *The Collected Shorter Plays,* 16.

14. Beckett, *The Collected Shorter Plays,* 220.

15. Samuel Beckett, letter to Linda Ben-Zvi, November 26, 1988.

16. Samuel Beckett, *Company* (New York: Grove Press, 1980), 7.

17. Beckett, *Company,* 57.

18. Samuel Beckett, *Ill Seen Ill Said* (New York: Grove Press, 1981), 20.

19. Beckett, *Ill Seen Ill Said,* 59.

20. Beckett, *Ill Seen Ill Said,* 59.

21. Samuel Beckett *Worstward Ho* (London: John Calder, 1983), 7.

22. Samuel Beckett, *Waiting for Godot* (New York: Grove Press, 1956), 58.

23. Samuel Beckett, *First Love and Other Shorts* (New York: Grove Press, 1974), 1.

24. Samuel Beckett, *Murphy* (New York: Grove Press, 1957), 2.

25. Steven Connor, "Over Samuel Beckett's Dead Body," in *Beckett in Dublin,* ed. S. E. Wilmer (Dublin: Lilliput Press, 1992), 101.

26. Elaine Scarry, *The Body in Pain* (New York: Oxford University Press, 1985), 4. Scarry's theories prove useful in discussing Beckett's work. Her central argument, that the experience of pain cannot finally be communicated by the one who experiences it to the one who does not, is illustrated in the "It hurts" exchanges between Didi and Gogo in *Waiting for Godot.* Scarry's description of the nature of torture also parallels what Beckett stages in *What Where:* "Torture . . . consists of a primary physical act, the infliction of pain, and a primary verbal act, the interrogation. The verbal act, in turn, consists of two parts, 'the question' and 'the answer,' each with conventional connotations that wholly falsify it" (35). She writes, "the 'it' in 'Get it out of him' refers not just to a piece of information but to the capacity for speech itself" (49). In her book Scarry uses the case of Winnie in *Happy Days* to make her point about aging and the possibilities of "self-extension" (33). She also discusses Beckett's writing in *Resisting Representation* (New York: Oxford University Press, 1994).

27. Samuel Beckett, "Dante . . . Bruno. Vico.. Joyce," in *Our Exagmination Round his Factification for Incamination of Work in Progress* (London: Faber and Faber, 1972), 16.

28. Beckett, "Dante," 14.

29. Beckett, "Dante," 16–17.

30. Samuel Beckett, "Letter to Axel Kaun," in *Disjecta: Miscellaneous Writings and a Dramatic Fragment,* ed. Ruby Cohn (London: John Calder, 1983), 172.

31. Beckett, "Letter to Axel Kaun," 173.

32. Fritz Mauthner, *Beiträge zu einer Kritik der Sprache,* 3rd ed., 3 vols. (Hildesheim: Georg Olms Verlag, 1967).

33. Beckett's notes on Mauthner can be found in a notebook now in the possession of Trinity College and available to readers, TCD MS 10971/5. A catalog of these and other holograph notes by Beckett held in Trinity College Dublin Library is published in *Samuel Beckett Today/Aujourd'hui* 16 (2006), ed. Matthijs Engelberts and Everett Frost with Jane Maxwell.

34. For a discussion of Mauthner's relation to Beckett's writing, see Linda Ben-Zvi, "Samuel Beckett, Fritz Mauthner, and the Limits of Language," *PMLA* 95 (1980): 183–200; and Daniel Albright, *Beckett and Aesthetics* (Cambridge: Cambridge University Press, 2003).

35. Samuel Beckett, "Three Dialogues," in *Samuel Beckett: A Collection of Critical Essays,* ed. Martin Esslin (Englewood Cliffs, N.J.: Prentice-Hall, 1965), 16–22.

36. John Pilling, *Beckett before Godot* (Cambridge: Cambridge University Press, 1997), 228.

37. Although I use the word *marked* here, it is possible, in performance, to imagine Beckett's decrepits as somehow refusing "marking," by their very indeterminacy as performed by actors whose bodies become the "raw material" (Chabert, "Body in Beckett's Theatre," 23) for such indeterminacy. In this sense, the work of Peggy Phelan, in *Unmarked: The Politics of Performance* (London: Routledge, 1993) offers interesting possibilities for a reading of Beckett's late theater. See also Richard Begam, "How to Do Nothing with Words, or Waiting for Godot as Performativity," in *Modern Drama* 50.2 (Summer 2007): 138–66.

38. Connor, "Beckett's Dead Body," 101–2.

39. Samuel Beckett, *Three Novels: Molloy / Malone Dies / The Unnamable* (New York: Grove Press, 1977), 137.

40. James Knowlson, *Damned to Fame: The Life of Samuel Beckett* (London: Bloomsbury, 1996), 407, 264–65.

41. Knowlson, *Damned to Fame,* 382–83.

42. Frederick Smith, *Beckett's Eighteenth Century* (New York: Palgrave, 2002), 90.

43. Knowlson, *Damned to Fame,* 58, 609.

44. Beckett, *Three Novels,* 318.

45. Samuel Beckett, *Endgame* (New York: Grove Press, 1958), 53.

46. Samuel Beckett, *More Pricks Than Kicks* (New York: Grove Press, 1972), 41.

47. Beckett, *More Pricks Than Kicks,* 39, 47.

48. Beckett, *More Pricks Than Kicks,* 39, 47, 41, 15.

49. Pilling, *Beckett before Godot,* 230.

50. Beckett, *Collected Shorter Plays,* 1–6.

51. Samuel Beckett, *Proust* (New York: Grove Press, 1931).

52. Ruby Cohn, *Just Play* (Princeton: Princeton University Press, 1980), 145.

53. Knowlson indicates that the 1931 parody of Pierre Corneille's *Le Cid,* entitled *Le Kid,* sometimes attributed to Beckett, was the work of Beckett's Trinity College friend Georges Pelorson, Beckett supplying only the title (Knowlson, *Damned to Fame,* 123–25). See also Deirdre Bair, *Samuel Beckett: A Biography* (New York: Harcourt Brace, 1978), 126–28.

54. Knowlson, *Damned to Fame,* 536.

55. Samuel Johnson, *Rasselas,* in *Eighteenth-Century English Literature,* ed. Geoffrey Tillotson et al. (New York: Harcourt, Brace, 1969), 1031.

56. On his first trip to France, in the summer of 1926, Beckett visited the homes of Ronsard, Rabelais, Descartes, and Balzac (Knowlson, *Damned to Fame,* 64).

57. Smith, *Beckett's Eighteenth Century,* 110–31.

58. Knowlson, *Damned to Fame,* 755, n. 35.

59. Pilling, *Beckett before Godot,* 163.

60. For a discussion of Johnson's dependence on friends and associates, see Hugo Reichard, "Boswell's Johnson, the Hero Made by a Committee" *PMLA* 95 (1980): 225–33.

61. James Boswell, *Boswell's Life of Johnson,* ed. G. B. Hill, rev. L. F. Powell (London: Oxford University Press, 1934), 1:277.

62. W. Jackson Bate, *Samuel Johnson* (New York: Harcourt Brace, 1977), 357.

63. Smith, *Beckett's Eighteenth Century,* 125.

64. Bate, *Samuel Johnson,* 72, 106.

65. Smith, *Beckett's Eighteenth Century,* 114; Knowlson, *Damned to Fame,* 269.

66. One of the interesting questions that arises about Beckett's travels throughout

Germany at this time was his reactions to the growing influence of Nazism. Knowlson's summary of the diary Beckett kept has relatively few references to the tightening Nazi stranglehold on the country, save its effects on the art community. However, one comment is telling. Beckett, bemoaning his lethargy, writes, "I am always depressed and left with [a] sense of worthlessness at the beautifully applied energy of these people, the exactness of documentation, completeness of equipment . . . and authenticity of vocation" (Knowlson, *Damned to Fame*, 252).

67. Bair, *Samuel Beckett*, 253–54.

68. Smith, *Beckett's Eighteenth Century*, 113.

69. Bate, *Samuel Johnson*, 554.

70. John Wain, *Samuel Johnson* (New York: Viking Press, 1974), 355.

71. Knowlson, *Damned to Fame*, 482.

72. Ruby Cohn in *Just Play* provides the most detailed description of these notebooks and analyses of their contents. N. F. Löwe comments on them and on "Human Wishes" in "Sam's Love for Sam: Samuel Beckett, Dr. Johnson and 'Human Wishes,'" *Samuel Beckett Today/Aujourd'hui* 8 (1999): 189–203. See also Smith, *Beckett's Eighteenth Century* and Linda Ben-Zvi, *Samuel Beckett* (Boston: Twayne, 1986) and "Beckett and Johnson: Two Sams Abroad in Hamburg."

73. Cohn, *Just Play*, 158. Löwe provides the complete sentence: "Sent to hell, sir, and punished everlastingly" (Löwe, "Sam's Love for Sam," 197).

74. Cohn, *Just Play*, 159.

75. Bate, *Samuel Johnson*, 502.

76. Bate, *Samuel Johnson*, 554.

77. John Wiltshire, *Samuel Johnson in the Medical World* (Cambridge: Cambridge University Press, 1991), 210.

78. Leslie Stephen, *Samuel Johnson* (New York: Harper and Brothers, 1878), 147.

79. Cohn, *Just Play*, 159.

80. Wiltshire, *Samuel Johnson*, 210–11.

81. "Human Wishes" was published in Cohn, *Just Play*, in 1980, republished in *Disjecta*, ed. Cohn. In the latter, however, the date is erroneously given as April 14. It should read April 4, 1781, the date of Henry Thrale's death, on which Beckett chose to set his scene.

82. Beckett, "Human Wishes," 295.

83. Beckett, "Human Wishes," 300.

84. In a touch that will amuse Beckett students, it should be noted that Taylor's collected writings appear under the title *The Whole Works*.

85. Beckett, "Human Wishes," 299.

86. Beckett, "Human Wishes," 300.

87. Löwe, "Sam's Love for Sam," 193.

88. Ruby Cohn, *A Beckett Canon* (Ann Arbor: University of Michigan Press, 2001), 107.

89. Bair, *Samuel Beckett*, 255–56.

90. Cohn, *A Beckett Canon*, 106.

91. Löwe, "Sam's Love for Sam," 193.

92. Knowlson, *Damned to Fame*, 271.

93. See Cohn, *A Beckett Canon*, 85, about questions of dating the poem.

94. Samuel Beckett, *Collected Poems, 1930–1978* (London: John Calder, 1984), 29.

95. Knowlson, *Damned to Fame*, 270.

96. Anne Atik, *How It Is: A Memoir of Samuel Beckett* (London: Faber and Faber, 2001), 76–77.

97. Knowlson, *Damned to Fame,* 785.

98. Harmon, *No Author Better Served,* 25.

99. Wiltshire, *Samuel Johnson,* 13.

100. Wiltshire, *Samuel Johnson,* 23.

101. Boswell, *Boswell's Life of Johnson,* 1:463.

102. Hester Lynch (Thrale) Piozzi, *Anecdotes of Samuel Johnson,* ed. S. C. Roberts (New York: Arno Press, 1980), 52.

103. Johnson, *Rasselas,* 140.

104. Boswell, *Boswell's Life of Johnson,* 1:53.

105. Boswell, *Boswell's Life of Johnson,* 1:394.

106. Piozzi, *Anecdotes of Samuel Johnson,* 62; Smith, *Beckett's Eighteenth Century,* 126.

107. Smith, *Beckett's Eighteenth Century,* 117.

108. Samuel Beckett, *Watt* (London: John Calder, 1976), 124.

109. Beckett shifted from English to French in the middle of the story. (See Cohn, *A Beckett Canon,* 128.) The first part of the story was entitled "Suite," and was published in 1946; the entire story appeared in 1955.

110. Cohn, *A Beckett Canon,* 129.

111. Knowlson, *Damned to Fame,* 352.

112. Shenker, "Interview with Samuel Beckett," 148.

113. Beckett, *Watt,* 62.

114. See, for example, Carol Houlihan Flynn, *The Body in Swift and Defoe* (Cambridge: Cambridge University Press, 1990); Veronica Kelly and Dorothea von Müke, *Body and Text in the Eighteenth Century* (Stanford: Stanford University Press, 1994); and Wiltshire, whose book *Samuel Johnson in the Medical World* details prevailing attitudes of the period concerning the body and Johnson's contributions to the discourse.

115. Flynn, *The Body in Swift and Defoe,* 1.

116. Anna McMullan, "Virtual Subjects: Performance, Technology and the Body in Beckett's Late Theatre," *Journal of Beckett Studies* 10 (2002): 172.

117. Leslie Hill, *Beckett's Fiction: In Different Words* (Cambridge: Cambridge University Press, 1990), 117.

118. Smith, *Beckett's Eighteenth Century,* 90.

119. George Tabori, *Unterammergau oder Die guten Deutschen* [Unterammergau, or the Good Germans] (Frankfurt am Main: Suhrkamp, 1981), 202.

120. Chabert, "The Body in Beckett's Theatre," 27.

Terry Eagleton

Beckett and Nothing

In Flann O'Brien's novel *The Third Policeman,* policeman MacCruiskeen fashions with tools so tiny as to be invisible a box so small that it is, as the narrator remarks, nearly half a size smaller than ordinary invisibility. "The box I am making now," observes MacCruiskeen proudly, "is nearly as small as nothing. Box number one would hold a million of them at the same time and there would be room left for a pair of woman's horse-breeches if they were rolled up. The dear knows where it will stop and terminate." To which the narrator replies, "Such work must be very hard on the eyes."[1]

What is at stake here, one might claim, is sublimity. We usually think of the sublime as vast, perilous, shattering, ravishing, excessive, traumatic, dwarfing, exhilarating, uncontainable, overwhelming, boundless, obscure, terrifying, and enrapturing. Because it is frightful and exuberant together, it's an image, sexually speaking, of sado-masochism, or what the Lacanians might now call the obscene enjoyment of the Real; and it's thus no accident that Ireland's foremost theoretician of sublimity, Edmund Burke, is also, as far as I know, its first analyst of sadomasochism, the ambiguous mixing of pleasure and pain, in the very same text. For Burke, the Law works as well as it does because we reap secret delight from being chastened and daunted.[2] The sublime is an infinite void that turns us not outward to the starry heavens but inward to that unfathomable, unrepresentable gulf known as the self. Its ambivalence, as at once life-giving and annihilating, is a secular version of the Almighty, whose terrifyingly unconditional love threatens to shrivel us to nothing; indeed there's scarcely an aesthetic concept that isn't a displaced version of a theological one.

It was, I think, Saint Augustine who first came up with the idea of the self as a vertiginous abyss—who recognized that we are, so to speak, shot through with nothingness from one end to the other. There's an abyss at the very heart of the universe, a joker in the cosmic pack, an illegible nonentity, and its name is the human subject. And there is a vacancy at the very core of our being, for which a modern name is desire. This, for both Augustine and Aquinas, is because the self is created, which means it's a form of being that is radically contingent. The self is pure gift, with no smack of iron necessity to it at all; and in this sense it resembles God's creation as a whole, the scandal of which is that it might just as well never have come about. What we do, then, is overshadowed, hollowed out, by the perpetual possibility of its own nonbeing. The twentieth-century modernists will belatedly reinvent this sense of the pure contingency of things, Samuel Beckett not least, but now as sickening fragility and ontological anxiety rather than as gift. Gratuitousness is now less a matter of free self-giving than of absurdity.

Yet the sublime isn't just enormous. Burke reminds us that it can be microscopic too—the link between the two conditions being that they both defeat representation. I've argued elsewhere that the central trope of Irish writing in English is bathos[3]—that deflating or debunking swoop from high to low which one might expect from a society that inherits lineages of high learning but is incongruously aware of the contrast between them and the sheer dinginess of everyday colonial existence. From Stephen to Bloom, as it were. Beckett's father's dying words to him were a rousing "fight, fight, fight," followed with remarkable understatement by "What a morning!"[4] But it's not just that from the sublime to the ridiculous is a small step, rather that—like policeman MacCruiskeen's disappearing boxes—the sublime *is* the ridiculous. It's the farcically meager as much as the portentously boundless. That which slips beneath the signifier in its extreme attenuation is on speaking terms with the kind of Kantian immensity that beggars the imagination; indeed it was Swift who remarked in *A Tale of a Tub* on how near the frontiers of height and depth border on each other.[5] Samuel Beckett's degree-zero writing, which is as thin as is compatible with being just perceptible, and which shares with Swift a savage delight in diminishment, is sublime in just this sense. It seems continually surprised to find itself doing anything as importunate as actually existing, and manifests a Protestant animus against frippery and excess (though not at all against *ritual*).

The greatest of Irish medieval philosophers, John Scottus Eriugena, of the ninth-century Carolingian renaissance, was a connoisseur of negativity. He formed the nucleus of a learned Irish coterie at the court of Charles the Bald, a figure perhaps soon to be reincarnated on the throne of England. Renowned for his Hibernian eloquence and erudition, Eriugena was evidently also a bit of a joker, though his end was grim enough—stabbed to death by a group of his students with their stiles or sharp pens: a warning to all lecturers to keep it lively. Deeply marked by the negative theology of Pseudo-Dionysus, Eriugena grasped the fact that God is not any kind of megabeing, indeed is no kind of being or entity at all, and certainly not a person in the sense that Al Gore is arguably a person, but an abyss of pure emptiness; and this (since subjectivity is itself a kind of void or a lack of being) is what it means to say that God is a person or subject.

Long before Nietzsche and Derrida, Eriugena saw the world as an ungrounded play of self-delighting difference, an infinity of partial perspectives or anarchy of unbridled nonidentity. Creation is a great spiral of self-referential signs with a void at its center, rather like Joyce's *Ulysses*. Eriugena was an early deconstructor of Augustinian ontology, a kind of Romantic Idealist *avant la lettre* with his notion of a nonlinear, utterly gratuitous world in which an infinite play of signifiers communicates ceaselessly with itself. Subjectivity, the image of God within us, is endlessly elusive, so that, as he comments, we have perfect self-knowledge when we don't know who we are. The I for Scottus Eriugena is also a Not-I—and this Beckettian title, incidentally, is anticipated by that most exotically depleted and decentered of all Irish subjects, James Clarence Mangan, who speaks in one of his prose writings of the self as a *Nicht-ich,* a Not-I, a non-ego,[6] a view he attributes with flamboyant inaccuracy to Immanuel Kant.

God is thus entirely unrepresentable, utterly beyond cognition or comprehension. As Pseudo-Dionysus observes of this "infinity beyond being" with Beckettian brevity in *The Divine Names:* "He was not. He will not be. He did not come to be. He is not in the midst of becoming. He will not come to be. No. He is not."[7] It isn't all that far from such negative theology to Berkeley's celebrated comment that for the Irish, something and nothing are near allied,[8] where I suppose something and nothing, or identity and nonidentity, can be translated among other things into Britain and Ireland. Berkeley's clerical colleague Archbishop King wrote that "all finite beings partake of nothing, and are nothing beyond their bounds."[9] This tradition of Irish negativity, which deserves a lot more investigation than I'm giving it here, has culminated in our own day in an impressive work by the Irish philosopher Conor Cunningham entitled *Genealogy of Nihilism.*[10]

Eriugena's views are of course theologically perfectly proper, and will lead straight to Aquinas's notion of theological language as analogical, that's to say as authentic only when it doesn't really have a clue what it's on about. Only in the glare created by its implosion upon itself can theology illuminate something of its elusive object, rather like the self-canceling modernist work of art. There can be no graven images of God, because the only image of God is human beings; and to say that they are God's creations is to say that human subjectivity is as elusive and non-self-identical as he is—which is to say, in a word, *free*.

Any culture in which theology plays a dominant role, then, is bound to harbor a suspicion of representationalism. And this is one clear philosophical distinction over the centuries between the Irish and the English, one that caused Berkeley to inscribe in his copy of Locke, for whom language is indeed representational, his famous "We Irish do not think so," a gesture that delighted the heart of W. B. Yeats.[11] In a striking anticipation of the later Wittgenstein, Berkeley sees that language is not a matter of representing mental images—what mental image does "perhaps" or "cor blimey" represent?—and substitutes for this realist perspective a performative or pragmatic one. Swift sends up linguistic representation in his portrayal of the communicative habits of the Laputans, a kind of ne plus ultra of empiricism. Edmund Burke's insistence on the necessary fuzziness, opacity, and indeterminacy of poetic language, its suggestive rather than pictorial status, is another instance of this case.

Indeed, one might claim that eighteenth-century Irish theology in general elevates the conative over the cognitive, the rhetorical over the real, and this because the object of such discourse is a sheer nothingness to which no signifier could conceivably be equal. Eighteenth-century Dublin divines like Peter Browne, Edward Synge, and William King emphasize the fraught relations between image and object, and at the center of this semiotic crisis lies our knowledge or nonknowledge of God.[12] If you allow an empiricist gap between image and thing, you open up a space in which the thin end of skepticism may be inserted; so Berkeley will close this gap by assimilating the world itself to signs, seeing objects themselves as the articulate language of the Almighty.[13] Yet since God is that groundless nonentity beyond all imagining, this means that the world itself, not least our perceptions and sensations, is made out of nothing, ridden with negativity, like some Einsteinian universe that is solid and stable only to the unregenerate eye.

Theological discourse is thus performative rather than representational, fostering certain appropriate attitudes in us such as deference or awe, rather than proffering accurate descriptions. This performative theory of language lingers on at least as late as Wilde's rejection of artistic

reflectionism, Yeats's mind-fashioned universe, and Beckett's antiex-
pressive aesthetics. (Yeats's poetry pivots on grandly performative gestures: summoning, blessing, invoking, mourning, cursing, commemo-
rating, and the like.) In 1916, a piece of literary rhetoric ushers a new
nation into existence.[14] In sacramental fashion, the sign participates in
what it denotes; but as what it denotes becomes in modernity more and
more meager, fractured, and obscure, this becomes pretty well equivalent to claiming that what the sign denotes is itself. For modernism, it is
by the sign putting itself into question, flaunting its own nothingness or
non-self-identity, that its problematic relation to the real can be most
faithfully portrayed.

Speaking of spiraling constellations of self-referential signs with a
void at their center, I suppose there could be worse descriptions than
that of one of the finest of all Irish antinovels, *Tristram Shandy*—a cock-
and-bull story or tale about nothing, or rather perhaps a tale of a *missing*
cock, of an absent or castrated phallus or transcendental signifier, certainly in the case of the mutilated or semi-impotent Toby, Tristram, and
Walter. This most extraordinarily Lacanian of literary texts, one that is all
about that grievous lack of being which is the linguistic animal, was produced by a man who remarked that there was no harm in nothing, considering what worse things there are in the world.[15]

If there's an oddly Freudian resonance to that remark, it's because
nothing for Freud is what *keeps* us from harm, from the vindictive fury
of the death drive. Battered by the aggression of the superego, the frenzied demands of the id and the ravages of the reality principle, the poor
old pitiable ego seeks to revert to the nothingness from which it arose, a
process of reversion which is that long disease or chronic disorder
known as life. Nothing is less vulnerable than nothing, and by playing
dead you can always hope to avoid being killed. To be hollowed out like
Beckettian man, adrift between life and death, means aspiring to shed
guilt, sinfulness, and political terror by the desperate device of shedding
subjectivity itself, in a world where agency means aggressivity, and sub-
jecthood itself is now a nameless crime or primordial transgression. To
jettison memory is to be free of history. There is much of this in Arthur
Schopenhauer, as Beckett was keenly aware, and Schopenhauer's voracious Will is certainly the origin of Freud's implacable death drive or
Thanatos.

For Beckett's eviscerated figures, of course, death would be far too
definitive, too grandiose an event to be coped with; even suicide requires more agency than they are capable of mustering. You have to

have some sense of identity in order to abandon it. Death would risk being—that most portentously hyperbolic, ideological thing of all—*tragic*. In such a situation, these men and women would only fluff their lines or bungle their big moment. Anyway, how can there be tragedy in a world as utterly indeterminate as this? An indeterminate universe must logically leave room for hope. If there are no absolutes, simply a truth-shaped hole at the center of things, then there is absolutely no assurance that Godot will not arrive, is not always-already arriving. If reality is provisional, then this must apply to our knowledge of it as well. Like Freud and Adorno, Beckett knew that the sober, bleak-eyed realists serve the cause of human emancipation more faithfully than the bright-eyed utopians, bearing witness as they do to a suffering so unremitting that it cries out for redemption. The problem is that there is no redemption in Beckett, but that his world looks like the sort of place where the term still has meaning. Modernism is still tormented by the memory of such things. We are not yet in a postmodern age too young even to remember that there was once, so the rumor has it, a thing called truth, meaning, and reality, and which simply admonishes us not to scratch where it doesn't itch.

Simply to exist, to differentiate oneself by a hair's breath from nothing, to crawl forward an inch or two in the mud, to preserve that paltry surplus over the inanimate that some might laughingly call life, is in Beckett's world a sweated labor of Herculean achievement. We are dealing here with a chronic case of colonial *perversity*—with an artist who sets himself the self-punitive task of conjuring a whole evening's entertainment out of the most calculatedly exiguous of materials—who in quasi-structuralist fashion spins out his impoverished stuff by combining these few scraps and leavings into ever more ingeniously pointless permutations, so that the rift between the elaborate pedantry of form and the parsimoniousness of content becomes comically, grotesquely evident. The reader or spectator is packed off poorer but more honest.

I'm tempted to see this pedantry both as a sort of hardheaded Protestant rationalism (one very rare in Irish culture, where there's no major rationalism, but that's another essay), but also perhaps as a mad caricature of a very Irish scholasticism, which like some Lévi-Straussian myth is all category and scarcely any substance. What's surely so distinctive about Beckett is the meticulous exactness with which he weaves the wind, his crazedly clear-minded attempt to eff the ineffable, the monkish scrupulousness with which he plucks ever more slender nuances from what seems mere shapelessness. One thinks of Swift's lunatic projectors or Sterne's mad rationalist Walter Shandy. If this is vacancy, it is one that is exquisitely sculpted. Like Yeats's magic, it is at once completely off the wall and lucidly systematized. As so often in Anglo-Irish writing, the author's triumph over the world's importunity is known as form.

We know that Beckett was interested in Democritus's theory that nothing is more real than nothing. Nothing is attractive not only because it is blessedly invulnerable but because it is entirely unblemished. There is, to be sure, a paradox here: the Apollonian seeks perfection, but since nothing is more perfect than nothing, it rejoins the very Dionysian void that it seeks to fend off. Thomas Mann's *Death in Venice* is among other things about this irony of Eros and Thanatos. From the viewpoint of a certain nihilistic austerity, creation and the Fall are simultaneous events, since the lapse from pure nothingness is known as matter. As Danton cries in Georg Buchner's drama *Danton's Death,* "Nothingness has killed itself, and creation is its wound."[16] One is reminded of the *symboliste* notion of the pure poem as a blank sheet of paper: for modernism, language is the stuff that binds your poem to a degraded modernity, the nexus or shared medium between the two; and this is why language must be purged, warped, dislocated, slimmed down, cut loose, tightened up, for fear it proves the medium of conveying the virus of untruth and ideology into the only phenomenon left—art—that seeks to be inoculated from it.

In this sense, nothingness is a profoundly political notion. It is an implicit critique of a social order obscenely bulging with matter. In Beckett's case, of course, it has a more particular political resonance as well, as a riposte to what he takes to be the rhetorical flatulence of nationalism, whether Irish or otherwise. Yet it isn't hard to detect a subliminal memory of famished Ireland in those starved, stagnant landscapes, with its disaffected masses waiting listlessly on a redemption that never quite comes. Perhaps there's a particular irony in this respect in the name Vladimir. Negativity is the way Beckett, whose art is profoundly antifascist without needing to speak of the Nazis, maintains a secret pact with failure and finitude, of which the prime signifier is the material body; and without such a pact no political order will endure for very long. The fact that so boldly avant-garde an art is also so scant, modest, humdrum, and quotidian is one of the most striking ironies of his work, as it is of Joyce's. If it is an art after Auschwitz, it is that because it keeps faith with silence and terror by paring itself almost to vanishing point. The world will not of course be destroyed by bleak-eyed cynics and hardheaded pragmatists. It will be annihilated by starry-eyed vision-aries stuffed with hope and prating of freedom and democracy. It is hubris we have to fear, not nihilism—though as I've argued in a recent book, *Holy Terror*,[17] the two are in some ways sides of the same coin. When the ancient Greeks heard this Faustian talk of infinite striving and sublime potential they trembled and looked fearfully to the skies, aware that such blasphemous overreaching would have its comeuppance. And it is from the skies that the comeuppance has come.

NOTES

1. Flann O'Brien, *The Third Policeman* (London: MacGibbon and Kee, 1967; reprinted London: Paladin, 1993), 76–77.

2. Edmund Burke, *A Philosophical Inquiry into the Origin of Our Idea of the Sublime and the Beautiful* (1757), ed. James T. Boulton (London: Routledge and Kegan Paul, 1958).

3. See Terry Eagleton, *Crazy John and the Bishop and Other Essays on Irish Culture* (Cork: Cork University Press in association with Field Day, 1998), 25.

4. James Knowlson, *Damned to Fame: The Life of Samuel Beckett* (London: Bloomsbury, 1996), 170.

5. Jonathan Swift, *A Tale of a Tub & Other Works,* ed. Angus Ross and David Woolley (Oxford: Oxford University Press, 1986), 76.

6. *The Prose Writings of James Clarence Mangan,* ed. D. J. O'Donoghue (Dublin: O'Donoghue and Co.; London: A. H. Bullen, 1904), 285. The concept of the *nicht-ich* was posited by Johann Gottlieb Fichte (1762–1814), a disciple of Kant.

7. Pseudo-Dionysus, *The Complete Works,* trans. Colm Luibheid (New York: Paulist Press, 1987), 98.

8. George Berkeley, *Philosophical Commentaries* (London: Nelson, 1944), 124.

9. William King, *Sermon on Predestination* (1709), ed. Andrew Carpenter (Dublin: Cadenus Press, 1976).

10. Conor Cunningham, *Genealogy of Nihilism* (London: Routledge, 2002).

11. W. B. Yeats, *Explorations* (London: Macmillan, 1962), 333.

12. See David Berman, "The Irish Counter-Enlightenment," in *The Irish Mind: Exploring Intellectual Traditions,* ed. Richard Kearney (Dublin: Wolfhound Press, 1985), 119–40.

13. *The Works of George Berkeley DD,* ed. Alexander Campbell Fraser (Oxford: Oxford University Press, 1871), 98.

14. W. B. Yeats, "Easter 1916."

15. Laurence Sterne, *Tristram Shandy,* vol. 9, chap. 25.

16. Georg Buchner, *Danton's Death: A Play in Four Acts,* trans. Stephen Spender and Goronwy Rees (London: Faber and Faber, 1939), 3.7.43.

17. Terry Eagleton, *Holy Terror* (Oxford: Oxford University Press, 2005).

Terence Brown

Yeats and Beckett: The Ghosts in the Machines

All the dead voices

—Estragon in *Waiting for Godot*

The twentieth century was the first full century in human experience in which the species had both aural and visual records of the individual person. This dual inheritance began of course in the nineteenth century when toward its end the photographic record, which had since earlier in the century increased the possibilities of portraiture, was joined by the crackling recording machines that allow us a dim sense of how, for instance, Alfred Lord Tennyson actually sounded in his last years. Before this, all is silence. We may have portraits and photographs of the luminaries of the past, but of the distinctive timbre of their voices we have not the slightest idea. So when we speak of the "voice" of a poet from before the end of the nineteenth century we are speaking about a tone that characterizes the poetry itself, not the living resonance of the actual speech organ. From the twentieth we have of course that sense of poetic "voice," but also the tape recordings, the films, the videos, the DVDs and downloads that allow the dead their say in a way denied to the dying generations that preceded them. And not only the mighty dead have this strange power in our time, but each one of us can leave aural traces to accompany the family photo album—a talking will, a last message, the camcorder record of life's occasions.

Yet this quite new human capacity, made available by machinery of one kind or another, in Western culture has coexisted, paradoxically, with a disturbing sense that the human person is an unstable phenomenon, lacking substance, integral being. The ready availability of human record in so many diverse forms (photograph, film, radio and TV broadcast, recorded telephone message, tape recordings, e-mail, text messages, downloaded Internet material) has been experienced as a dispersal of subjectivity rather than its confirmation, so that selfhood, the very ground of our being as persons in the world, has come to seem a fragile thing, phantasmal, lost amid performative acts and texts made possible by technology. Inasmuch as the human self could be allowed any "real existence" in all of this it would be as a ghost in the machines, a quick of being lurking in the electronic ether, in the nondimension of cyberspace. To discover the bedrock of individual identity in the media that represent it in so many forms can begin, therefore, to seem an occult thing, the task of a medium indeed. A medium amid the media.

W. B. Yeats was of course famously concerned with ghosts. Indeed, one recent biographical study was provocatively titled *George's Ghosts,*[1] highlighting that a turning point of the poet's life was that moment on his honeymoon with his new bride Georgie in the autumn of 1917, when her automatic writing began to bring him a cornucopia of messages from the spirit world. This extraordinary turn of affairs that led to five and more years of intensive spiritualist investigation was not, however, an anomaly in Yeats's mental life, but a culmination. For since his late teens the poet had been fascinated by occult phenomena, and from about 1909 he had been attending seances regularly in Dublin, London, Paris, even the United States when on tour there, in hopes of finding an answer to the question that he had asked so dramatically and so poignantly in his poem "The Cold Heaven": "Ah! when the ghost begins to quicken, / Confusion of the death-bed over, is it sent / Out naked on the roads, as the books say, and stricken, / By the injustice of the skies for punishment?"[2] In other words, does the self survive death intact, even if in its naked vulnerability it must then face the challenge of personal judgement?

Curiously enough, machines and technology played their own part in the spiritualist experimentalism of late Victorian and Edwardian mediumship in which Yeats immersed himself. The poet who had once, as a very young man, told a famous Irish medium Eileen Garrett, in her girlhood, that he had invented a spool-like gadget with threads and corks, which when attached to a windowsill would summon fairy music from the vasty deeps, was a habitué of a world of spirit photos, planchettes for automatic writing, speaking trumpets, ectoplasmic cabinets, and other mechanical paraphernalia that might allow the spirits to communicate with mortal men and women. One of the most surprising communications that he received through the power of a medium before the flood of his wife's revelations, involved a primitive machine. At a séance in 1912 in London a voice came through, speaking from a long tin trumpet that the American medium always kept with her during her work. This was Leo Africanus, the writer and explorer, who possessed,

Yeats noticed, "a strong Irish accent" that one participant at the sitting thought was like enough to Yeats's own. This spirit came through repetitively at subsequent séances and encouraged Yeats to write a dialogue in which he, the spirit, would obligingly participate. And the same Leo was involved in the most preposterous of Yeats's flirtations with machinery. For a time in 1917 he became interested in the spiritualist experiments of a David Wilson of St Leonard's-on-sea. Wilson had invented a talking Homunculus or Metallic Medium. The machine apparently could answer questions addressed to it. Yeats consulted this coastal oracle several times. On one occasion when he went to Wilson's house to inspect the machine, it began to talk "about 11 incoherent words from an alleged 'Leo' who presently said he did not know who he was & that he might be Yeats. When I said I was 'Yeats'. [*sic*] He said 'no Yeats has gone.'"[3] Later Yeats bent over the machine "arm on a table to speak mentally to it." The only response was "a curious trembling or pulsing under [his] arm."[4] When Yeats "told pulsing to stop"[5] the apparatus did so and refused to perform again.

At the same time as Yeats's haunting transaction with Leo was being established, the poet was also at work with a young English girl named Elizabeth Radcliffe in the production of automatic script. Her revelations seemed for a time to offer "irrefutable proof that the messages she received were not the product of telepathy or unconscious memory but came from a supernatural source."[6] And they seemed to establish the survival after death of an intact selfhood, a soul. Yet in all this trafficking with spirits Yeats was troubled by two things. First, as he admitted at the end of his lengthy exchange with the ghost of Africanus, he was "not convinced that in this letter there is one sentence that" had "come from beyond [his] own imagination."[7] And second, he was aware as he confessed at the end of a document he prepared on the Radcliffe case, which seemed to prove after death survival, that "Another hypothesis is possible. Secondary & tertiary personalities once formed may act independently of the medium, have ideoplastic power & pick the minds of distant people & so speak in tongues unknown to all present. If we can imagine these artificial beings surviving the medium we can account for haunted houses & most of the facts of spiritism."[8] In this he was coming close to the conclusion reached indeed by Eileen Garrett on her own powers, when she averred that the "controls" of mediumship are "principals of the sub-conscious"[9] and the spirits themselves "entities . . . formed from spiritual and emotional needs of the persons involved."[10] (Her book is titled *Many Voices: The Autobiography of a Medium*.) And in so doing he was encountering a crucial fact about spiritualism and the occultist movement in general that so preoccupied him. Their altered states of consciousness, their moments of mediumistic possession, challenged the very basis of individual identity. As Alex Owen, a historian of the subject, astutely comments, mediumship "helps to lay bare the paucity of an analysis based on the often unacknowledged notion of the unified subject. Mediumship, because it so often involved the disclosure of a multivalent and disruptive consciousness, revealed the inconsistency, heterogeneity, and precariousness of human identity."[11]

So Yeats among the spirit mediums with their photographs of ectoplasmic apparitions and of spirit auras (a photograph exists of Yeats himself with his shadowy daimon as a face floating eerily rightward from the top of his skull) and their ramshackle machines was encountering not the evidence of personal survival he hoped to discover but indications that selfhood itself was an echo chamber of conflicting voices. The machines of spiritualism were not rescuing voices from the vast silence of the human past (out of which Leo Africanus seemed to come), but revealing, almost, it might seem, in anticipation of the ensuing century, what machines would do to the concept and experience of a unified human subjectivity.

An aspect of Samuel Beckett's great achievement as an artist that I want to highlight in this essay is that he was wonderfully alert to how modern media with their machines were altering the ways in which human beings would experience selfhood in a century that allowed so various and so new representations of the human subject. More contentiously and speculatively, I want to suggest, too, that whereas Yeats at the last feared he had found no secure individual human identity in what he despairingly symbolized as "the foul rag-and-bone shop of the heart," Beckett hints at an irreducible ghostlike presence of the human in his late works for television, which on the face of it suggest that selfhood is an illusion, wistfully clung to in defiance of the dark. There are ironies involved here. The invincibly religious, if heterodox Yeats, in his long quest, finds only detritus when he contemplates in "The Circus Animal's Desertion" the source of all the self's contradictory performances. Beckett, the atheist, if such he truly is, the avowed disbeliever, finds in some of his late works, it may be, a vital ghost in the machine—that ghost being consciousness as ineluctable suffering.

There is no record as far as I know of Beckett ever attending a séance or of having any truck with spiritualism's summoning of all the dead voices. Curiously, however, at the point in his life when he came closest to the mixture of pseudoscience, mythology, and occultism that is psychoanalytic theory he also spent time in the company of a famous medium. For in the 1930s when he attended the Tavistock Institute in London to undergo psychotherapy at the hands of Wilfred Ruprecht Bion, his friend the poet and art historian Thomas MacGreevy was lodging in a house owned by one Hester Dowden at 15 Cheyne Walk Gardens. Dowden was a famous spiritualist, described by her biographer Edward Bentley as "medium and psychic investigator." Among her claims to fame had been that the spirit of Sir Hugh Lane came through to her before news broke of the sinking of the *Lusitania*. Unfortunately she had been unable to help in the matter of the disputed codicil to his will. Beckett, who lived nearby his friend MacGreevy, occasionally played duets with Dowden on her grand piano and enjoyed the musical evenings she arranged. However, as Knowlson reports in his biography of Beckett, he was repelled by Dowden's spiritualism: "he got 'terribly tired of all the psychic evidence [and] wonder [*sic*] what it has to [do] with the psyche as I experience that old bastard.'"[12] Had he cared to enquire, at a time when, under Bion's guidance, he was exploring his own dream-life, he might have learned that most serious spiritualists and psychic investigators were troubled, as Yeats had certainly been, about the possibility that mediumship merely unlocked the unconscious mind when it thought it had penetrated more deeply into the silence.

In the cultural context I am evoking in this essay, it can be suggested that something of the atmospherics of the séance pervades Beckett's play of 1958 *Krapp's Last Tape,* in which the dramatist most brilliantly exploited the strange power electronic tape has bequeathed to humanity to record the human voice. Indeed Yeats insisting to that Metallic Medium in St Leonards-on-sea, that he is Yeats and has not left, Yeats bending over the machine, has its odd echo as an image in the mind in the stage spectacle of Krapp crouched over his tape recorder to catch the voice of his dead selves.

Krapp's Last Tape is of course only one of Beckett's works that actually makes a specific machine part of the cast, as it were. There are a good few others, as well as plays that draw attention to how technology is being exploited to make them possible: *Play,* where a spotlight functions as a kind of interrogator; *Film,* where, as Stanley Gontarski has it, "part of the self is represented by the camera and so the machine itself is drawn into the perceptual frame, although like Godot it never physically appears";[13] *Eh Joe,* where the TV camera interrogates as the spotlight had done in *Play,* and *A Piece of Monologue,* where an electric standard lamp, skull-sized, a white globe, begins to fail and then goes out, as a single speaker ponders:

> The dead and gone. The dying and the going. From the word go. The word begone. Such as the light going now. Beginning to go. In the room. Where else? Unnoticed by him staring beyond. The globe alone. Not the other. The unaccountable. From nowhere. On all sides nowhere. Unutterably faint. The globe alone. Alone gone.[14]

Then there is the TV piece *Ghost Trio,* which like *Krapp's Last Tape* exploits a tape recorder as a participant in the action, but it is also a work, like the radio play *All That Fall,* that signals self-referentially to the technology-generated medium by which it is being brought into existence. *Ghost Trio* begins tantalizingly with a fade up to general view on screen with a female voice-over repeating, as if a tape had malfunctioned: "Good evening. Mine is a faint voice. Kindly tune accordingly. [*Pause.*] Good evening. Mine is a faint voice. Kindly tune accordingly."[15] And in *All That Fall* the human voices that ape animal sounds in the original BBC production of 1957, highlighted the use of mechanically produced sound effects in the play, though Beckett would have preferred, Clas Zilliacus informs us, "natural sounds; their brevity and incongruousness would [have been] enough to keep conventional realism at a distance."[16] Sound effects suggest the noise of a bicycle bell, a motor engine, the arrival of the mail train, the eerie wail of wind, and the ponderous, rhythmically mesmeric dragging of footsteps (the experiments in sound production for this play at the BBC, as Zilliacus again reports, "started the era of radiophonic drama in Britain"; the radiophonic workshop was founded in 1958, the year after the broadcast of *All That Fall.*)[17] And as if to highlight that this is a work of an era of mechanical production and reproduction, the play is framed by the playing on a gramophone of a piece of music, Schubert's "Death and the Maiden." "All day," observes Maddy Rooney, "the same old record. . . . She must be a very old woman now."[18] In *Rough for Radio I* there is even the use of what seems to be some kind of radio set to a channel that delivers music and another that delivers voice. This piece also allows us to hear a telephone being answered and one side of a brief conversation (an odd-enough radio moment when we image the existence of someone at the other end of the line, who is doubly not there, a fiction within a fiction).

It is notable that in each of these machine plays, as I shall call them, the self is forced to occupy a zone of being that relates it to the machine, as unitary, originary human subjectivity itself is cast in radical doubt. In *Play,* bursts of rapid, essentially toneless utterance are wrested from three figures in their urns by the relentless, peremptory spotlight, which Beckett himself compared to the sudden activity of a hand-driven lawnmower. In this work dialogue as conventionally understood on stage has died, and the three figures are reduced to acts of repetitive utterance as if they are themselves "switched on" immediately when the light fixes on them. Beckett in the directions is insistent on that mechanical sense of immediacy. It is by the stream of particles and wave field of electric light itself that the three figures are "provoked" (Beckett's word) into their less than fully human speech that scarcely releases them from the dehumanized condition of their existence, with "faces so lost to age and aspect as to seem almost part of the urns."[19] So it is as if the dead urns speak, provoked by the sudden demand of the spotlight. Indeed the spotlight is the most alive thing in a theatrical space Beckett insisted must include the single light itself, not "situated outside the ideal space (stage) occupied by its victims."[20] Billie Whitelaw, who acted in one production, compared its insistence as participant in the piece as an "instrument of torture."[21] Similarly in *Film* the self is reduced in significance and made to seem mechanically producible, since self-consciousness—the self contemplating the self in perplexity and perhaps in awe—is represented by the camera as experienced presence, in a work that is based on Berkeleyan conundrums about being and perception. In *A Piece of Monologue* the references by the speaker to lamps being lit and faded draws the audience's attention to the standard lamp on stage that fades out in the last thirty seconds of the monologue. Who in fact is speaking? Is it the fading "skull-sized white globe" or the ghostly figure "white hair white nightgown"? Is death merely the dying electrical charge in a standard lamp, however lyrically the power fails? In *Ghost Trio* emotion itself seems a mechanically produced thing. For in that piece for television the voice-over at the outset introduces itself as a mechanical phenomenon and the image on the screen as a composition ("Keep that sound down," it instructs the viewer and auditor, "Now look closer").[22] Part 2 of the Trio offers a set of actions, which is then repeated with additions in part 3. Here the music that has been heard faintly as a kind of accompaniment to the piece (Beethoven's Fifth Piano Trio, known as *The Ghost*) now evidently has its source in the tape cassette the solitary old man on screen clutches to himself. The emotion he feels as he hopes for a meeting with someone who does not materialize, is part of a mechanical

world of production, repeats, and camera-generated images. At the end
the directorial instructions read: "With growing music move in slowly
to close-up of head bowed right down over cassette now held in arms
and invisible. Hold till end of Largo."[23] Man and machine, emotion and
revolving tape have become one. In *Rough for Radio I* a woman visits a
man who lives alone with that strange machine which delivers at the
turn of a knob both voice and music. The woman can scarcely believe
it's not "live," the word referring both to biological and electrical energy
and "real time" broadcasting. At the end the man is convinced that voice
and music are becoming one. Something is ending. He shouts down the
telephone when the human voice and the mechanically produced music
become one in a machine. He is told by a nurse that the doctor will not
be coming since he is required at two confinements, one a breech birth,
an image of unwillingness to enter human life that has become indistin-
guishable from the life of machines.

In Beckett's machine plays, man and machine share, therefore, the
same order of being. The terrible consequence of this is that the human
self, for all our ability to record our voices and images, begins to seem
insubstantial, ghostly, lacking any firm ground upon which to stand in
knowledge of the self. A ghost in the machines. It seems as problematic
an entity as those ghosts of the dead the spiritualists, among them the
poet Yeats, sought to summon at their séances, with their suspect paraphernalia. Yeats at his séances was uncertain whether the ghosts that
were summoned were merely inchoate aspects of his own unconscious.
All that Krapp can do as he listens on his tape recorder to the "voices"
of his past selves is to sense the contrast between his current self and his
earlier self, as he mockingly avers: "Just been listening to that stupid bastard I took myself for thirty years ago, hard to believe I was ever as bad
as that. Thank God that's all done with anyway."[24] He cannot, however,
gain access to any essential selfhood, no more than Yeats could be as-
sured that at St Leonard's-on-sea he was contacting himself in a former
incarnation. Nor can he apprehend that what he is committing to tape
in his sixty-ninth year is no more a fully realized selfhood that he could
subsequently identify as his essential self, than that in any of the tapes he
might have chosen to play. It is just another recording, to be recorded in
his ledger. Selfhood becomes the equivalent of a representational montage, mechanically produced and reproduced, endlessly deferring the
moment when self might be fixed in some final definition of itself. On
stage the contrast with the kinds of definitional fixity that print culture
seemed to offer in the past and the near random permutations of identity

electronic media can generate (on tape the voice says, "Just been listening to an old year, passages at random. I did not check in the book"),[25] is imaged by the written ledger, with its ordered dates and records and the dictionary with its precise entries on a word like *viduity*.

The stage moment in which Krapp looks up that word in his dictionary is an especially telling one. He has been listening to his voice recounting an earlier occasion when he had been exploring the contents of old tapes. Krapp present joins in the laughter of Krapp past as if they were one and the same person. They are not. He stops the machine on the phrase "when I look." He broods, refreshes himself offstage from his bottle, slipping out of the light into the dark that surrounds this play, and he then restarts the machine that runs on sequentially "back on the year which is gone" to arrive at the word *viduity*. Krapp stops the tape, winds it back a little and then fetches the dictionary, reading out the elaborate definition with its formal description of a constant condition: "State—or condition—of being or remaining—a widow—or widower."[26] "Being or remaining," Krapp reflects quizzically, as if he cannot quite grasp a distinction that would have been meat and drink to his philosophic mind in the past. He restarts the machine, which because he has rewound the tape somewhat, does not as before, follow sequentially, but breaks into a passage where on a park bench he awaited the sign of his mother's death when a blind went down in a window. The impression is of the senile mind jolting incoherently from recollection to recollection, suffering obviously from memory lapses. A word once used with bold self-confidence has no current meaning, and a dictionary definition seems troublingly opaque. The interruptions in the tape, the back-and-forward trawling through its contents suggest ruptures in selfhood itself. Consciousness is a set of tapes that Krapp finds increasingly difficult to run in meaningful sequence as he winds the tape back and forward, without recourse to his neatly kept rational ledger. At one point Krapp sweeps the ledger and the boxes, which hold his collection, to the ground in an image of consciousness disordered. Increasingly emotional, the banana- and drink-addicted old man seeks to suppress memories the machine provokes, with which he cannot deal. As the play ends, it is difficult to know who Krapp in fact is. Is he the voice on the tape declaring, "Perhaps my best years are gone. When there was a chance of happiness. But I wouldn't want them back. Not with the fire in me now. No I wouldn't want them back."[27] Or is he the old wearish man, motionless, staring before him, transfixed by his memory of a love affair, as the tape runs silently on.

A similar sense that consciousness functions like a machine and that the human subject has the machine's mechanical properties pervades Beckett's television play *Eh Joe* with similar problems raised for the notion of the self as a source of being, knowable by the self. In this work a man is seen on screen, sitting on a bed, moving about a room, opening a door and shutting it, opening a cupboard and shutting it, and performing anxiously other habitual actions. Beckett then instructs the director: "After this opening pursuit, between first and final close-up of face, camera has nine slight moves in towards face, say four inches each time."[28] In between these nine camera moves are ten paragraphs of a female voice-over. The camera only moves in when the voice has stopped for an extended pause. Does the camera move stimulate a new wave of speech? Or does the voice, intensifying its accusation that Joe has treated all his women disgracefully and driven one to suicide, pull the camera closer and closer to register Joe's increasing distress. The voice-over is obviously a voice Joe is hearing in his head (that familiar cliché of television technique, where voice-over is reckoned, where one figure is concerned, to be the expression of subjectivity). She is one of his former lovers, who for some reason Joe chooses to make his accuser, so that he can strangle her voice in his mind (he calls this process "mental thuggee"), thereby ridding himself of guilt. So he imagines her in possession of the details of the suicide's last night, of the woman evoked as "the green one." For it cannot be imagined that the woman who speaks in this play was actually present to witness the terrible events that she inflicts in her monologue on Joe. So the voice is understood to be a product of Joe's subjectivity, chosen by him since, if he can destroy it in "mental thugee," he can perhaps destroy any voice, even the judgmental voice of God to whom his former lover is made to refer. But the camera with its deliberate moves does not seem simply a tool to represent this psychological state of feeling about a seducer's emotional life, but a mechanism with a peculiar life of its own. It has its own time rules, carefully laid out in the directions: "Camera does not move between paragraphs till clear that pause (say three seconds) longer than between phrases. Then four inches in say four seconds when movement stopped by voice resuming."[29] There are time gaps between the paragraphs of about seven seconds, "i.e. three before camera starts to advance and four for advance before it is stopped by voice resuming."[30] And the voice itself is to observe rules: "Low, distinct, little colour, absolutely steady rhythm, slightly slower than normal. Between phrases a beat of one second at least."[31] (In the Jackie MacGowran version of the piece the voice of Sîan Phillips "was picked up by a long, slim microphone almost in her mouth, high and low frequencies were cut off. This resulted in a kind of posthumous vocal colourlessness, as suggested by the author's directions.")[32] The effect of all this is to make what Joe seems to experience as subjectivity and the kind of controlling involvement in his own thought processes he believes he possesses, appear as mechanical as his anxiety-induced movements about his room, with which the piece had begun (when Beckett is insistent we see "Joe full length in frame throughout," entirely apprehended by the camera/machine, before we hear the voice of his subjectivity).

Oddly however, it is in Beckett's plays for television, which are so manifestly mechanical productions—deploying camera, lighting, electronically broadcast images on a box screen—that the human self begins to seem more than simply a set of performative acts made available through technology. The minimalism of the production values may have something to do with this. Beckett works essentially in black and white (with telling shades of gray). *Eh Joe,* of course, dates from a pre-color era, but of the later pieces for television only the first version of *Quad* uses a rather muted color (and in its second version this was rendered in black and white). The many opportunities for visual pleasure TV usually affords, what might be termed the erotics of the screen—montage effects, cross-fades, vivid color sequences, tricksy camera angles—are eschewed for intense concentration on a few fairly simple techniques. We have a figure alone in a room, a voice-over, camera movements, in *Ghost Trio* a faint strain of music and in . . . *but the clouds* . . . (first broadcast 1977) an image of a woman's face that fades in and out. In the flood of televisual imagery that is now the context in which we watch these late Beckett works, they possess a mysterious austerity, as if the artist is intent on making us aware of the medium in which he is working, as he employs the TV screen as a flat plane upon which he can dispose his images with accompanying sound. Yet this highly self-referential austerity of practice has the paradoxical effect of endowing these works with a sense of awesome significance, as if in the endless flow of TV trivia, sensation, and commercial urgency, Beckett has demarcated a space and temporal zone to present images of iconic status, a space in which televisual time is slowed down to permit the atemporal mysteries of consciousness, especially consciousness in pain, to register in the viewer's awareness. For Beckett's television works are ghost plays (even *Quad* with its obsessive rhythmic walkers stepping in and out of existence as they enter and leave the force field of their mathematical compulsion is a kind of ghost play). And in his ghost plays, even for human consciousness that shares so much with the machines that allow it representation, time is a medium that allows past and present to come together in what can seem an irreducible moment of suffering. The ghost in the machine is consciousness at its most substantial, lost to sequential, quotidian time, rapt, as the power of memory fills the present moment.

    . . . *but the clouds* . . . is the short work where Beckett permits the memory of the past, of the dead, so to take over consciousness that it seems to dwell in the realm of the spirit. James Knowlson has informed us that this work in which, as he puts it, Beckett "made an attempt to materialize a beautiful face that seemed to him to incarnate spirit"[33] was written shortly after he received a "family group photograph . . . with the faces of all the Beckett forebears, long since dead."[34] It takes its title and a key set of phrases from Yeats's poem "The Tower," which had poignantly asked of an imaginary ghost: "Does the imagination dwell the most / Upon a woman won or woman lost?"[35] Beckett would seem to reply that lost love is the source of obsession. The work presents a highly self-conscious individual whose own voice is heard setting the mise-en-scène of his own action, supplying the directorial instructions, as it were. He describes how he tries each evening, when he returns from tramping the roads, to set the conditions for the "appearance" of a dead woman. Her appearances, however, do not seem to be in his control. As his love for her in the past was unrequited (he invokes "those unseeing eyes I so begged when alive to look at me"),[36] her ghost does not come easily at his bidding. And when she comes, it is only as eyes and a mouth, scarcely the full face. Yet at moments there is synchronicity between the man, his voice, and the ghost, whose lips have inaudibly murmured the phrase ". . . but the clouds . . ." At the last we hear the man's voice join with the ghost as they recite the final lines of Yeats's great poem as man and woman become suffering ghosts in the dark that lasts for five seconds as the piece ends: ". . but the clouds of the sky . . . when the horizon fades . . . or a bird's sleepy cry . . . among the deepening shades . . ."[37]

NOTES

1. See Brenda Maddox, *George's Ghosts: A New Life of W. B. Yeats* (London: Picador, 1999).

2. W. B. Yeats, *The Poems,* ed. Daniel Albright (London: Everyman's Library, 1992), 176.

3. *Yeats's Vision Papers,* gen. ed. George Mills Harper, vol. 1, ed. Stephen L. Adams, Barbara Frieling, and Sandra L. Sprayberry (London: Macmillan, 1992), 9.

4. *Yeats's Vision Papers,* 9.

5. *Yeats's Vision Papers,* 9.

6. George Mills Harper and John S. Kelly, "Preliminary Examination of the Script of E[lizabeth] R[adcliffe]," in *Yeats and the Occult,* ed. George Mills Harper (London: Macmillan 1975),133.

7. Stephen L. Adams and George Mills Harper, "The Manuscript of Leo Africanus," *Yeats Annual* 1 (1982): 38.

8. Harper, *Yeats and the Occult,* 171.

9. Eileen J. Garrett, *Many Voices: The Autobiography of a Medium* (New York: G. P. Putnam's Sons, 1968), 9.

10. Garrett, *Many Voices,* 94.

11. Alex Owen, *The Darkened Room: Women, Power, Spiritualism in Late Nineteenth Century England* (London: Virago Press, 1989), 226.

12. James Knowlson, *Damned to Fame: The Life of Samuel Beckett* (London: Bloomsbury, 1996), 191.

13. *The Theatrical Notebooks of Samuel Beckett: The Shorter Plays,* ed. S. E. Gontarski (London: Faber and Faber, New York: Grove Press, 1999), xvi.

14. Samuel Beckett, *The Complete Dramatic Works* (London: Faber and Faber, 1990), 429.

15. Beckett, *Complete Dramatic Works,* 408.

16. Clas Zilliacus, *Beckett and Broadcasting: A Study of the Works of Samuel Beckett for and in Radio and Televsion* (Åbo, Finland: Åbo Akademi, 1976), 70.

17. Zilliacus, *Beckett and Broadcasting,* 73.

18. Beckett, *Complete Dramatic Works,* 197.

19. Beckett, *Complete Dramatic Works,* 307.

20. Beckett, *Complete Dramatic Works,* 318.

21. Beckett, *Theatrical Notebooks,* xix.

22. Beckett, *Complete Dramatic Works,* 408.

23. Beckett, *Complete Dramatic Works,* 414.

24. Beckett, *Complete Dramatic Works,* 222.

25. Beckett, *Complete Dramatic Works,* 218.

26. Beckett, *Complete Dramatic Works,* 219.

27. Beckett, *Complete Dramatic Works,* 223.

28. Beckett, *Complete Dramatic Works,* 361.

29. Beckett, *Complete Dramatic Works,* 361.

30. Beckett, *Complete Dramatic Works,* 362.

31. Beckett, *Complete Dramatic Works,* 361–62.

32. Zilliacus, *Beckett and Broadcasting,* 198.

33. Knowlson, *Damned to Fame,* 634.

34. Knowlson, *Damned to Fame,* 634.

35. Yeats, *The Poems,* 242.

36. Beckett, *Complete Dramatic Works,* 420.

37. Beckett, *Complete Dramatic Works,* 422.

Marina Warner

"Who can shave an egg?": Foreign Tongues and Primal Sounds in Mallarmé and Beckett

About twenty years ago, a friend from Paris gave me a copy of *Premier Amour* (1945), one of Beckett's very early works in French. This friend, who was a great lover of Beckett, especially treasured this little-known short *récit,* but there was a word he did not understand. The protagonist does some kind of business with a "panais," he said, and added:

"Qu'est-ce que c'est qu'un panais?"
"It's a parsnip."
"Yes, so the dictionary says. But what is a parsnip? The French do not eat parsnips. They feed them to animals."

So I went to the greengrocer's and bought a handsome, phallic, rustic parsnip such as Buster Keaton or Krapp or other Beckettian clown would have used for a surrogate banana or carrot, and posted it to my friend in Paris.

The appearance of the *panais* in *Premier Amour* is ruefully comic; it brings into play in characteristically Beckettian style the cryptic, the abject, and the theatrical. It hints, according to punning dream logic, at the acute proverb, "Fine words butter no parsnips." Beckett was finding his way out of fine words. *Panais* would not condense quite so many tones and meanings if *Premier Amour* had been in English. Beckett's use of it can tell us several things about his writing in French: the decision to reject his mother tongue illuminates his particular music and his turn toward silence. It is interesting to think of Beckett's precursors in adopting a foreign language: one of these, the poet Stéphane Mallarmé, like Beckett a supreme artist of linguistic, syntactical music, can throw a particular light on the Irishman's decision. Mallarmé translated and taught English, and was so involved in aesthetics and semantics that he composed three rare and eccentric works on the language. It is in one of these, *Thèmes anglais* (English lessons) that Mallarmé offers, as a phrase that falls from the lips of any English speaker born and bred: "Who can shave an egg?"[1]

I had never heard this before, but then that is true of most of the sayings in Mallarmé's weird and wonderful English phrase book, but it did strike me as clownish, a little alarming, and a minimalist's maxim.

Mallarmé's love of English was not rooted in fluency or familiarity, but rather in something literally other or alien in the language used by the writers he admired—by William Beckford,[2] Edgar Allan Poe, Alfred, Lord Tennyson,[3] Robert Louis Stevenson, and some rather lesser-known authors, such as Mrs. Elphinstone Hope, whose forgotten story, "The Star of the Fairies," Mallarmé translated in 1880. He also left unfinished a mammoth anthology of English literature.[4] What is entirely seductive about Mallarmé's lists of English words and phrases remains their irreducibly foreign flavor. This strangeness, removing them from English as you or I know it, turns his collection into a kind of prose poem, an aleatory nonsense sequence of phrases—sometimes beautiful, sometimes weirdly comic.

The Fiction of French

When Beckett was asked why he wrote in French, he gave a celebrated answer: "Pour faire remarquer moi." Like the word *panais,* this is a phrase that is not-quite-French but purposely askew; it draws attention to itself on purpose to say, "to make people take notice of me." The turn of phrase is "pidgin," the critic Michael Edwards has commented, adding that this deliberate clumsiness establishes "a gap, a confusion, and we find ourselves conversing in Babel."[5]

Beckett thus shares with Mallarmé a pleasure in unfamiliarity and also a sought-for *dépaysement* and estrangement through the foreign tongue. For Beckett did not assume French *identity* in the trilogy of novels in which he first adopted the language: the man himself might have come back from Paris and shocked his parents in the respectable suburb of Foxrock in Dublin by wearing a beret and smoking Gauloises, but his literary personae stick to Irish caps or vaudeville toques. His characters continue to have names like Molloy or Malone. In *En Attendant Godot,* also first written in French, the cast are named in motley—but the motley nods more to Grockian circus clowning (Vladimir and Estragon) and to the Italian *commedia dell' arte* tradition and their American metamorphoses in the routines of Charlie Chaplin and Buster Keaton. The transition into a different language helps estrange the characters and their setting—strands them somewhere else, somewhere their speech and their own labels do not match exactly. In philosophical terms, this draws attention to the made-up character of Beckett's scenes and tales, and allows the artifice free development. He breaks with representation by this foundational severance of the word from the world. As Edwards comments, "a foreign language is already a kind of fiction."[6]

In a recent intense and inspired lecture, the Irish writer Colm Tóibín remembers the two actors whom Beckett most admired and loved as friends, as drinking partners, as interpreters of his work: Patrick Magee and Jack MacGowran, and he observes that they had both shed their Irishness in different ways in order to make a stage career beyond Dublin; the sounds they made, like Beckett's own, were pieced and patched from different fonts—the mother tongue's pure music scrambled and jangled.[7] Making an analogous point, a critic reviewing Fiona Shaw's recent, compelling brave and funny Winnie in *Happy Days* remarks that she too now speaks in a multilayered accent, inflected by many places beyond her native Cork, and that this hybridity and instability mingle and reverberate to render more intense Beckett's bleak and homeless landscapes.[8]

When my sister, who is four years younger than me, was first learning to speak, we were living in Brussels, and so growing up with English and French side by side. We all laughed happily when she asked crossly one day, "Why won't anybody tell me *in English* what ladybird is in French?" But she was right, about the way languages mean things. As Saussure observed, we learn the words for things in another language by learning the vocabulary: the ladybird-thing is always a ladybird really, if *ladybird* is the original name in the mother tongue. But as Beckett often explores, "coccinelle" somehow sounds more tellingly: being a new word to my sister it did not dissolve into the thing it named, but hung there, resonating with factitious, but fresh, ladybird-like qualities. Newfangledness makes an English speaker take more notice of it—*il fait remarquer soi,* you could say. Or you might also say that the foreign word takes you to a different level, where the embodied character of the term, chiefly conveyed through its sound and shape, acts more directly on our physical receptors because they are freed from intelligibility. The physicality of a word grows lighter and less substantial when we know what it means without having to think.

How to avoid this attenuation, with its corresponding drying up of the *rasas,* the living juices of aesthetic response, becomes the writer's task.

Mallarmé once remarked that poetry should make air and silence hang around a word, and Beckett also likes to give a character a particular word to hold, with a pause, as it reverberates. He does this when he began to write again in English, for the radio, as if his characters were now acquiring English as a foreign tongue. Toward the beginning of *All That Fall,* broadcast by the BBC in 1957, Mrs Rooney says:

> I use none but the simplest words, I hope, and yet I sometimes find my way of speaking very . . . bizarre.[9]

Though her words are indeed simple, they are often rare or archaic: *weasand* for throat, and *pismire* for ant, and the lovely, precise designation *hinny,* with its oral echoes of the animal's cry. Beckett sends us to the English dictionary, where *hinny* turns out to be "the offspring of a she-donkey and a stallion."[10] Beckett also sends characters to the dictionary: in *Krapp's Last Tape,* Krapp himself bundles a huge tome on to the stage to look up the word *viduity,* another unfamiliar usage and one that allows Krapp to linger and savor it, turning the syllables round his tongue, assaying their precise weight and the associations that arise, and then finding, with a surprise that perhaps takes us into Beckett's own when he found this for the first time:

> Also of an animal, especially a bird . . . the vidua or weaver-bird . . . Black plumage of the male . . . [*He looks up. With relish.*] The vidua-bird![11]

Krapp recognizes himself in this state, names himself by another name and so edges toward becoming that little bit more present to himself.

Making a detour through French, Beckett was refreshing language itself, including his native Irish-English, and effectively sharpening its sensory powers of precise naming.

Beckett also switches tone by picking an exact, unfamiliar term and allowing it to bob like unidentifiable flotsam in the broken stream of his characters' monologues—or dialogues—a new shard, as it were, from *Echo's Bones:* the "hog's setae," for example, the authentic material of Winnie's toothbrush in *Happy Days,* again needs to be explained—for most of us—by recourse to the dictionary. Another would be *emmett,* the unusual word for ant that Winnie chooses. Michael Edwards remarks, "Beckett . . . disengages himself from memory [and] . . . signals the danger of familiarity. One can feel so much at home in one's language and in the world which that language enters, illuminates, and sweetens, that one forgets one's exile, and the writer in particular needs to mistrust the wontedness of words and to experience at times, or maybe on a particular occasion, the foreignness of his own tongue."[12]

Estrangement, and through estrangement, reknotting of the threads between naming and the named: this is the first reason for Beckett's writing in French. But he also famously remarked that he had made the decision "pour avoir moins de style"—or, in the English version reported, to write "without style." His first novel in French, *Mercier et Camier,* was finished in 1946 and only published in 1970; his first play in French, *Eleutheria,* was written in 1947, and performing rights remain unavailable. So after the great turning point in the wake of his father's death and the ordeal of the war, the first writings in the new tongue were experiments—apprentice works, he said. *Eleutheria* was published only recently for the first time. But *En Attendant Godot* followed this, and was composed in a fugue of inspiration over a few months only (October 1948–January 1949)—the manuscript, in a school exercise book, shows hardly a revision. The famous masterwork, the trilogy—*Molloy, Malone meurt,* and *L'Innommable*—was then completed in a frenzied burst of creativity, and published in 1951–1953 during a time of extreme hardship when Beckett was living in Paris. Beckett recognized that this new, French *soi,* or voice, could offer him a precious way of slipping from the shadow of Joyce. Compared to *Murphy* and *Watt* and the earliest *Poems in English,* the earliest poems in French are pared down, austere, and plain. For example, the simple closing lines of a 1948 lyric are

> sans voix parmi les voix
> enfermées avec moi

They could be rendered literally: "without a voice / among the voices enclosed with me" (or "shut up with me," with a pun implied not present in the French), but they are in fact translated from the more metaphysically inflected:

> Among the voices voiceless
> that throng my hiddenness[13]

Beckett's French continued to cultivate surprise in its phrasing and lexicon, by often picking an unfamiliar, even obsolete term. In *Fin de partie* (1958), for example, during the exchange between Hamm and Clov and Nagg about the last rat and the last sugar plum, they begin to pray but soon give up, and the failure of this sacred performative speech form leads them to expostulate:

> Hamm: Bernique! (à *Nagg*) Et toi?
> Nagg: Attends *(Un temps. Rouvrant les yeux.)* Macache!
> Hamm: Le salaud! Il n'existe pas.
> Clov: Pas encore.
> Nagg: Ma dragée!
> Hamm: Il n'y a plus de dragées.
> *Un temps.*[14]

I had to look up *bernique* and *macache* in a dictionary of French slang. Mine gives "No dice" and "Not bloody likely" for the first and "Bugger all" for *macache*.[15] English could have offered Beckett some vivid and mimetic words for the same thoughts—*poppycock* and *gibberish* and *balderdash*—but they do not have the same street cred as *bernique* and *macache,* nor the particular mystery of the proper noun. Without the dictionary, you can catch the drift of the French, and respond to the intrinsic rhythm of dismissal and contempt—these are terms that seem to spit in derision.

In English, this succinct comic repartee goes like this:

> Hamm: Sweet damn all! *(to Nagg.)* And you?
> Nagg: Wait! *(Pause. Abandoning his attitude.)* Nothing doing!
> Hamm: The bastard! He doesn't exist!
> Clov: Not yet.
> Nagg: Me sugar-plum!
> Hamm: There are no more sugar-plums!
> *Pause.*[16]

It is funny and rueful and deft in performance, but it does not work with the ring and shape of words to the same perfect pitch as the French.

Performance touches on ritual at one end of the spectrum, at playing at the other, as Beckett recognized with his characters' ceremonious and repetitive procedures. In a letter he wrote in 1937, Beckett raises the question of the ritual power of words when he wondered if there might not be "something paralysingly holy in the vicious nature of the word that is not found in the elements of the other arts,"[17] while toward the beginning of *Malone Dies,* he connects the power of words with play. Malone tells us, "People and things ask nothing better than to play, certain animals too."[18]

Sound Sense

Mallarmé's interest in English as a language never became as central as Beckett's use of French, nor did his command of the foreign tongue reach Beckett's supreme artistry. But both men were language teachers: Mallarmé taught English at various lycées, first outside Paris, then in the capital, while Beckett taught French at Campbell College in Belfast for seven miserable months in 1928. After two years as a *lecteur* in English at the École Normale Supérieure in Paris, Beckett became a lecturer in French at Trinity College, Dublin. Neither writer liked teaching— Beckett, who was nocturnal, was reproached for his timekeeping;[19] Mallarmé was under constant criticism for his distracted and chaotic classes.[20]

But the formal understanding of languages that comes through teaching and through translation tells in Beckett's writing; and in Beckett's case he continued to apply himself to the task even after *Waiting for Godot* had brought him fame and the wherewithal to survive. In 1958, for example, he published a rather unremarked volume in his oeuvre: a full translation of Octavio Paz's *An Anthology of Mexican Poetry* (1958). Nowhere in this unexpected book does Beckett comment on his reasons for undertaking to render into English five hundred years of lyric poetry in Spanish, a language he shows little sign elsewhere of knowing; nor does anyone else—editor, publisher—offer insight into how the collaboration came about. But such absorption in foreign languages which the poets did not know at all or knew only a little opened their own more fully. The formal understanding of languages that comes through teaching and translating tells in Beckett's writing; it gives both Mallarmé's poetry and Beckett's prose and poetry exactitude, translucency, control, compression, depths of resonance, and in Beckett's case especially, stirring emotion under the lucid syntax and the pitch perfect lexicon— qualities sought by any writer perhaps, but above all by those who do not seek to apply language to representing a world out there, but are attempting to create worlds with language in texts made as literature.

There are further reasons as well for looking through Mallarmé's English at Beckett's French. Beckett made frequent references to the famous line "le vide papier que la blancheur défend" (the empty page that whiteness defends),[21] and in 1932, when Beckett was reading Mallarmé's famous achievements of formal perfection, he railed in a letter to his friend Thomas MacGreevy in most revealing terms:

> I don't know why the Jesuitical poem that is an end in itself and justifies all the means should disgust me so much. But it does— again—more & more. I was trying to like Mallarmé again the other day, & couldn't, because it's Jesuitical poetry . . . I suppose I'm a dirty low-church P.[rotestant] even in poetry, concerned with integrity in a surplice. I'm in mourning for the integrity of a *pendu*'s emission of semen, what I find in Homer & Dante & Racine & sometimes Rimbaud, the integrity of the eyelids coming down before the brain knows of grit in the wind.[22]

Maybe Beckett did not consistently hold this view of Mallarmé, and indeed Mallarmé's occasional writings take him close to the nervous and visceral immediacy that Beckett craves: that integrity of the body's thought (the hanged man's involuntary emission, the eyelids coming down) responding automatically before rationality transmits signals openly to consciousness. Mallarmé shows an analogously surreal desire for this erotics of language, a sense of language as sound, as music, as havoc, as nonsense, an understanding of modes of communication that defy semantics and prick and kick with life, as in Beckett's drama and fiction—however much his theme remains the ebbing of vitality: the limits of sense stand for the limits of being in his restless rueful inquiries into the running out of life and of time.

Mallarmé tried various approaches to overcoming his difficulties teaching English to his pupils. Thinking to capture the attention of his class, he turned to English literature's near unique rattle bag of nursery rhymes and made versions of them in French prose—with extended, mock earnest commentary and scrupulous grammatical notes, solemnly expanding on each rhyme's possible significance.[23]

But his efforts did not meet with approval. In 1880, a government inspector, making the rounds of the classrooms, happened to enter M. Mallarmé's when the pupils were chanting a variation on "Tell Tale Tit":

> Liar liar lick spit
> Your tongue shall be slit

And all the dogs in the town
Shall have a little bit.[24]

The inspector was scandalized, reported that the teacher must be out of his wits to teach such wretched rubbish: "Since M. Mallarmé remains a professor of English," he wrote, "Let him learn English . . . it's tempting to ask oneself if one is not in the presence of someone sick."[25]

It is a clue, however, to Mallarmé's other pedagogical masterpieces that "Liar liar lick spit" is not the opening of the version that most English children know, which opens more usually, "Tell tale tit . . ."[26]

Mallarmé's failures in the classroom did not stem from lack of effort: *Thèmes anglais* contains a wondrous gathering of a thousand English phrases, proverbs, adages, and saws, all conscientiously marshaled in order to illustrate a rule of English grammar: first the definite article, then the indefinite, first the possessive pronoun, then the relative pronoun, and so on. The contrast between the austerely dry objective of the examples and their fantastical oddity, the disjunction between the scrupulous lexical and grammatical rigor and the free-association lexical chain of words, achieve an exhilarating absurdity of effect. A native speaker of English would know precious few of these locutions at the very most, and use them—never. The ones that you might know you would find stale; and you would have done so then in the 1880s. Mallarmé was using an anthology he'd come upon in Truchy's bookshop to glean a myriad equivalents to "My postilion has been struck by lightning," regardless of current usage.[27]

What is entirely seductive about his lists is their irreducibly foreign character (some of the proverbs he cites were already archaic by the seventeenth century):

Under water, famine; under snow, bread.
Prettiness makes no pottage.[28]

These rare enigmas are offered to illustrate how, where French uses a definite article, English does without.

Besides "Who can shave an egg?" phrases such as "You can't hide an eel in a sack" are included in order to illustrate the use of the indefinite article. The quirkiness of these rules inspires a riddling sequence:

It is hard for an empty bag to set upright.
To cut down an oak and set up a strawberry.

Undone, as a man would undo an oyster.
You ask an elm tree for pears.
You shall ride an inch behind the tail.[29]

These adages—proverbs or whatever—teeter on the verge of incompre-
hensibility. But their cumulative effect is melancholy: failure stalks them,
regardless of syntactical exactitude.

The third work Mallarmé wrote on the English language, *Les Mots
anglais,* was compiled in 1877. It begins with a long essay on linguistics,
which discusses relations between sound and sense, and Henri Mondor,
Mallarmé's editor, rightly points out how fascinating it is to watch a poet
of this intense aesthetic stringency explore the topic.[30] Mallarmé sets out
a theory of correspondences in line with Rimbaud's famous sonnet
"Voyelles," and reveals his excitement in the potential of alliteration, as-
sonance, onomatopoeia, and, again, a version of linguistic mimicry that is
not quite expletive or vociferation, but a kind of semantic synaesthesia.

Beneath common English parlance, Mallarmé was questing for an
Adamic language, which would match the essence of the referent to the
signifier without friction, without separation. Unlike Rimbaud, he de-
cides to cluster his poetic associations around a dominant consonant or
diphthong, in order to point out the natural semantic wake of certain
particular English sounds. He delights in the slitheriness of "snake" and
the flatness of "flat" and the liquidity of "glide." He proposes joyfully
that "wr" authentically marks "torsion" or twisting, since so many
words cluster around it: wry, awry, wrist, wrest (which he translates as
torturer), wrestle, wreath, wring, writhe, and wrong.[31] He includes exclamations: "Ugh!"

He makes lists: acoustic chains with variations. Not unexpectedly,
the rich mimicry in words about speaking captures his attention: "babble" and "blab" lead off the Bs; "gabble," "gibberish," "jabber," the Gs;
he brings in "tittle-tattle" and "chit-chat";[32] he makes a small independent cluster round "jangle jingle jaw chew chin cud" and "jumble." Is
this an exercise in jest—wordplay, a puzzle?[33] The group of words in D
takes an excursion into little marked territory ("to daggle," writes Mallarmé [in Beckettian mode] signifies "s'humecter" [to dampen oneself]).

D takes a more serious turn when Mallarmé comments : "Seul, il
[D] exprime une action suivie et sans éclat, profonde, comme plonger,
creuser, ou tomber par goutte, ainsi que la stagnation, la lourdeur morale
et l'obscurité" (on its own [D] expresses a continuous action of no

lustre, deep, like sinking, hollowing, or falling in drops, as in stagnation, moral heaviness, and darkness).[34] The resulting list offers the closest Beckettian miniature from Mallarmé's English words—this is the left-hand column:

Day
Damp
Dear
. . .
Deal
Dew
Dip
Die
Dig
Dim[35]

G has its importance, he adds, signifying "a simple aspiration, to a point where the spirit goes . . ." as in "God."[36] C denotes vivid acts, such as clinging, cuddling, cutting, climbing, crashing, crushing, and crying—for food.[37]

These lists read like Beckettian dramaticules.

In one of his books on the poet, Roger Pearson reflecting on Mallarmé's theory of language, illuminates the poet's drift from intelligibility to noise, from conscious referents to unconscious associations, from patent to latent meaning:

Language is a mysterious universe, a strange place in which pre-existing patterns, dimly perceived, seem to bespeak some original harmony. As we follow the threads of its labyrinthine lace, the everyday meanings of language become obscure. Homophony comes to haunt it with the spectres of other meanings, and the skeletons of etymology begin to rattle in their cupboards [note they *rattle*]. Syllables break loose from their verbal context, and, like the sibyls of old, call up the shades from an other, spirit world. In the ensuing darkness new constellations of meaning begin to glimmer. The former, seemingly unproblematic representational function of language has sunk beneath the horizon to be replaced by the non-representational Idée, by Mallarmé's music of the spheres . . . The reader's task (and the critic's) is to listen to this "music."[38]

Beckett's play scripts with their precise notations recall musical scores; and Mallarmé's semantic and psychological synaesthesia also treats verbal expression as if it were music. To the French poet's ear, D leads subjects to dreariness and darkness as B-flat changes the mood of a musical theme that began brightly in C major. Beckett also employs phonemes in this way—like the pianist he was (and he preferred playing the sonatas of Mozart composed in a minor key).

Beckett found in his chosen French a way to poise himself both inside literature and outside it; he also found in the language an intrinsic music, and in its literature experimental precursors in nuance, wordlessness, pulse, and fugitive image-sounds. And, as mentioned before, soundings on the ear gain salience when meanings have been consciously acquired. Also, when sound produces sense as if organically as its own pith, then the gap that gapes between the live thing in the world and its name can be closed—or almost. As Beckett wrote about this elusive ideal, "Watt set to trying names for things, almost as a woman tries on hats."[39]

In 1930, in one of her most free-associating fugues of an essay, *On Being Ill,* Virginia Woolf meditates on the relation between sounding and meaning:

> In illness words seem to possess a mystic quality. We grasp what is beyond their surface meaning, gather instinctively this, that, and the other—a sound, a colour, here a stress, there a pause—which the poet, knowing words to be meagre in comparison with ideas, has strewn about his page to evoke, when collected, a state of mind which neither words can express nor the reason explain. Incomprehensibility has an enormous power over us in illness, more legitimately perhaps than the upright will allow. *In health meaning has encroached upon sound.* Our intelligence domineers over our senses. But in illness, with the police off duty, we creep beneath some obscure poems by Mallarmé or Donne, some phrase in Latin or Greek, and the words give out their scent and distil their flavour, and then, *if at last we grasp the meaning, it is all the richer for having come to us sensually first, by way of the palate and the nostrils, like some queer odour.* Foreigners, to whom the tongue is strange, have us at a disadvantage.[40]

Mallarmé and Beckett were "foreigners" in relation to English and French respectively, and they used their advantage with a difference: Mallarmé's English lessons exhibit a scrupulous, chaste fastidiousness with language that Beckett profoundly shares; a near-pedantry, the grammarian's niceties. But Mallarmé's writings in English sever language from subjectivity, and syntax from referential or experiential significance; the subject's voice does not circle around its own imminent, baffling disappearance. They do not possess Beckettian poignancy, or his sense of personal hebetude.

Babel Babble

The naming of characters consistently inspired Beckett to nursery-style babble: Didi and Gogo in *Waiting for Godot,* M. et Mme. Saposcat in *Malone meurt;* Krim and Kram in *How It Is,* Winnie and Willie in *Happy Days,* Flo, Vi, and Ru in *Come and Go,* Pim in *How It Is,* Bim, Bam, Bem, and Bom in the very late *What Where* (1983). In the French version of *Happy Days,* Beckett abandons monosyllables for the Ubu-like rigmarole, "Monseigneur le Réverendissime Père en Dieu Carolus Chassepot."

In what has become a legendary piece, Lucky's speech at the end of act I in *Waiting for Godot,* Beckett has the hitherto tongue-tied character pour forth a torrent of words . . . words that lie the other side of intelligibility, held to an underlying time signature by nonsense syllables punctuating the flow, such as *quaqua. Quaqua* recurs in *How It Is,* too—one of Beckett's nonsense words that mark senselessness of rational discourse.[41] On the one hand *quaqua* picks up the Latin casuistry of the Schoolmen, while on the other, through its quacking echoes, it evokes the mysterious communications of animals. Lucky is largely parodying Scholastic pedantry with his scatological, punning, trifling, highly theological ruminations, but the phrase harks back precisely to a famous scene in Ovid's *Metamorphoses:* after the goddess Leto has given birth to the divine twins, Apollo and Diana, she goes to bathe in a pond but is driven away by men cutting rushes by the shore. In revenge, she turns them into frogs. Ovid mimicks alliteratively the subhuman, "Ca-Ca-Caliban"-esque noises that the men make after the metamorphosis takes hold of their human bodies and deprives them of human speech:

*qua*muis sint sub a*qua,* sub a*qua* maledicere temptant.[42]

(However much they lie underwater, they struggle to curse underwater.)[43]

Ovid's monstrous frog-peasants, their words turning to croaks as they choke on lake mud, were not the only slime-dwellers to attract Beckett's darkly comic and desolate imagination; others are found in the *Inferno,* where those sinners who were disaffected and listless and suffered from anomie—with whom Beckett no doubt felt some affinity—are plunged into cold "black filth" so deep that their mouths are stopped.[44]

Beckett took from Dante the art of the dramatic tableau involving bodies in torment, in mud, in eternal repetitive cycles of impaired and diminished existence that goes on, that keeps going on in the eternal present of hell.[45] He also found there a language for inner states written on the body, for vices emblazoned in exterior, physical conditions, and mimicked by sound and gesture and mien: in the *Inferno* especially, language sometimes collapses altogether as devils and sinners return to the elements that imprison them and torture them. The flaying hail and freezing rain of the Third Circle sets the gluttons howling like dogs ("Urlar li fa la pioggia come cani . . . ," Canto VI, line 19). At other times, Dante's characters articulate through their bodies—not through their mouths and lips—but communicate most vividly through their eyes and beetling brows. But the monstrous body in Dante also speaks through nether orifices, most unforgettably through the anus, as when Malacoda rallies his troop of demons at the close of Canto XXI:

Per l'argine sinistra volta dienno;
  ma prima avea ciascun la lingua stretta
  coi denti verso lor duca per cenno;
ed elli avea del cul fatto trombetta.

(They [the devils] wheeled round by the dike on the left; but first each pressed his tongue between his teeth at their leader for a signal and he made a trumpet of his rear.)[46]

At this, in the opening of the next canto, Dante launches into a military simile, enumerating the different trumpet sounds and drum rolls and bugles calls he has heard, none so "different" as this signal of the devil Malacoda, whose name means "bad tail."

The episode made a lasting impression on Beckett: he responded to Dante's chosen vulgar tongue and his somatic uses of it. Writing *The Divine Comedy,* Dante had broken with classical decorum, mixing styles and registers with a scandalous, deliberate use of the vulgar and its resources; he deploys medieval Italian's raucous, rough music to summon the monstrous company of devils and takes the language to its very limits as a semantic system. After the devils march off with Virgil and Dante, the brutal expressiveness of their leader's trumpet replicates the inventive *brutte parole*—Italian for swear words—of the names the poet dreamed up for them: Scarmiglione, Calcabrina, Cagnazzo, Barbariccia, Libicocco, Draghignazzo, Graffiacane, Farfarello, Rubicante.

With rasping onomatopoeia, these names evoke the devils' monstrosity, character, and their actions. But the words are also made-up hybrids—nicknames—that sound farouche and terrible apart from their associations, and demand a kind of violent tonguing in order to pronounce them at all.

Beckett reprises the name Malacoda, the farting demon, in one of his early poems where he figures the undertaker who came to prepare Beckett's father for burial.[47]

This aspect of Beckett's writing does of course keep him tightly connected to Joyce, but it leads us to another reason for his choice of a foreign language, one that returns us to the vital relation between sound and sense.

The key concept here is Babel: babel as babble, babble as a word—*babiller* in French—that itself imitates exactly the first sounds of a baby learning to speak, and speaking at that stage of development a kind of nonsense that brings joy in the utterance, that fills both speaker and listener with delight, and causes echoing, answering babble in the mother or father or grandparent or nurse or friend playing with the infant as he or she stumbles out of infancy, out of the state of speechlessness (*infans* in Latin) into speech and begins to try to express for the first time the voice that throngs the hiddenness inside them.

But babble also connotes the failure of powers—in senility and in mortality's triumph. The "tristi" of Canto VII are the only sinners whom Dante encounters who have no voice of their own, as Virgil explains to the poet:

> "e anche vo' che tu per certo credi
> che sotto l'acqua è gente che sospira,
>   e fanno pullular quest' acqua al summo,
>   come l'occhio ti dice, u' che s'aggira.
> Fitti nel limo, dicon: 'Tristi fummo
>   nell'aere dolce che dal sol s'allegra,
>   portando dentro accidïoso fummo:
>   or ci attristiam nella belletta negra.'

Quest' inno si gorgoglian nella strozza,
chè dir nol posson con parola integra."

("I would also like you to understand
That underneath the water are people sighing;
It is they who make the water bubble on top . . .
They say, 'We chose to be sad
In the sweet air enlivened by the sun,
And our hearts smouldered with a sullen smoke:
Now we are sad instead in this black filth.'
That is the hymn they gurgle in their throats
And cannot even get the words out properly.")[48]

This landscape of mud and of mangled or abolished utterance keeps bubbling in Beckett's ear, resonating in *How It Is* above all. He draws out the sense of the sounds, through onomatopoeia and alliteration and also through other kinds of rhyme, not simply oral and phonetic, but semantic, physical, and visual: Krapp croons and mutters "spooool" in English, a word that mimics its referent to the extent of spooling out on the page as if the ooos were materializing the machine's very component turning parts. In French, this effect of visual mimicry fades, but the word "bobiiiine" miraculously returns us to the sound of babel as Krapp begins to listen in and babbles in accompaniment. And as we listen to Krapp, we are entangled in those associations: *crapuleux* is more common in French than English *crapulous,* but *crap* is English for nonsense as well as for excrement. Sometimes Beckett is tuning our ear to both languages at once, and he is always listening to the primal sounds, to the coughs, hawking, wheezing, and croaking that pass for laughter (*Embers,* 1959), to the groans and sighs between words, to the footfalls, trudging, and even unexplained blasts *(Happy Days)* in the soundscape of the plays. Leslie Hill conjectures that for Beckett "'m' words [the first letter of his characters Molloy et al.] are incorporative and 'gi' and 'c' words ('cracher', 'crever') are expectorant."[49] Beckett's energies continually expand his powers to discover non-sense and denounce utterance, to reiterate phrases until, like a familiar word repeated again and again, meaning drains and something infinitely strange, mysterious, potent, and otherwise secretly meaningful replaces it. Think of tongue-twisters: the pleasure in the gradual disappearance of the words leaving only the trace of the sounds, like the knowing smile of the Cheshire Cat.

Such words are formed of inarticulate cries and sighs, groans and growls, howls and whimpers, of fizzles (another Beckett word), farts, snorts, and whistling in the wind. What is the proper term for these kinds of words—expostulations, ejaculations, exclamations? Beckett uses the word *vociferations* for Lucky's incoherent shouts when Vladimir and Estragon and Pozzo succeed in quelling him at the end of act 1 of *Waiting for Godot*. Vociferation is a good term; vociferations are close to the springs of language and are formed of inarticulate cries and sighs, groans and growls, howls and whimpers—all those sounds that punctuate Beckett's music and weave the texture of its poignancy and its sorrowful humor. They are expressive and hold emotional meaning, but without referring to anything one could put into significant words. They turn into pure sign—acoustic sign. They are close to animal noises; they reveal human beings' intimacy with the animal, again something Beckett makes play with in his conception of bodies on stage and his dramatization of relations between a person and his or her body.

It is interesting that Beckett remarked to Patrick Bowles in 1955, "It is as if there were a little animal inside one's head, for which one tried to find a voice; to which one tries to give a voice. That is the *real* thing. The rest is a game."[50] The natural habitat of such animal babble is the nursery or dotage, the termini so often telescoped by Beckett. Such words come close to magical naming, when the word gives life to the thing, becomes the thing. They therefore represent the child's omnipotent dream that by saying "Mummy," Mummy or her breast will come back. Mmm . . . the sound of a child suckling lies at the root of words for mother and for breast—*mamme* in Greek from which comes our *mammal*. Such words are oral spells, shaping objects in the image of desire, stamped with the referent's intrinsic qualities and at the same time forming them by their own powers of impression. They can also act apotropaically, uttered to ward off an unwelcome presence or turn of events, and to expel something unwanted, to obliterate it, make it disappear. These words are oral spells, shaping objects in the image of desire, both stamped with the referent's intrinsic qualities, and forming them by their own powers of impression. Steven Connor has commented, "the principal form of magic in Beckett's work [is] aversive."[51] Ourobouros-like, infancy meets decrepitude in Beckett's meditations on existence, and he often casts scenes in the past, in which characters retrospectively evoke a recess of images, set one inside the other. In these scenes, feelings elude naming: as we know, this is the essence of Beckett's created inscape, something that hovers beyond the grasp of words, even of sounds. As Winnie says, "Words fail, there are times when even they fail. . . . Is that not so, Willie? . . . Is that not so, Willie, that even

words fail, at times? . . . What is one to do then, until they come
again?"[52]

Again in *On Being Ill,* Virginia Woolf ruminates on this deep
stratum of expressive inarticulacy, shifting its grounding in childhood to
its connection with sickness:

> Finally, to hinder the description of illness in literature, there is the
> poverty of the language. English, which can express the thoughts of
> Hamlet and the tragedy of Lear, has no words for the shiver and the
> headache. It has all grown one way. The merest schoolgirl, when
> she falls in love, has Shakespeare or Keats to speak her mind for her;
> but let a sufferer try to describe a pain in his head to a doctor and
> language at once runs dry. There is nothing ready made for him. He
> is forced to coin words himself, and, *taking his pain in one hand, and
> a lump of pure sound in the other (as perhaps the people of Babel did in the
> beginning), so to crush them together that a brand new word in the end drops
> out.* Probably it will be something laughable.[53]

This brings us to Beckett for whom the physical presence of things
requires that we listen to their voice somewhat like a child animating a
roomful of toys: however far they lie from ensoulment . . . entombed,
less than alive, inert, they register their existence through the sounds
they make: sighs and whispers, groans and burbles. Beckett once
changed the name of a character from an "Observer/Eye-Mind" to a
"Hearer-Creature." A "Hearer-Creature" rather than an "Eye-Mind"
can pick up the stirrings of other signs of life more surely. The "eye-
mind" does not guarantee that sheer materiality of embodiment on
which his imagination fastened.[54]

In Beckett's language, nursery nonsense joins sound music through
the noises of the body: he called his tiny last poems "Mirlitonnades,"
from *mirliton,* a reed pipe or primitive whistle (a kazoo), suggesting a
ditty, a trifle.[55]

These scraps of music—Beckett himself referred to them as
"gloomy . . . doggerel"—have attracted a great deal of attention recently
from translators and inspired a correspondence about rival suggestions in
the *Times Literary Supplement.* The Irish poet Derek Mahon interestingly
renders *Mirlitonnades* as "Burbles," thus catching at its nonsensical, even
monstrous, Jabberwocky side;[56] several other writers made different
proposals (Raymond Bell suggested "Flitters,"[57] John Crombie

"jingling,"[58]) until the exchange reached a splendid climax with the learned comments of Adam A. Watt:

> Derek Mahon observes that the best of Beckett's verse "speaks, or rather whispers . . . to the inner ear." This is undoubtedly so. Beckett's neologistic title, *mirlitonnades,* however, suggests a noise a little less reserved than a whisper . . . I would like to suggest a further interpretation founded in another set of little-read Beckett texts, written more or less contemporaneously with the *mirlitonnades.* The latter, in their idiom, themes and the morphology of their title share much with the prose *foirades* ("fizzles" in English). Both title words can refer to an expulsion of air, but one which is rather more forceful than a whisper. . . . The *Petit Robert* illuminates: "foirade" derives from "foirer": "1. Evacuer des excréments à l'état liquide [evacuate excrement in a liquid state] 2. Mal fonctionner [function badly] 3. fam [familiar] Echouer lamentablement" [fail miserably]. *The Faber Companion to Samuel Beckett* reliably informs us that Beckett's preferred understanding of "foirade"/"fizzle" was "a wet fart" or "the act of breaking wind quietly." When we look at the mirlitonnades alongside the foirades, the two sets of texts are mutually illuminating. It seems as if certain mirlitonnades are the precipitates or residua that would have derived from the foirades had Beckett continued to pare back and refine their structures. To think of the mirlitonnades as foirades in miniature, quiet breakings of philosophico-linguistic wind, fizzles reduced to the confines of the backs of envelopes, beer mats, the label of a whiskey bottle, takes us some way towards understanding the problems they pose to readers and translators. There is little that is less harmonious than the nasal squeals of a kazoo, little that is serene about a fart, quietly passed, failed, or otherwise.

After this rather Beckettian mock solemn paragraph, the appropriately named Dr. Watt concludes feelingly that "Beckett's attempts, in language, to approach the state of these *inarticulate expulsions* provide us with a valuable and highly rewarding entry into what we might call his late style."[59]

"Inarticulate expulsions"—these are the cries and sighs of the mud-locked sinners, the spluttering and stuttering drooling of Krapp and the other geriatrics in Beckett's solemn comedies, the vociferations of the cartoon victims. For not everything is fizzling out, and wind is not mere wind, at least not quite or otherwise we would not feel the tragic-comic involvement that Beckett inspires. There is something to the fizzle itself.

In this sense Beckett summons a preverbal relation to love and to loss in disguise as a postverbal diminution of powers. The time when words shall fail meets the time before they were at our command. He consciously wanted to recapture this state because he considered it existentially true of all consciousness: "That point at which words break down because in life, there are wordless situations, where words shatter, or where words fail you."[60] The angle of view in so many of his works opens onto elusive glimpses of the dim past, but that past itself often belongs to Beckett's childhood, to his mother, his father, their parents, and their sisters (Beckett's beloved aunts)—their customs, clothes, diction, and doings haunt his works. As the title *Rockaby* evokes, the pain and plangency and occasional bliss of these echoes rising from the obscurity of forgetting return their declining, impaired subjects to a time of lullaby, while the rocking chair in which they sit or even the boat that moves from side to side in *Krapp's Last Tape* recalls another motion that seeks to soothe restless, unnameable discomfort: the rocking of the cradle that settles the anguish of the baby.

Magic Play

These strands fuse in Beckett's writing—lexical estrangement, organic sound tending to the comic, sense relations (the color of consonants), and the language of physical suffering as age meets infancy in a loop of half-remembered fragments from the past of his own early life; and they take us to the zone where words are magic, performative magic. W. R. Bion, the analyst at the Tavistock Institute in London who treated Beckett for two years in 1934–35 during the growing crisis after his father's death the year before,[61] was later analyzed by Melanie Klein, whose thinking emphasized the child's imperious way with utterance.[62] Words summon presence—the mother, the mother's breast (as mentioned before), and they also possess the power to animate the inanimate, to quicken toys with imaginary life, to throng the playroom with imaginary company and breathe into empty space the living form of an imaginary friend.

Charles Baudelaire commented on childhood imagination long before the British psychologists placed it at the center of clinical treatment for depression. His memoir essay is called "Morale du joujou"

(Moral of the plaything)—where *joujou* (not the usual word for toy, *jouet*) is almost a pet name with a nursery ring like a "teddy" or a "dolly." Baudelaire recalls in pleasurable detail the miniature worlds conjured by Victorian nursery games and child's-play, and muses in wonder at children's ability to play without props or models, through fantasy alone: "All children talk to their toys; toys become actors in the great drama of life, reduced by the *camera obscura* of their small brains. Children bear witness through their games to their great faculty of abstraction and their high imaginative power. They play without playthings."[63] Significantly, Baudelaire goes on to say children also want "to see the soul" of a toy, and Baudelaire remembers how they will turn it about and shake it and scratch it and hurl it to the ground, baffled, even enraged, by the stubborn inanimateness of the thing. His meditation hints that the primal loss brings with it an understanding of mortality, and that this takes place when make-believe fails and the vitality of toys vanishes: "But *where is the soul?* It's here that vacancy sets in—and bewilderment."[64]

Around sixty years after Baudelaire, Rilke meditated in similar terms on the passions aroused by this relationship in his essay on playing with dolls: he describes play as a process of animation—of the doll and through the doll—of the child playing, dreaming the doll into life. He broods on his memories of trying to feed and coddle and . . . yes, *animate* it. It became "a confidant, a confederate, like a dog, not however receptive and forgetful like a dog, but . . . a burden." His efforts turned to fury when confronted by the doll's mute obstinate solidity. But he then invokes the onrush of compensatory fantasy: "[A doll] made no response whatsoever, so we found that we needed to split our personality. . . . The incomprehensible things which were happening to us we mixed together in the doll as in a test tube and saw them . . . change colour and boil up. Really, we invented the doll: a doll was so abysmally devoid of phantasy that our imagination became inexhaustible in dealing with it."[65] Rilke then passes on to other things that have become saturated with hopes and dreams, and have through human handling and love acquired a soul.

A more ludic writer than either Baudelaire or Rilke, the artist Kurt Schwitters also played with dolls—and well into adulthood, and he mischievously intimates his pleasure with them in a poem of 1944, very adroitly done into English by Jerome Rothenberg. It starts:

The dollies doll with little dollies,
The little dollies doll with tiny dollies . . .

And later closes with the latent harmony of language:

> Oh thou my darling dolly,
> I get to feel so jolly
> When I do press my muzzle
> Against your guzz—and guzzle.
> Dolly jolly
> Jolly dolly
> Dolly guzzy.
> Guzzly dolly dolly lady
> First they muzzle then they guzzle.[66]

This ambiguity about the soul of the toy—the doll or other object—haunts the psychology of play and through play, the theory of language's relation to the world, and the impact of imagination: is the state of animation which the power of thought can conjure sufficient to make reality present? This question at first invites a quick dismissal. But when it comes to art and art's own ways of make-believe, it becomes far harder to reject. Beckett's work probes this puzzling boundary of consciousness, of animation and inanimateness, with ceaseless patient forensic fingers. In his case, by contrast, the stress often falls in his work on the disappearance of things: not so much "Abracadabra" as "Vamoose . . ."

Colette, writing the libretto for Ravel's *L'Enfant et les sortilèges,* the opera that premiered in 1925, dramatized a significant variation on a primal scene or, if you like, a child's original sin: in her protagonist's nursery, the naughty little boy has a tantrum. He smashes the teapot and teacup in his room, torments his cat and pet squirrel, slashes the curtains, swings on the pendulum of the grandfather clock, and generally plays havoc with his world, all of this mimicked vividly and wittily by the orchestra. But his toys and things are not things, it transpires: they retaliate. Unlike Rilke's dolls, they are sensate, curious, and alive, and they are outraged by the child's violence. So they take their revenge, punishing him in a variety of ways, until he feels utterly desolate faced with their vitality and autonomy:

> "Ils s'aiment . . . Ils sont heureux . . . Ils m'oublient . . ." he cries.
> "Ils s'aiment . . . ils m'oublient . . . Je suis seul . . ."[67]

> (They love each other. They're happy. They have forgotten me.
> They love each other. . . . They've forgotten me . . . I'm alone.)

"In spite of himself" *(malgré lui)*, Colette writes in the stage direction, the child finds himself calling out "Maman." This is the Magic Word, and with this summons, he changes, and they change too: it gradually brings about the conclusion of the opera in reconciliation and hope and love.

Terry Eagleton has placed Beckett in a tradition of eighteenth-century Protestant theology about negation-as-presence, about the gulf between the word and the world, and commented on the performative actions in the plays, on their uses of blessings, curses, and expletives.[68] By contrast Colette's sensibility is saturated with a Catholic feel for language as a performative as well as voluptuous instrument. Beckett's austerity rejects precisely this function of linguistic art/enactment, and with it, holds at bay the insistent coming into being—incarnation—of images, verbal and visual, as well as wishing to stifle symbolism, to speak it instead "How It Is." ("No symbols where none intended," he writes.)[69] This difference in use of language deserves greater attention, but for the moment, let's return to the delinquent child and Colette's affecting, poetic drama. It presents us with a play about playing that takes up thinking about childhood, and the power of naming; it also tells a story that Beckett's only film effectively inverts.

This condensed and marvelous enigma—twenty-one minutes simply called *Film*—was made in New York in 1964 by his longtime collaborator Alan Schneider, and stars Buster Keaton, one of many great comics who haunt Beckett's writings, whom he brought out of retirement to make the film. It is a silent movie—apart from one harshly uttered and highly emblematic "Shush!" near the beginning—and it is set in 1929, and styled in the tradition of both Expressionist films of the time and Keaton's own masterpieces. It takes us back to the years when Beckett was first learning to write—and speak—in French, and the film's muffled and elusive melancholic comedy catches something of Beckett's desires, desires that turn upside down Colette's easy, potent sentimentality and Mallarmé's trust in sound-words. Instead, it communicates a dream of solitude, silence, inanimateness, absence, and stillness, with the exception of the rocking of the chair in which Keaton sits. Here it is the very vitality and autonomy of other things—things that have consciousness of him—that distresses the protagonist. Designated as O for Object, this protagonist (Keaton) is first caught by the camera, which is designated as E for Eye. *Eye* was the original title of the film itself, and is the other principal actor in the unfolding of the film. In the script, Beckett quoted Bishop Berkeley's principle, "esse est percipi" (to be is to be perceived) and the things—animate and inanimate—seem to disturb the object of their attention. "Ah yes, things have their life, that is what I always say, *things* have a life." This is Winnie in *Happy Days,* and then after a pause, adds, "Take my looking-glass, it doesn't need me."[70] Far from wanting to call things into symbiotic existence with his active appetites and feelings, Keaton plays O, a person-object who wishes to quell their energies, to stop himself existing in their consciousness, constituted by their gaze.

The sequence of actions the central figure undertakes focuses on the life in things beyond the life conveyed by naming: the room that the Keaton character enters is sparsely furnished, but he strips it further, just as Beckett's own use of language seeks to pare down to the *haecceitas* of things.[71]

O keeps his face averted from E throughout, and also huddles and sidles and crouches and shrouds himself in order to retreat from everything in the room—from the view in at the window, and the reflection in the mirror, and from the living things, like the cat, the dog, the goldfish, the parrot. He ejects the cat and the dog, performing gentle comic routines of timing as the animals refuse to be set outside. He covers the goldfish bowl and the parrot's cage. Inanimate things also turn their gaze on him: the rocking chair seems to stare with blazing devil eyes from its ornamental crest; he notices the huge orbs of an Assyrian god on the wall and tears up the picture; later, when he settles in the rocking chair and takes out a well-thumbed wallet, its twin clasps also seem to be looking at him. He looks through a sheaf of photographs, and contemplates himself and others in a sequence of his own life from cradle to the decrepit present: he tears up the pictures.

In this room, there are no words and there will be no images either—no eye-objects. Verbal and visual representations must go, only bare existence remains. But in that mute and bare existence, the perceiver cannot escape self-perception. Even when nothing is left to hold you in its mind—there is your own sense of yourself. At the end the camera Eye circles round O (Keaton) and for the very first time looks him full on; Keaton is wearing a patch over one eye, the blind eye with which the film begins, the mirror of the camera's single lens. Seeing himself from the camera's point of view, thus beholding himself as an Other who is his double, his jaw drops, and then his face settles, Beckett's script prescribes, into a "very different expression, impossible to describe, neither severity nor benignity, but rather acute *intentness. . . .*

Long image of the unblinking gaze."[72] Then he covers his face. "Image of O rocking, his head in his hands but not yet bowed."[73] Eventually he sinks down, still rocking.

This is a picture of the ineluctable cogito: his inner eye goes on. Beckett brilliantly and often movingly crystallizes in *Film* his thinking about the gaze, the camera, and the self. His title draws attention to the simple fact that this film refers to nothing outside its own boundaries.

In the notes to the script Beckett writes, "It may be supposed it [the room] is his mother's room, which he has not visited for many years and is now to occupy momentarily, to look after the pets, until she comes out of hospital." He then adds, "This has no bearing on the film and need not be elucidated."[74]

The mood in the film is, however, valedictory, not hopeful; it does not anticipate the return of the room's occupant, but rather conveys strongly that O is returning to it and opening it after her death. Here, there is no magic word that will make her come back; like so much of Beckett's work, the pain of elegy lies within reach of consciousness, perception, and art through a language that hovers on the brink of its own nonbeing; that dissolution he conveys through languages from the start of speech, as when first learned. Words arrived then like music, sense coming up behind the sounds, and seemed to have power both to still and to quicken loved things and loved ones into being there and then again, into not being there. Babel/*babil* captured the bubbling and flux of consciousness, before perception formed, hardened, and became an impediment, a stasis.

NOTES

My profound thanks to Anne Holmes for her help with Mallarmé; and to Philip Terry, Steven Connor, Patricia Scanlan, Christopher Reid, Jean Khalfa, Roy Foster, Bill Prosser, Sarah Blair, and Thierry van Eyll for advice and comments with regard to Beckett. Also to the *British Journal of Psychotherapy* for help with Beckett's Bion analysis. A shorter version of this paper was published as "Babble with Beckett," *TLS*, February 29, 2008, and "Beckett, Mallarmé, and Foreign Tongues," *Raritan*, 27 (2008): 62–89.

1. Stephane Mallarmé, *Les Mots anglais*, in *Oeuvres complètes*, ed. Bertrand Marchal, vol. 2 (Paris: Gallimard, 2003), 1220.

2. Mallarmé wrote a lavishly enthusiastic, long introduction to *Vathek* for the French edition of 1876, *Oeuvres complètes*, 3–20.

3. Mallarmé made a prose translation of *Mariana* and of two other poems by Tennyson, *Oeuvres complètes*, 825–33.

4. He wrote to Catulle Mendès in 1871 that he knew "de l'Anglais que les mots employés dans le volume des poésies de Poe." But this is not quite fair to himself, of course, *Lettre du 1er mars 1871*, quoted *Oeuvres complètes*, eds. Henri Mondor and G. Jean-Aubry

(Paris: Pléaïde, 1945), 1124. This is the edition I was using, when I first began this research, until the Marchal ed. of 2002 became available through the London library. For Mallarmé's shaky command of idiom of English, see also his letter to Edmund Gosse, August 1875, in Mallarmé, *Correspondance,* vol. 2 (1871–75), ed. Henri Mondor and L. J. Austin (Paris: Gallimard, 1965), 69–70.

5. Michael Edwards, "Beckett's French," *Translation and Literature* 1 (1992): 69. My thanks to Philip Terry for bringing this article to my attention.

6. Edwards, "Beckett's French," 70.

7. Colm Tóibín, "My Darlings: On Beckett's Irish Actors," *London Review of Books,* April 5, 2007, 3–8.

8. John Stokes, "The Raven Herself is Hoarse," *Times Literary Supplement (TLS),* February 2, 2007.

9. Samuel Beckett, *All That Fall,* in *Collected Shorter Plays* (London: Faber and Faber, 1984), 13.

10. Paul Muldoon in his paper at the Centenary Conference, Dublin, on April 7, 2006, displayed with bravura ingenuity how *Watt* can be glossed by rich excursions to the Oxford English Dictionary.

11. Samuel Beckett, *Krapp's Last Tape,* in *Collected Shorter Plays,* 59.

12. Edwards, "Beckett's French," 72.

13. Samuel Beckett, *Poems in English* (London: Calder, 1961), 51.

14. Beckett, *Fin de Partie* (Paris: Les Éditions de Minuit, 1961), 76–77.

15. René James Hérail and Edwin A. Lovatt, *Dictionary of Modern Colloquial French* (London: Routledge, 1987), 27, 183.

16. Samuel Beckett, *Endgame* (London: Faber and Faber, 1958), 38. In *Molloy,* Beckett uses another term, *charabia,* indeed rendered by him as "gibberish" in the English translation—and in this case, both terms vividly mimic their meaning.

17. Letter of 1937, trans. Martin Esslin, in *Disjecta: Miscellaneous Writings and a Dramatic Fragment,* ed. Ruby Cohn (London: Calder, 1983), 172, quoted by Philip Terry, "Waiting for God to Go: *How It Is* and *Inferno* VII–VIII," *Samuel Beckett Today/ Aujourd'hui: Beckett versus Beckett* (1998): 352.

18. Samuel Beckett, *Malone Dies* (Harmondsworth: Penguin, 1965), 6.

19. See Brigitte Le Juez, *Beckett Before Beckett: Samuel Beckett's Lectures on French Literature,* trans. Ros Schwartz (London: Souvenir Press, 2008).

20. Gordon Millan, *Mallarmé: A Throw of the Dice: The Life of Stéphane Mallarmé* (London: Secker and Warburg, 1994), 214–15.

21. James Knowlson and Elizabeth Knowlson, eds., *Beckett Remembering, Remembering Beckett: Uncollected Interviews with Samuel Beckett and Memories of Those Who Knew Him* (London: Bloomsbury, 2006), 217.

22. Quoted by Dan Gunn, "'Until the Gag is Chewed': Samuel Beckett's Letters: Eloquence and 'Near Speechlessness,'" *TLS,* April 21, 2006, 14.

23. Mallarmé included 106 nursery rhymes and eight nonsense songs, mostly taken from Mrs. Barbauld, Walter Crane, and Kate Greenaway: Mallarmé, *Recueil de "Nursery Rhymes,"* *Oeuvres complètes,* 1254–1329 (1798), which reprints the first published edition: Stéphane Mallarmé, *Recueil de "Nursery Rhymes,"* ed. C. P. Barbier (Paris: Gallimard, 1964); John Ashbery has introduced and translated a selection: see "The Secret Lives of Children," *Conjunctions* 45 (2005): 370–77. I am grateful to the poet Daniel Tiffany for bringing this work to my notice, and for lending me his own "Mother Goose and the Proverbial Mallarmé," forthcoming in *Infidel Poetics: Riddles, Nightlife, Substance* (University of Chicago Press, 2009).

24. Mallarmé, *Recueil de "Nursery Rhymes,"* 1281.

25. Carl Paul Barbier, introduction to Mallarmé, *Recueil de "Nursery Rhymes,"* 13.

26. Iona Opie and Peter Opie, in *The Lore and Language of Schoolchildren,* record its first appearance in 1744, as "Spit Cat Spit, . . . etc." ; "Tell tale tit" appears in *Mother Goose's Melody* (1780), 45, and in *Juvenile Amusements (1797),* no. 2.; the Opies give many variants, 189–90. When I gave this essay in Dublin on April 8, 2006, Prof. David Simms remembered that in India in the late thirties his ayah taught him a variation beginning, "Liar liar lip stick . . . ," which strongly suggests that the version Mallarmé quotes circulated very far afield.

27. Mallarmé's source was *A Handbook of Proverbs, Comprising an Entire Republication of Ray's Collection of English Proverbs* (London, 1867); see notes to "Dossier des 'Les Mots anglais,'" *Oeuvres complètes,* 1796.

28. Stéphane Mallarmé, *Thèmes anglais,* in *Oeuvres complètes,* ed. Henri Mondor and G. Jean-Aubry (Paris: Pléaïde, 1945), 1128.

29. Op. cit., 1130; in a letter to *TLS* (March 14, 2008), Martin Smith suggested that Mallarmé was back-translating from French into English, e.g., from the proverbial phrase "tondre un oeuf" describing a skinflint. He gave other examples, but his theory is not borne out by the French translations that Mallarmé provides for the English phrases; e.g., gives, "Qui peut *raser* un oeuf?"

30. Mallarmé described it in a letter to Verlaine as the kind of task he would undertake in moments of frustration and "pour acheter de ruineux canots" ("to buy rotten canoes [for his children]"), *Oeuvres complètes* (1945), 1643.

31. *Oeuvres complètes* (1945), 931.

32. *Oeuvres complètes* (1945), 973.

33. See Terry Eagleton, "Beckett and Nothing," in this volume.

34. Mallarmé, *Oeuvres complètes* (1945), 969.

35. Mallarmé, *Oeuvres complètes* (1945), 949–50.

36. Mallarmé, *Oeuvres complètes* (1945), 938.

37. Mallarmé, *Oeuvres complètes* (1945), 939–40.

38. Roger Pearson, *Unfolding Mallarmé: The Development of a Poetic Art* (Oxford: Oxford University Press, 1996), 5; see also a fine study by Adam Piette, *Remembering and the Sound of Words* (Oxford: Oxford University Press, 1996).

39. Paul Muldoon, discussing the many efflorescences of the sound "watt," explored how it conceals hat within it.

40. Virginia Woolf, *On Being Ill,* intro. Hermione Lee (Ashfield, Mass.: Paris Press, 2002), 22–23; emphasis added.

41. Beckett, *How It Is* (New York: Grove Press, 1964), 7.

42. Ovid, *Metamorphoses,* Book VI, ll. 370–76; emphasis added. See interesting note by Michael Hendry, "Improving the Alliteration: Ovid, *Metamorphoses* 6.376," in *Mnemosyne* 49 (1996): 443–45.

43. In the Royal Shakespeare Company production of *The Tempest,* the director Rupert Goold created tableaux of Caliban's servitude to Stephano the butler that suggestively reflected the domination of Lucky by Pozzo, seen Albery Theatre, London, March 2007.

44. Terry, "Waiting for God," 352.

45. Terry, "Waiting for God," 349–60.

46. Dante Alighieri, *Inferno* XXI, 136–40, *The Divine Comedy,* 3 vols., trans. and ed. John D. Sinclair (London: Bodley Head, 1958), 1:266–67.

47. Beckett, *Poems in English,* 35–36.

48. Dante, *Inferno* VII, 117–24, *The Divine Comedy*, 1:104–5.

49. Leslie Hill, *Beckett in Different Words*, quoted by Steven Connor, personal communication, August 14, 2006.

50. Knowlson, *Beckett Remembering*, 111.

51. Personal communication, August 14, 2006.

52. Samuel Beckett, *Happy Days* (London: Faber and Faber, 1962), 20. The French here has *lacher*, to let go, not as in Lacan's favored "le mot me manque" for "words fail me."

53. Woolf, *On Being Ill*, 6–7; emphasis added.

54. Samuel Beckett, *That Time* (1975, unfinished ms.), Samuel Beckett Archive, University of Reading, quoted by Andrew Renton, "Dwelling on a Ray: Long Observation of the Ray—Samuel Beckett's Intractable Text," *Lovely Jobly*, March 1990 (special issue on Samuel Beckett), 23–25, kindly copied for me by Patricia Scanlan, founder and editor of the magazine.

55. The catalog of Beckett manuscripts at Reading gives this alternative meaning: "a set of child's brightly coloured ribbons, associated with fairgrounds" (I am grateful to the artists Bill Prosser and Sarah Blair for this reference, personal communication, August 22, 2007). *Mirlitonnades*, exhibited in "All This This Here: Samuel Beckett Manuscripts at Trinity College Library," Dublin, April–June 2006; published in French in *Poems, 1930–1989* (London: John Calder, 1978); a complete English translation is forthcoming from David Wheatley, NB, *TLS*, July 7, 2006; Daniel Tiffany has pointed out that Aristide Briant opened a café, *Le Mirliton*, in Paris, which Beckett certainly knew about, and that the word was also associated with lighter-hearted conviviality. Personal communication, May 2008.

56. Derek Mahon, "Burbles" and "Watt Is the Word: The 'brief scattered lights' of Beckett's Poems," *TLS*, November 3, 2006; see also NB, *TLS*, March 30, 2007, for other translations by Mahon of a *Mirlitonnade*.

57. NB, *TLS*, June 9, 2006.

58. NB, *TLS*, June 23, 2006.

59. NB, *TLS*, November 10, 2006; emphasis added. *Foirades* is available in French in *Pour finir encore et autres foirades* (Paris: Minuit, 1976); in English in *Samuel Beckett's Complete Short Prose, 1929–1989*, ed. S. E. Gontarski (New York: Grove Press, 1995).

60. Knowlson, *Beckett Remembering*, 114.

61. See a most illuminating paper by David Mayers, "Bion and Beckett Together," *British Journal of Psychotherapy* 17, no. 2 (2000): 192–202, from conference "Beckett/Bion: The Emergence of Meaning," University College London, September 18, 1999; see also Helen Taylor Robinson, "'The Bespoke Universe': Shakespeare, Freud and Beckett, Tailors and Outfitters," 181–91, presented at the same conference; and Didieu Anzieu, "Beckett and Bion," *International Journal of Psycho-Analysis* 16 (1989): 193–99.

62. See D. W. Winnicott, *Playing and Reality* (1971; Hove: Brunner-Routledge, 2001), 38–64; and Mary Jacobus, *The Poetics of Psychoanalysis: In the Wake of Melanie Klein* (Oxford: Oxford University Press, 2005) for a fine study of this movement.

63. Charles Baudelaire, "Morale du joujou," in *Oeuvres complètes*, ed. Marcel A. Ruff (Paris: Seuil, 1968), 358–60.

64. Baudelaire, "Morale du joujou."

65. Rainer Maria Rilke, "Puppen: Zu den Wachspuppen von Lotte Pritzel," in *Werke: Kommentierte Ausgabe in 4 Bde,* ed. Manfred Engel und Ulrich Fülleborn (Darmstadt: WBG, 1996), 4:685–92; compare with Rainer Maria Rilke, "Some Reflections on

Dolls," in *Rodin and Other Prose Pieces,* trans. (slightly altered) G. Craig Houston (London: Quartet, 1986), 121–22.

66. Kurt Schwitters, "She dolls with dollies" (1944), in *Poems, Performance Pieces, Proses, Plays, Poetics,* ed. and trans. Jerome Rothenberg and Pierre Joris (Philadelphia: Temple University Press, 1993), 102.

67. Deutsche Grammophon recording, with LSO and André Previn, 457–589–2, 69.

68. Eagleton, "Beckett and Nothing."

69. Samuel Beckett, "Addenda," *Watt* (London: John Calder, 1976), 255.

70. Beckett, *Happy Days,* 40.

71. Cf. Terry Eagleton, *The Meaning of Life* (Oxford: Oxford University Press, 2007), 110–11: "The other side of Beckett's work, however, is a kind of postmodern positivism, for which things are not endlessly elusive but brutely themselves. . . . This reflects the side of Beckett for which the world just is whatever is the case, the artist who is fascinated by the sheer inert materiality of objects like pebbles or bowler hats . . . ('No symbol[s] where none intended.')."

72. Samuel Beckett, *Film: Complete Scenario Illustrations Production Shots with an Essay 'Directing Film',* by Alan Schneider (London: Faber and Faber, 1972), 47–48; see also Katherine Waugh and Fergus Daly, "*Film* by Samuel Beckett," *Film West* 20 (1995), http://www.iol.ie/~galfilm/filmwest/20beckett.htm.

73. Beckett, *Film,* 48.

74. Beckett, *Film,* 59.

Antony Tatlow

Samuel Brecht and Bertolt Beckett: Schopenhauer and Nietzsche as Educators

Beckett and Brecht have been so frequently read against each other that surely nothing more can be said about them. Many books, more chapters, and countless articles have juxtaposed and above all contrasted their work. What one had in abundance, the other lacked. One offered the antidote or counterpoison to protect against the other's enticement.

As BBC head of drama, Martin Esslin worked closely with Beckett. Though not emotionally or politically close to Brecht, he nevertheless had a lively sense of his talents and his work's capacity.[1] But he also contrasted the two dramatists, and where we might have expected more searching comparisons, in Esslin's book whose title bears their names, they are taken separately.[2]

The word *dichotomy* might have been invented to describe their positions, in the dictionary sense of a division into two parts or classes, especially when these are sharply distinguished or opposed, and reinforced by its use within biology, where the division establishes two equal parts. Yet astronomers call the moon dichotomous when half its surface is illuminated. This metaphorical image suggests that appearances can be deceptive, that at least half of what is substantial may be concealed even from superficial inspection. All is perhaps not as clear-cut or as transparent as it may seem.

There are as many parallels as differences in their use of metaphor, in personal behavior and attitudes, and in the responses these invoked. The coldness of the earth, a founding metaphor for both, can be given a convergent as well as a divergent reading. For both, a "vulture" metaphorizes a complex, overdetermined response to the conditions of life. The images radiate beyond their particular contexts into the rest of their work. "The Vulture," said to have derived from reading Goethe's poem *Harzreise im Winter,* is the first poem in Beckett's *Echo's Bones,* published in 1935.[3] Esslin finds the poem anticipates "the future argument of Beckett's complete *oeuvre*."[4]

Compared with Brecht, Beckett wrote little poetry, but a poetic imagination infuses all his work. Brecht's "vulture" figures in a verse of the *Hymn of the Great Baal* that opens his first play, the only verse then repeated within the play itself.[5] It could well be considered fundamental to the project that is Brecht's work. These "vultures" metaphorize the imagination as a soaring, circling bird of prey, figuring the life of the mind that must nourish itself upon that of which it is itself a part, upon death in nature. These philosophical poems are acts of exorcism, probing destiny, focusing loneliness; they are all close to the person of their authors. The self-identification with this insatiable, transcendent, immortal/mortal murdering force is as evident in Beckett's "dragging his hunger through the sky / of my skull shell of sky and earth" as it is for Brecht's Baal, who, by shamming death in the form of its prey, then catches the swooping vulture in order to devour it and internalize its soaring immortality. Baal, in the last words of the verse, eats it "zum Abendmahl," a word that means both "dinner" and the Holy Sacrament that recalls the Last Supper.[6] Both Beckett and Brecht materialize the spiritual or sacramental by facing, or facing up to, by ingesting death.

Sensitive to music, no matter how differently it resonates, both feared it might overwhelm them, so even as they needed it, they kept it at a distance. In 1947 Brecht gave Lotte Goslar an outline for a pantomime, *From Circus Life* (GBA 20:184), whose story of a "silent subject" was comparable to a Beckettian *Act Without Words*.[7] Both meticulously documented their innovative practice in the theater. The behavior of their estates was virtually identical in believing that these practices had to be protected. Beckett is a sharp observer of class-specific behavior, and survival is at the center of Brecht's project. Both focused on the small and the ordinary. When power confronts the powerless, Beckett has recourse to a flawed detective, Brecht to a flawed judge. Both invoked intense loyalty among their advocates and followers, who stylized them as paragons: Beckett as secular saint, Brecht as embodied practical friendliness.

Two recent books engage with their subjects from different critical, professional, and cultural perspectives, but reveal surprising congruities. As his publisher, John Calder had unique access to Beckett and offers unusual insight into the person and his work.[8] The German translation of Fredric Jameson's *Brecht and Method* is aptly entitled *Pleasure and Terror at the Ceaseless Transformation of All Things: Brecht and the Future*.[9] It might just as well have been called *The Philosophy of Bertolt Brecht,* because he reads the work as articulating a fundamental attitude, triangulating language, narrative, and thought. Attempts to derive abstract meanings or to extrapolate political positions respond to it below the level of its complexity. Both books affirm the importance of a particular kind of philosophical reflection upon the conditions of existence, upon ways of living, which we could describe as ethical and which touches upon stoic values. They show how such reflection both informs this writing and provides perspectives upon it, and why all of this should be taken seriously. Jameson sees in Brecht's reflections on the nature of identity, given the inescapable flow of time, "a Beckett-like drift scarcely held in place by the afterthought of a situation and response framework." This may "from a post-contemporary position . . . seem a mode of containment, and a way of managing the otherwise frightening chaos of psychic flux that threatens individuality's dissolution."[10]

Calder and Jameson draw attention to Buddhist philosophy. We are invited to reflect on the concept of "nothing" in their work, though Beckett's is maybe closer to Sartre's *néant* than any Buddhist Nirvana, which, if the relationship is properly expounded, is indeed pertinent to Brecht, for whom the term *Nichts* is just as suggestive, if not more so, than it was for Beckett. Calder traces Beckett's "nothing" from Geulincx through to Buddhism. Brecht's "nothing" resonates with Nietzsche. If Beckett held, as Calder reminds us, that the key word in his writing is *perhaps,* we can see an equivalent to this in Brecht's call to actors to embody in their performance what the character does not do, which he called "fixing the 'not/but'" ("Fixieren des Nicht-Sondern," GBA 22.2:643), provided we do not read this as advocating a loaded binary opposition between right and wrong but as an opportunity to reflect on the construction of a restrictive "identity" that is confronted by multiplicity, as Jameson suggests.[11] Their work is infused by paradox, doubleness, and contradiction, which accounts for the importance of laughter to both, though Beckett's is also the *risus purus,* which laughs at laughter.

The Beckettian *perhaps* is a word that certainly applies to Brecht, and especially to his political and philosophical activity, since the physical/metaphysical flow of the "river of things" and of time will not cease. This "perhaps" surrounds his work like the discernible circle of the moon before its visible half is fully illuminated. And "perhaps" we can say that there is a "not/but" in Beckett too, a grimmer one, since consciousness could not be obviated, and he wanted to be both forgotten yet remembered. In Clov's words, more affirmation perhaps than denial of this thought: "It's not certain."

Academic disciplines tend to compartmentalize attention and to neglect their own borders by ignoring what transcends or undermines them. Since we have left "Beckett and the absurd" or "Brecht and behaviorism" behind us, we must account for the compatibilities within their differences. What follows is an attempt to do so.

I.

Genealogies are problematic and certainly impure. Nietzsche also held that *endings* are *un*scripted. The Eternal does *not* return, not because what is unchanging cannot repeat itself within time, but because the idea of the same is a *verbal* illusion. *Eternal return* means *process* never ends. What is eternal is recurrence itself: *life* everlasting. The challenge is not how to become strong and constant enough to overcome the world, but how to live in a world without end that never stays the same.[12] *Will to Power* means the act of accepting that everything changes, including yourself. The later Nietzsche also employs another rhetoric, of dominance and exclusivity, which is unconscionable. It influenced many artists and had a certain social effect but was historically limited compared with his other writing.

Since we speak of impure origins and repetitions, let me hazard: In the beginning was the lecture. Or rather: In the beginning were the lectures, and they clashed. The truth has already split in two. We are into a dialectic, and that sounds more promising. But what lectures, and what truths? The story is well known. When Schopenhauer became a *Privatdozent* at the University of Berlin he deliberately scheduled his lecture at the same time as Professor Hegel's, with predictable results. At the back of Hegel's class Bert Brecht could be heard *talking*. He called Hegel one of the great comic writers because in his system everything kept changing into something else. Sam Beckett was definitely *listening* to Schopenhauer. But because nobody else came, Schopenhauer discontinued the course and, like his student, put academic life behind him: the essential step, according to Nietzsche, for a serious professional career.[13]

It seems you had to choose between Hegel and Schopenhauer, and to do so from the start: either a rational, outward-looking, history-encompassing, and teleologically benign system, or the opposite to all of that. Brecht's and Beckett's work was and is routinely described as divergent, even incompatible. But those lectures clashed not because they were so different, and certainly not just because they were scheduled concurrently, but because they had so much in common. Nobody is so like me as my own worst enemy. *Constructing* oppositions means they can be thought together. Brecht and Beckett stood for antitheses. Dominating theater for decades, their work seemed to cover, without overlap, the range of possible expression. It was used to place, not deconstruct, its opposite, a sure sign that criticism was caught within the episteme as, at first, it always must be. Epitomizing opposed possibilities, they relativized anyone assigned to either camp: the theater of the absurd that, recognizing aspects of himself, Brecht disparaged (GBA 23:239–40); the theater of political engagement or Schiller's moral institution, which Beckett rejected.[14] Sartre was eclipsed by Brecht, Ionesco by Beckett. It is scarcely any longer possible to imagine two artists and dramatists so dominating the cultural discourse.

There is a danger of talking at cross-purposes. It is not easy to have the full range of their texts and interventions in mind. Then we use the same names but mean different authors. Brecht is perhaps half, maybe only a quarter, known in English, his prose virtually unopened, though it is as aesthetically, if differently, innovative in respect of identity construction as Beckett's. Brecht mostly stands for an aesthetically difficult corrective to dramatic conventions, and for a sharp focus on the politics of art. Yet that dramatic work, never mind the rest, is more differentiated than is appreciated by either the standard political readings, which I will not recapitulate, or those that seek to reverse them, taking his early writing as pre-postmodernist but the rest as dustbin-of-history stuff.[15]

Beckett unfolds into a spread of language texts, self-fashioned or self-approved, producing culturally distinct resonances. A French or German Beckett is differently nuanced from his Irish namesake, though confusions can be creative. We may prefer one author to the other, and can legitimately take sides, intellectually and emotionally, in any contest of excellence, but a good holding assumption might be that we really do not know either Brecht or Beckett that well.

Of the two, I suspect Brecht is less understood, naturally so in Dublin, London, or Sydney, though perhaps also, for other reasons, in Berlin. I wonder, for example, how many who read Brecht in English know why a German critic once said: "He feels chaos and putrefaction physically. Hence the incomparable vividness of his language. You feel this language on your tongue, in the roof of your mouth, in your ear, in your spine."[16] Were I to speak in detail about their texts, whatever I said would be all-too-familiar to at least half the audience. You would face unpalatable alternatives: boredom or suffering, as Schopenhauer predicted, and Beckett feared. So I will say little about the texts themselves.

Instead of reading Beckett, for example, as the last "essentialist" and Brecht as the last "Marxist," we could see both as deconstructing the dilemmas of these paradigms. For Parmenides transubstantiates into Beckett's paradoxical Zeno—why otherwise worry about that impossible heap? And the Heraclitean flux of *Mann ist Mann* (GBA 2:189)—we cannot step twice into the same river—is transformed into the *longue durée* of a Brechtian Zen or Dao.[17] Beckett once spoke, in German, of passing through "das Nichts" and, whether or not anyone could follow him, creating poetry on the other side.[18] We can say something similar of Brecht. But where does this come from and where does it lead us?

II.

So with apologies, which I shall not repeat, now primarily to the Brechtians, I want to summarize some critical views. When these seem authorially indexable, but have been taken out of their contemporary discourse and thereby necessarily more abstractly placed in other contexts, the subtexts and overtones get lost. What was culturally astute suddenly looks much cruder. Words on their own are never enough. It is a problem of cultural translation.

If we set aside anxiety of influence, why did Howard Barker so scorn Brecht as "The One Who Knows," and why does this irascible rejection of a claim to knowledge still reverberate, as whoever followed the Brecht centennial will have noticed?[19] That "knowledge" was grounded in political struggle: against Fascism, for socialism and, finally, located within the deeply insecure East German state. What may look, later and from outside, like a government policy statement was virtually always formulated in resistance to official dogma. I am not thinking of the unambiguous—"Would it not be simpler if the government dissolved the people and elected another?" (GBA 12:310)—but rather of formulations within quieter theoretical writing.

If we have no ear for the language of resistance, we read naively, and take a stronger moral stand. In his suggestion that "Creative realism in art can only be developed in conjunction with the rising classes,"[20] Brecht hardly expresses a Broadway or a Beckettian ethos, but every term here has a subversive meaning. Read in the 1950s this amounts to a shrewd, prophylactic declaration of war against cultural policies. The East German government wanted a controllable, not a rising working class. It was terrified of creativity. Brecht's realism turned the official script upside down. Listen to his 1955 public description of Soviet art: "inhuman, barbaric, superficial, bourgeois, that is to say petit-bourgeois, slipshod, irresponsible, corrupt, etc., etc."[21] Enough said. English-speaking feminist dramatists and critics value Brecht's deconstructing of the subject but dislike what they see as his putting people in place, and associate this with a male authority reflex. These responses seem contradictory.[22] I will return to the subversive counterknowledge of the one who knows.

Part of this adverse reaction may well be indirectly connected with perceptions of Brecht's response to *Waiting for Godot*. The play was originally bad news in East Berlin and shunned by officialdom. "Without substance and without humor," was a typical critical comment.[23] Brecht recognized a challenge to his own project. For a possible Berliner Ensemble production, he began making changes in the German translation, but they are minimal and soon peter out: Vladimir, an intellectual; *von* Pozzo, a landowner, social concretizations that hardly move that far from Beckett.[24] Heiner Müller argues it was only the start of what might have looked very different, had he pursued it.[25] But that was not to be. Brecht was in hospital with four months to live. It would certainly have ended in disaster, had the idea communicated by one of his assistants prevailed. Clas Zilliacus quotes Käthe Rülicke-Weiler, who observed that since the "magnificently written" play contradicted the purpose of Brecht's theater, projected film scenes should show people changing the world, while Vladimir and Estragon wait for Godot.[26] A counterplay was not then possible.[27]

Adorno thought Beckett the *greater* realist, of a totally reified world for whom there is "no more nature." For him, Beckett's absolute refusal of commodified language was the only possible post-Auschwitz political intervention, exemplifying Adorno's negative dialectics. Adorno opposed Beckett to the positive dialectics of Lukács and Brecht, about whom he held contradictory views, not based on any real understanding of Brecht's work, which Brecht reciprocated. Since Lukács was the greater enemy for Brecht, it is both not surprising and fascinating that the Marxist Lukács objected to Beckett in language virtually identical to conservative West German academic criticism of Brecht. Beckett, Lukács complained, reduces human beings to the state of animality, the charge made against Brecht. The political extremes meet in aesthetic conservatism that, as Adorno once argued, marks political regression more accurately than abstract statements of social intent.[28]

If Lukács and Brecht represented "official optimism" for Adorno,[29] Beckett mythologized disenchantment, offering "realism . . . minus reconciliation" (127). Using Schopenhauerian language, Adorno argues that communication rests on the principle of sufficient reason, but Beckett alone shows that reason masks interest (139–40). In effect, Adorno argues that Beckett's play is the *Endgame* of the subject, and therefore parodies the master/servant dialectic. When history has been annulled, what is left is compulsive repetition. Because Beckett does not mention the specific historical danger, the nuclear threat, Adorno calls him the "simplifier of horror," adding however that "unlike Brecht he refuses simplification."[30] But Adorno also maintains they were "not so dissimilar . . . insofar as [Beckett's] differentiation becomes sensitivity to subjective differences, which have regressed to the 'conspicuous consumption' of those who can afford individuation. Therein lies the social truth."[31] Beckett's images also represent the historical form of his society: "Because there was no other life than the false one, the catalogue of its defects becomes the mirror image of ontology" (133). Adorno saw Beckett within the post–Second World War, post-Holocaust balance of terror, but had himself described the consequences of instrumentalizing nature in *Dialectic of Enlightenment*. In such a reading Beckett offers the vision not of local but of total catastrophe, and he becomes the realist of planetary destruction.

III.

It is easy to construct a Beckettian Brecht from the early work. This passage in Foucault could apply to either:

> From within language experienced and traversed as language, in the play of its possibilities extended to their furthest point, what emerges is that "man has come to an end," and that, by reaching the summit of all possible speech, he arrives not at the very heart of himself but at the brink of that which limits him; in that region where death prowls, where thought is extinguished, where the promise of the origin interminably recedes.[32]

Beckett could have written this dialogue from *Baal:*

Baal: What's wrong with you?
Gougou: Bronchitis. Nothing bad. A little inflammation. Nothing
   serious.
Baal to *Bolleboll:* And you?
Bolleboll: Stomach ulcers. Won't kill me!
Baal to the *Beggar:* There's something wrong with you too, I trust?
The Beggar: I'm mad.

He would have underwritten what follows:

Baal: Here's to you! We understand each other. I'm healthy.
The Beggar: I knew a man who said he was healthy too. He believed it. He came from the forest and one day he went back
   there as there was something he had to think over. He found
   the forest very strange and no longer familiar, he walked for
   many days. Always deeper into the forest, because he wanted to
   see how independent he was and how much endurance there
   was left in him. But there wasn't much. *He drinks . . .*
Ekart: Did it cure him?
The Beggar: No. He had an easier death, though.
Maja: I don't understand that.
The Beggar: Nothing is understood. But some things are felt. If one
   understands a story it's just because it's been told badly.[33]

If Brecht stands for political and Beckett for ontological metaphor,
we can construct a Brechtian Beckett. The master/servant dialectic may
be parodistic but is still in use. Some plays are amenable to political readings: *Catastrophe, Rough for Theatre II, What Where,* no matter what
Beckett may have said.

But much in the later Brecht undoes Adorno's political "simplification": a dislike of what he called *Weltbildhauer* or world systematizers
(GBA 21:349); his suspicion of the "myth" of a continuous ego (GBA
26:476, 682); a rejection of correspondence in favor of relational or coherence theory (GBA 21:428; 22.1:458);[34] his questioning of rational art,
whether he really wanted "to do away with the space where the unconscious, half conscious, uncontrolled, ambiguous, multipurposed could
play itself out" (GBA 22.1:468), and the unstated answer is obviously:
No!

I wish to dehistoricize readings whereby Beckett's ontology becomes an expression of frozen history, of the historically created malaise of the bourgeoisie, of an immobility and functionalization closer to Max Weber than Karl Marx, and also Brecht's Marxist solution for historical problems. I then wish to rehistoricize the emerging conjunctures on another level of analysis. The trajectory through Schopenhauer and Nietzsche is necessarily roundabout. But we need to understand why there are such contradictory movements in their work: a strong disintegrative undertow in Brecht, and a powerful integrative desire in Beckett. Before I get into these central arguments, I first want to inspect what we might call their parallel lives. The method is partly anecdotal, like Plutarch's, but the information interesting, though some may find this reviewing distasteful.

IV.

Hans Mayer, professor of literature in Leipzig, worked with Brecht, though he was never part of the theater's inner circle. Beckett liked him enough to present him a poem in French written in 1976, which Mayer only let go when he published it in 1995.[35] Mayer found them both "very lonely men." In respect of Brecht, this observation may have been retrospectively constructed after understanding the disproportion between Brecht's hopes and the realities of his last years. But it connects with an aspect of Brecht's mind that Mayer knew less about, and does not describe, but is apposite to our topic: what I term the *longue durée* of Brecht's thought.[36] Brecht spoke in Berlin of "Chinese exile," not meaning, as some have thought, that he wished he were in China, but rather that he felt shunted aside, his views not welcome.[37]

Beckett told Mayer that he knew Brecht's work. Since there seems no very obvious response to it, all the more reason, we might think, for sticking to those antitheses, which set Brecht's "interventionary thought" against Beckett's epiphany for his life's work: man is the "non-knower, non can-er."[38] But there is a "non-knower, non can-er" in Brecht as well. Siegfried Unseld published both and tells a story that bears on *longue durée*.[39] During one of their meetings in Paris Beckett quoted his poem—"en face / le pire / jusqu'à ce / qu'il fasse rire"—and described it as continuing the spirit of Goethe's "Xenien" or his *Chinesisch-Deutsche Jahres- und Tageszeiten*. (These are philosophical-satirical, or short late lyrical poems loosely but interestingly connected with

China.) Beckett then offered a German version. Unseld later brought him another translation, by Elmar Tophoven, improved by Karl Krolow, a poet Beckett admired: "bis zum Äußersten / gehn / dann wird Lachen entstehn." According to Unseld, Beckett agreed this recalled a perception in Laozi (Lao Tse): "Eh' nicht das Äußerste erreicht ist, kehrt sich nichts ins Gegenteil." (Only when the extreme is reached, will something turn into its opposite.) Even the longest encounters will turn in the end. Brecht certainly absorbed that Daoist dialectic early on, and it remained fundamental to his work.

Beckett's second conversation with Georges Duthuit, on the painter Masson, ends abruptly when Duthuit asks if he really can "deplore the painting that admits 'the things and creatures of spring, resplendent with desire and affirmation, ephemeral no doubt, but immortally reiterant'. . . B:—(exit weeping)."[40] What interests me here is the emotional load, the depth of the repression, uncovered by Beckett's silence and weeping departure. Brecht's counterpart was to remark, in the poem "Schlechte Zeit für Lyrik," what terrible times he lived in when, in spite of the beauties of spring, only the horrors of history drove him to his writing desk (GBA 14:432).

Both had uncomplicated fathers, and a tortured relationship with their complex mothers. Both endured psychosomatic trauma, including real fear of heart failure. Both led complicated emotional lives with tangled relationships. Beckett to Pamela Mitchell in 1954: "Be fond of me but not too fond, I'm not worth it, it'll make you unhappy, you don't know me."[41] Brecht, in a poem: "Here you have someone on whom you can't rely."[42] Beckett to his wife: "As we both know that [love] will come to an end, there is no knowing how long it will last."[43] Brecht, in *The Threepenny Opera:* "For love will endure or not endure / Regardless of where we are."[44]

Both were musical, rejected Wagner, admiring students of Schönberg. Both preferred blackbirds to nightingales. They disliked Rilke. Both praised Brueghel, used Rimbaud, found German acting too emotional, disapproved of empathy and psychologizing. Both loved detective stories, especially Edgar Wallace, though Beckett also read Agatha Christie. Both were wary of Aristotle: for Beckett, "the master of those who know" (ironically exemplified in Watt).[45] Brecht's anti-Aristotelian theater was not really antiemotional, or even antinaturalist, but ultimately antiteleological. Brecht once remarked that in the interest of socialism, somebody should make a list of the questions they could not answer. Me-ti, Brecht's Chinese persona, "was against constructing too complete images of the world" (GBA 18:60). Both loved music hall and popular theater, beds disintegrating on stage: Brecht's *Die Kleinbürger-hochzeit;* in Beckett's case, affection for O'Casey's *The End of the Beginning,* when the two characters lie "in an agony of callisthenics, surrounded by the doomed furniture."[46]

Both drew extensively on the Bible. The index of biblical quotations in Brecht is in double columns over thirty pages long (GBA Registerband, 647–80). Knowlson speaks of Beckett's "grafting technique, and at times it almost runs wild."[47] He stitched Saint Augustine into *Dream of Fair to Middling Women,* and Knowlson observes: "It is not that he plagiarizes; he makes no attempt to hide what he is doing."[48] Apart from remarking that you cannot show quotation marks in the theater, Brecht's best comment on borrowing comes in a description of Zhuangzi in a Keuner story, "Originality":

> "Nowadays," Mr. K complained, "there are countless people who boast in public that they can write large books all by themselves, and this meets with general approval. As a grown man, the Chinese philosopher Zhuangzi composed a book of 100,000 words, nine-tenths of which consisted of quotations. We can't write such books any more, we haven't the intelligence." (GBA 18:18)

All writing is plagiarism, says Derrida. Thank goodness they both plagiarized. Chateaubriand has the last word on that topic: "An original writer is not someone who imitates nobody, but someone whom nobody can imitate."[49]

Both wanted to work with Eisenstein. Brecht met him in Moscow. Beckett wrote a letter.[50] What if Eisenstein had answered? In Berlin Beckett said he wrote *Waiting for Godot* as "a game in order to survive."[51] Brecht's early work is an encyclopedia of survival strategies. Of course they permeate what follows. He later answered a question about political content: "I'd have to admit, I'm not entirely serious."[52] Beckett met Karl Valentin in Munich and watched him in performance.[53] Brecht performed with Valentin. They also made a short film, *Mysterien eines Frisiersalons,* in 1923. Brecht wrote the script, and helped Erich Engel direct it. Engel worked in many later productions but said he had never had so much fun in his whole life.[54]

Beckett loved Chaplin too, and made a film with Buster Keaton. There is a strange parallel in what look, on the surface, like too quite different films, with Beckett's focused on the impossibility of escape into silence and invisibility, of hiding from self-perception, as the camera's eye closes on the protagonist's: *esse est percipi,* to be is always to be perceived.[55] Yet both films show the paradox of an essentialist claim to individuation, which can neither determine nor escape the conditions of existence. Both figure ultimate absence of control. There is a counteraesthetic, and ethic, in Brecht, often expressed through material from East Asian culture, which resists the ideological presuppositions that constrain in the name of a higher value. That is why Brecht's favorite Chaplin scene is when he closes the suitcase, picks up a scissors, and cuts off everything sticking out, everything that does not suit the case, in a graphic ideological *découpage* of the discourse.

Beckett remarked that Valentin was "reduced here and there to knockabout," but even if the Munich accent was hard to grasp, he records: "I was very moved."[56] And indeed there is much in Valentin's work that feels like Beckett, far more than the Laurel and Hardy act or the Irish and English music-hall repartee, to which criticism assimilates him in respect of any effect he had on Beckett.[57] Brecht said that Valentin enabled him to see "the inadequacy of all things including ourselves" (GBA 21:101). This is one reason why some of Brecht's early writing, including part of the one-act plays of 1919, sounds so like Beckett. When he was directing *Life of Eduard II* in Munich, Valentin showed up at the rehearsal, a highly unusual thing for him to do. Brecht asked him what the soldiers going into battle should look like. Valentin replied in his Munich accent: "Furcht hams, blass sans." (They're scared, they're pale.)[58] They got white face masks, in this defining production for the development of Brecht's theater.

Since Valentin is not well known outside Germany, I'll say something about his methods that carry through into Brecht and Beckett, whether or not anyone transported them. His stage was local accent, popular comedy sketches that he wrote himself. He was phenomenally talented and completely neurotic. He told Beckett he'd like to come to London, only the propeller would probably drop off the plane.[59] He also made a few halfhearted attempts to go to Berlin by train, but had to get off shortly after leaving Munich. Lucky the country whose popular culture can accommodate a parody of the Daoist Zhuangzi's celebrated *Butterfly Dream:* Valentin's *Ententraum (Dream of a Duck).*

He offered a form of physical farce in the sense that the scenes or stories were often physically ridiculous, but in Valentin this was guided, not by clowning but by an eccentric and impeccable logic, hence mostly by language, and language did not make sense of the world. In *Moving*

House (Der Umzug), he is asked why the wheels on the cart he is pulling are still chained, and replies: so that nobody can steal it.[60] The fish bowl is problematic. He pours the water from one receptacle into another, can't find a drain, and finally drinks it. When a long-lost document falls out of a drawer, he reads it: "Birth certificate, 1783, Great-great-grandmother, Catholic—kann uns nichts mehr passieren," which means both "this is the last straw," and "nothing more can go wrong after this." The predictions reinforce and contradict each other and neither is correct. Actions are circular, mystifying, funny, leading nowhere in terms of goal-directed behavior. The characters argue about pronunciation. Valentin says the word is "Katástrophé." His companion insists on the normal German "Katastróphe." I think of Beckett's "désert" and "desért," and also of *Endgame* when Valentin discovers a flea and hammers it with a rolling pin; his counterpart, Liesl Karlstadt, smothers everything with insecticide. The whole catastrophe, however you pronounce it, reiterates continuously, and when they reach the end, the script goes back to the beginning again. It is definitely a case of Hegelian "bad infinity," which only always returns us to the finite, rather than a Nietzschean "eternal return" that frees us from the illusion of a transcendental refuge.

Maybe this helps to explain how "Ein Hund kam in die Küche" (A dog came in the kitchen), which Kragler sings in the fourth act of *Drums in the Night,* the first of Brecht's plays to be performed, in 1922 (GBA 1:217), also appears, for the same circular reason, at the start of the *da capo* second act of *Waiting for Godot.* In Brecht's play, the act begins with Glubb, the bar owner, singing "Ballad of the Dead Soldier," the song that supposedly put Brecht at the top of the Nazi list of arrestees, in which the recruitment commission digs up the already dead and sends them off to a second death. Both songs are circularities, doomed attempts at survival, in which execution, burial, enforced resurrection, and execution continue forever. Such circularity is a reason why Beckett's and Brecht's work is haunted by ghosts from beginning to end, but that would be another essay.

Finally, in respect of these strangely parallel lives, they both read Fritz Mauthner, who in 1902 advanced positions we associate with Wittgenstein. Sweeping aside most of the tradition of Western thought, and following Nietzsche, he argued philosophy was only possible as a *critique* of language.[61] Mauthner concluded identity was caught up in the play of language and, therefore, fragile. Hence he also wrote on Buddhist philosophy. Brecht knew that, and Beckett read him for and pre-

sumably to the nearly blind Joyce.[62] Words are what we have, reality lies
beyond them.

Wolfgang Haug, professor of philosophy in Berlin, calls Brecht the
poet among the philosophers, perhaps that poet-philosopher Nietzsche
spoke of.[63] Because of its thorough critique of linguistically suggested es-
sentialisms, Brecht engaged with Buddhism. For example, in his own
copy of Luther's Bible, opposite the title page, he pasted in a Song dynasty bodhisattva.[64] I take this Buddhist figure as a metaphor of the alternative to a Western mind-set that would therefore be defined, and
circumscribed, by this very opposition. Against the revealed and written
word, he sets aesthetic gesture; against language's guarantee of substan-
tiality and its promise of ultimate and personal redemption, he implies
the refusal of an absolute self; against a belief in God the Father and a pa-
ternalistic state, he offers relational thought, consciousness of process. In
Buddhist terminology, having (in Chinese: *you*) cannot exist without
nothing *(wu)*. There can be no fullness without emptiness. Let me leave
it for now at this mythopoeic level.

What about Beckett on Buddhism? Apart from that very Buddhist
observation about passing through "nothing" and coming out on the
other side, there is an interesting complication, which I believe both de-
rives from Schopenhauer and is also a *definer* of his philosophical position, but for the moment let's recall a comment of Beckett's whose implications really take us into Brechtian territory: "Gautama . . . disait
qu'on se trompe en affirmant que le moi existe, mais qu'en affirmant
qu'il n'existe pas on ne se trompe pas moins."[65] The problem is how to
live under these circumstances.

V.

In *Untimely Reflections III,* "Schopenhauer as Educator," Nietzsche does
not describe Schopenhauer's philosophy. Instead he offers a coruscating
critique of contemporary cultural life against which he projects his own
intellectual autobiography.[66] He observes, for example: "The Schopenhauerian person accepts voluntary suffering for truthfulness, and this suffering helps to stifle self-willing and to prepare for that total overturning
and reversal of his being to which the real purpose of life leads us" (371).
"Many people," he notes, "see in negation the sign of evil. But there is
a way of negating and destroying that emanates from a powerful longing
for sanctification and deliverance, and Schopenhauer was its first philo-

sophical teacher among us disenchanted and thoroughly secularized human beings" (372). And he concludes: "A happy life is impossible: the highest we can achieve is a *heroic life*" at the end of which, following Schopenhauer, "the will, mortified throughout a whole life by strain and work, by failure and lack of gratitude, is extinguished in Nirvana" (373).

Since Nietzsche could not have written as he did without Schopenhauer, since Brecht absorbed a great deal of Nietzsche, and since Beckett unquestionably found in Schopenhauer a loadstone for his life, it is worth asking some questions about these interrelationships. Nietzsche transvalued Schopenhauer. Did Beckett do something similar, or rather take Schopenhauer straight? Is there perhaps even a Schopenhauer in Brecht? That is not so fantastic as it may seem. An argument has been made by Friedrich Dieckmann to which I will return, though it depends both on a particular view of Brecht's personality structure and on a Schopenhauerian understanding of Nirvana.

Because Schopenhauer said "No" to the *World as Will,* and Nietzsche first embraced negation and then radically transvalued it into a "Yes" for the *Will to Power,* my subtitle seems to imply that these educators animate the projects behind the masks of Beckett and Brecht, that Schopenhauer's Beckettian No is transvalued by Nietzsche's Brechtian Yes. Yet that would bring us close to Adorno's simplifications. To understand these processes, I therefore need to complicate them. The best way is through a defamiliarizing trajectory out of Western, into Asian culture. This is not a detour because it is substantial within their writing, no matter to what extent they were aware of it.

To ask what Schopenhauer meant for Beckett, or Nietzsche for Brecht, involves getting forensic in respect of texts and then stepping behind the discourses. By way of introduction, here are three short examples of complex genealogies:

1. Negation, says Nietzsche, is taken as a sign of evil, a word that Brecht internalized—in German, *böse*—provocatively stylizing himself as "B. B. REIN, SACHLICH, BÖSE" (GBA 13:266; "pure, matter of fact, evil"). For Nietzsche, however, "evil" was the only possible moral position in the face of what society considered to be "good." To choose "evil" is to embrace the pathos of opposition to a world on the path to the disasters he so clearly predicted. Hence he preferred the new and evil to the old and good, and Brecht followed here too in praising the "bad new" of any innovation. According to Nietzsche, Christ was crucified because he

was "evil," since he opposed those who ruled.[67] Nietzsche's "evil" is therefore a *pharmakon* or counterpoison to what Schopenhauer had described as the "evil" world, though using a less theological word—*Übel*—to define it.[68] One evil can only be fought by another. Schopenhauer seeks to counter his "evil" with equally strong medicine, and although it may be substantially different in Beckett's and Brecht's apothecary, the countermove is structurally analogous and no less difficult.

2. "Old stancher, you remain." Hamm replaces it on his reddened face, surely seeking, even if the verbal echo is not deliberate, "to staunch the eternal wound of Being," something Kafka's country doctor fails to do for his patient Rosa's life wound. It is a Schopenhauerian wound, of course, but this "eternal wound" occurs in *The Birth of Tragedy*. For Nietzsche the first of three illusions or beguilements is that knowledge can stay the pain of this wound. Did Beckett take some of his Schopenhauer through Nietzsche?[69]

3. Saying "Yes" was Zarathustra's and the child's sacred "Yes" to Life.[70] But in Brecht's *Der Jasager,* whose *title* clearly echoes Nietzsche, the child chooses self-*sacrifice,* and the play adapts a Japanese plot. The schoolchildren in the original production objected to this conclusion, thereby provoking a *Neinsager,* who rejects suicidal affirmation and so refuses a political metaphysics. Hence events took a hand in retransvaluing Brecht's transvaluation of Nietzsche. I doubt if he forgot that lesson.

But what about the Schopenhauerian presence in Brecht? Dieckmann attributes a fundamentally melancholic personality structure to Brecht, a secret desire for self-extinction. This reading assumes repressed psychological trauma, which other critics have also supposed, loss of unity, fear of abandonment, and guilt.[71] The only way of banishing this fear of chaos is to redirect the truncated sense of personal protection into hope and belief in a protecting system. Such unconscious conflicts are the source of poetry. Dieckmann therefore reads Brecht's poem "Gleichnis des Buddha vom brennenden Haus" (GBA 12:36; "The Buddha's Parable of the Burning House"), as a direct expression of a desire for "redemption from the burning will to live," which is sought in a "Schopenhauerian-Buddhist Nirvana."[72] Everything turns, however, on the meaning of Nirvana:

This seems more like Beckettian territory, and apart from the analogy I think here of a comment that denial of self and life is an expression of resentment against time.[73] That is Nietzsche, of course, so hypersensitive a psychologist that Freud, who destroyed all his notes three times, saying he wanted to make things difficult for his biographers, simply took over his theories, which were themselves reactions to Schopenhauer, so that passages in Freud map straight onto Nietzsche.[74]

Hence reaction to this fear of the flux of time passes, transvalued, from Schopenhauer, through Nietzsche and then Freud, to Brecht, who quotes from Freud's just published *Civilization and Its Discontents* in his 1930 "Notes to Mahagonny" that set out the differences between the old dramatic and the new epic theater (GBA 24:83); the image of a destructive (Dionysiac) flow that now must be contained recurs time and again within his later work, for example in the *Short Organon* (GBA 23:73). Perhaps we can speak, mixing Hegel's and Nietzsche's terminologies, of a sublated transvaluation, whereby what is apparently transformed continues to affect all thought in the new formulation that must therefore, through the act of reworking, be beholden to what it believes to have refuted.

Though Jacquette's book on Schopenhauer and the arts does not mention Beckett, Schopenhauer's importance to him is well known.[75] Yet I wonder about some readings. For example, in the only full study of Schopenhauer and Beckett, Ulrich Pothast considers his Proust essay the equivalent of *The Birth of Tragedy* for Nietzsche, meaning it summarizes or projects his later aesthetic.[76] Yet if Nietzsche's essay drew extensively on Schopenhauer, and reads like performance notes for *Tristan and Isolde,* Nietzsche later transvalued the positions, whereas the essay on Proust does indeed anticipate Beckett's later attitudes, and when they seem to differ, that is thinkable in terms of an even stronger reading of Schopenhauer. Nietzsche's celebrated essay not only glosses a Schopenhauerian Wagner, it also contains an uncanny anticipation of Brecht's aesthetic practice. Pothast reminds us how Wittgenstein noted that Schopenhauer distinguished what can be said from what can be shown.[77] Where philosophy cannot go, art begins. One could argue that in the Proust essay art, as a metaphysical activity, is stronger than philosophy because, in defamiliarizing reality, it captures the quality of "astonishment" *(Verwunderung)* that Schopenhauer sought.

That Beckett drew on Schopenhauer is incontrovertible; not only does he name him, he also uses Schopenhauerian language. Yet we must differentiate the Schopenhauerian effect. If habit dulls perception, there are moments, Beckett argues, when "the boredom of living is replaced by the suffering of being."[78] We suffer when facing "the spectacle of reality" and, reinforcing Nietzsche's resentment against time, because "the mortal microcosm cannot forgive the relative immortality of the macrocosm" (21). If Proustian involuntary memory is the expression of an unconscious desire to be taken out of the intrinsic flux (17) and unified with past experience, we then breathe the air of the only Paradise available: Paradise Lost (74). Significantly at that moment, "Time is not recovered, it is obliterated" (75). Krapp's experience falls short of the Proustian invocation of unity, because of a closer reading of Schopenhauer. But in the essay, the desire is still for an *achieved* stasis, the "exaltation of a brief eternity" (75). Where "the classical artist assumes omniscience and omnipotence" (81), allegory moves toward anagogy (80), and here we glimpse a distrust of all systematizers. Proust, however, "does not deal in concepts, he pursues the Idea, the concrete" (79). After a Schopenhauerian invocation of the power of music, Beckett concludes that "the Proustian stasis" is, and he uses these German words, "holder Wahnsinn"—let's say "beautiful madness" (91). He also cites a Spanish quotation in Schopenhauer: the original sin is the sin of having been born (67).[79]

Glossing Schopenhauer once again in his Proust essay, Beckett invokes "the wisdom of all the sages, from Brahma to Leopardi, the wisdom that consists not in the satisfaction but in the ablation of desire" (18). There is a slip here, in one sense trivial, except that it highlights a crucial divergence. Beckett names two *sages*. Yet Brahma is not a sage, but a *god,* personifying creation, sometimes confused with *Brahman,* Hinduism's ultimate, universal principle into which *Atman,* or individual soul, is finally absorbed. Beckett probably confused Brahma with *Buddha,* the enlightened one, as Gautama was indeed a sage, one of the greatest. My point is not just that Schopenhauer also confused Buddha and Brahma, but that this misapprehension was not accidental, because it reveals the impossible, *unconscious* agenda: not just a Buddhist ablation of *desire,* but the Hindu cessation of consciousness, as soul, or mind, and universe become an undifferentiated One, a possibility rejected by *philosophical* Buddhism.

It is the extinction of consciousness, not the ablation of desire, that guarantees the dancer's perfect gracefulness in Kleist's "Über das Marionettentheater," which Beckett so admired.[80] The invocation of such perfection, impossible to any human figure, if we accept the modalities of this thought, occurs in a passage where the angel ejects humanity from the gate of Paradise. We must travel round the world to see if there is perhaps a back door. Likewise, from the same text of Kleist mentioned by Beckett, the bear as perfect fencer stands for that unself-consciousness now forever lost, at least to Western culture.[81] It seems the ablation of desire will not alone suffice, but that the necessary loss of (self-)consciousness is impossible.

Schopenhauer addressed this problem as follows: "I owe what is best in my own development to the impression made by Kant's works, the sacred writings of the Hindus, and Plato."[82] Schopenhauer stressed the importance of the Upanishads, the final stage of the Vedas.[83] The teaching based on them, the Vedanta, in the first and most important school, promulgated Advaita, or nondualism. Atman was identical with Brahman, the Absolute, though the *empirical* ego reincarnates. The world, apart from Brahman, is maya or illusion. For the main teacher of this school, Sankara, there are two levels of insight: for the lower, the world and objects in space and time are real; for the higher, they are illusory as a result of a mystical experience of release and identification with Brahman, the undifferentiated One of ultimate reality.

Kant's thing-in-itself is unknowable; only the phenomenal world is given to consciousness. The title of Schopenhauer's main work, *Die Welt als Wille und Vorstellung,* is misleading, if taken to imply a Kantian dichotomy between idea, or representation, of the knowing subject and the separate, unknown and unknowable metaphysical life force called Will. For Schopenhauer: "we ourselves are the thing-in-itself," because we are not merely "knowing subjects," constructing the outside world according to the principle of sufficient reason, but also *willing* subjects, since everything in the world is an expression of Will. Hence "a way *from within* stands open to us to that real inner nature of things to which we cannot penetrate *from without.*"[84]

If the Will is, therefore, not absolutely impenetrable and unknowable, Schopenhauer nevertheless held that the best course of action was, where possible, to suppress it. There are two ways of doing this, even when the results are temporary: through art and through a religious-philosophical intellectual mortification. These paths culminate either in the work of the "genius," or in the behavior of the "saint." His description of the genius reads like a version of Beckett's position, provided we do not take it literally:

That pure, true, and profound knowledge of the essence of the world now becomes for him an end in itself; at it he stops. Therefore it does not become for him a quieter of the will, as . . . in the case of the saint who has attained resignation; it does not deliver him from life forever, but only for a few moments. For him it is not the way out of life, but only an occasional consolation in it.[85]

Unlike the genius, the saint can deny the Will. Schopenhauer says: "The Buddhist faith calls that existence Nirvana, that is to say, extinction."[86] He equates Nirvana with "the phenomenon of non-volition" or "denial of the will to live."[87] But Nirvana means something else. Schopenhauer, in effect, aligns the Buddhist concept of Nirvana with the Hindu obliteration of difference, or attainment of absolute identity between Atman and Brahman, and also equates Kant's thing-in-itself, the Will, and Brahman as sustainer of the world. Only Schopenhauer's is not a holy, it is a *catastrophic* monism: "the origin of the world (this Samsara of the Buddhists) is itself based already on evil; that is to say, it is a sinful act of Brahma. Now we ourselves are again this Brahma, for Indian mythology is everywhere transparent."[88]

What Schopenhauer proposes could be called a negative ontology of substance, which we cannot but affirm yet must try to deny: "That which in us affirms itself as will-to-life, is also that which denies this will and thereby becomes free from existence and the sufferings thereof."[89] Surely the effect is to place the empirical individual in a nonclassic, because not primarily psychological, double bind that is nevertheless infrangible, from which there is no escape. Schopenhauer sets up a contradiction in which Beckett, probably as no other writer, lived and had his being. For if consciousness is itself an expression of the will, it cannot then deny itself, since the act of denying is an intervention of what is to be denied. One consequence must be to create an ineradicable sense of guilt. The absolute unavoidability of this impossibility is also why Schopenhauer and Beckett have recourse to music.

Schopenhauer, famously, found music not just an "adequate objectification of the will," like the Platonic ideas reproduced in the other arts, but image or reproduction of the Will itself: "Abbild des Willens selbst." Therefore the world could just as well be called "embodied music as embodied will."[90] Leibniz called music "an unconscious exercise in arithmetic in which the mind does not know it is counting," and Schopenhauer changes this into "an unconscious exercise in metaphysics in which the mind does not know it is philosophizing."[91] Significantly, a repressed rationalism is surely revealed when Schopenhauer argues that since perfect pitch is impossible, a problem when tuning keyboard instruments, because no tuning system is mathematically impeccable, "a perfectly correct music cannot even be conceived, much less worked out; and for this reason all possible music deviates from perfect purity."[92] I see a parallel when Beckett, explaining to Duthuit why he admires Bram van Velde's paintings, says painting tries "to escape from this sense of failure [. . .] in a kind of tropism towards a light [. . .] as though the irrationality of pi were an offence against the deity, not to mention his creature."[93] This probably also needs a psychoanalytic reading since underneath it surely lies the strong and repressed desire for the disparaged rationality, because he continues, in respect of approaching van Velde's admired fidelity to "failure": "I know my inability to do so places myself . . . in what I think is still called an unenviable situation, familiar to psychiatrists."

But music, as embodied Will, could not be explained, it must just be listened to, and because it was also disembodied, not phenomenal, it was also painless. For Schopenhauer the bass notes embody the lowest form of the will's objectification, and the melody, corresponding to human intentionality, sets its course toward its own goal.[94] So music seems to offer a way out of that double bind, as if the will somehow came to an awareness of itself through goal-directed melody, rising over the lower music that, as embodied will, has no end or goal. Yet surely this double bind is then merely displaced, becoming the source of a philosophically ambiguous and temporary aesthetic pleasure, though the transaction relieves language of its burden of expression. Perhaps that explains why music takes over in Beckett where language cannot go, for example, in *Ghost Trio* or *Nacht und Träume*.

As for other Schopenhauerian constructions, Beckett's novels show the progressive collapse of the principle of sufficient reason, which secures the relationship between constructing subject and observed object. Murphy, seen from outside, may disintegrate, but the narrative does not. Moran, in *Molloy*, offers, in Schopenhauer's language, a "window to the real," as his body collapses. In *The Unnamable*, the Will is in dialogue with itself: "If only the voice would stop, the meaningless voice which prevents you from being nothing."[95] Though Schopenhauer could never have imagined the plays—after all Rossini was his favorite composer—they are visual translations of what he called "the essential nature of life," oscillating between boredom and suffering, and where the possibility of happiness is only contemplated as an abatement of suffering. In *Waiting for Godot*, Valdimir and Estragon both deny and affirm their existence, embodying what Schopenhauer called "the duplicity" of our being.[96] For Pothast this exemplifies Schopenhauer's metaphysical perception that individuality is denied, but my argument is that perception is here double: the will knows the will, and the subject is trapped. The conclusion must be that consciousness is Beckett's double bind. His avowed inability to express, together with the compulsion to do so, is hardly the mark of aesthetic incompetence for, if the words mean anything, Beckett was a master of his art, but is rather the effect of a displacement of the necessary but impossible self-suppression of the Will.[97]

But this contradictory rhetorical figure, when the music of the world as Will comes to consciousness of itself in melody, suggests why Schopenhauer's and Hegel's lectures clashed. Hegel secularized an eschatological teleology. History reveals the coming to consciousness of the World Spirit and, though conflictual, is itself the image and deed of Reason. The Schopenhauerian dialectic, however, sees the World Spirit as a morally malign force. Yet his blind Will is *also* self-divided, driven into ever new and competing forms of self-existence. Although it produces, in human intelligence, a higher form of itself, the ultimate telos is negative, and hence that intelligence must turn against it. Both Hegel and Schopenhauer theorize time, the emergent problem of their nineteenth-century episteme, by developing new metaphysical teleologies. For one, the ultimate process is good; for the other, it is evil. In Schopenhauer, Spirit goes underground and turns into libido or Drive. Then the enigma is no longer outside and above us, it is within and below. This is how Schopenhauer describes the dilemma of his dialectic:

> Every individual is on the one hand the subject of knowledge, i.e., the supplementary condition of the possibility of the whole objective world and, on the other hand, an individual appearance of the will, of that which objectifies itself in every thing. But this duplicity of our being does not rest in a separate unity: otherwise we would be able to become conscious of our selves through our self and independently of the objects of knowledge and of the will: yet this we simply cannot do, but rather as soon as we try to, and turn knowledge inward to really reflect upon ourselves, we lose ourselves in a bottomless void; we are like a hollow sphere of glass out of which a voice speaks, but whose cause cannot be found inside it, and as we try to lay hold on ourselves, we grasp, shuddering, nothing but an insubstantial ghost.[98]

Beckett turns this Schopenhauerian metaphysic and the impossibility of escape into the form of his art.

VI.

Brecht sought to escape from the Hegelianized Marx whose theory had been ontologized. In doing so, other concepts of time and process become evident in his writing. And this takes us back to Nietzsche. He absorbed much from Nietzsche and he transvalued, which was only possible because of what they had in common. In *The Birth of Tragedy* Nietzsche seeks an explanation why the extraordinary Greek form declined so suddenly. Created by the fusion of Dionysian intoxication and Apollonian illusion, it was destroyed through their mutual opponent: Socratic rationality. This destructive Socratic reason also found its voice *within* the theater: the voice of Euripides. Nietzsche's analysis of Euripides sounds like a description of Brecht's epic theater:

What in Euripidean, as compared with Sophoclean tragedy, has been so frequently censured as poetic lack and retrogression is actually the straight result of the poet's incisive critical gifts, his audacious personality. The Euripidean prologue may serve to illustrate the efficacy of that rationalistic method. Nothing could be more at odds with our dramaturgic notions than the prologue in the drama of Euripides. To have a character appear at the beginning of the play, tell us who he is, what preceded the action, what has happened so far, even what is about to happen in the course of the play—a modern writer for the theatre would reject all this as a wanton and unpardonable dismissal of the element of suspense. Now that everyone knows what is going to happen, who will wait to see it happen? [. . .] But Euripides reasoned quite otherwise. According to him, the effect of tragedy never resided in epic suspense, in a teasing uncertainty as to what was going to happen next. It resided, rather, in those great scenes of lyrical rhetoric in which the passion and dialectic of the protagonist reached heights of eloquence.[99]

Euripides . . . lays his dramatic plan as Socratic thinker and carries it out as passionate actor. So it happens that the Euripidean drama is at the same time cool and fiery, able alike to freeze and consume us. It cannot possibly achieve the Apollonian effects of the epic, while on the other hand it has severed all connection with the Dionysiac mode; so that in order to have any impact at all it must seek out novel stimulants which are to be found neither in the Apollonian nor in the Dionysiac realm. Those stimulants are, on the one hand,

cold paradoxical ideas put in the place of Apollonian contempla-
tion, and on the other fiery emotions put in the place of Dionysiac
transports.[100]

Some such combination of cold control and fiery emotions, of passion and dialectic, energizes Brecht's theater where, as in East Asian art,
the aesthetic strength in the representation of those emotions depends
upon the intellectual control exercised over the structures by which they
are contained. I am reminded here of an early comment in Brecht's diaries: "Meier-Graefe says of Delacroix that here was a warm heart beating in a cold person. And when you come down to it, that's a possible
recipe for greatness" (GBA 26:215).[101]

Nietzsche's impact on Brecht was considerable: elements of self-
stylization; the early Wagner infatuation; the rejection of religion in favor of a "strong" philosophy (GBA 26:272); the metaphor of coldness in
the early poetry; the remark—"Since Copernicus man has been rolling
from the center toward X"[102]—picked up in *Mann ist Mann* (GBA
2:206). There are countless echoes of his love of paradox and contradiction: "Only someone who changes is compatible with me" (KSA 5:243:
Nur wer sich wandelt, bleibt mit mir verwandt). Brecht's version, in the
Geschichten vom Herrn Keuner, is "A man, who hadn't seen Mr. K. for a
long time, greeted him with the words: 'You haven't changed a bit.'
'Oh!' said Mr. K. and grew pale" (GBA 18:21). Furthermore, Nietzsche
also had roots in the Enlightenment, visible in his identification with
Voltaire,[103] in his absolute disdain for anti-Semitism, in his disgust with
German nationalism, in his alarm over the destruction of personality in
modern culture, over what he called the "*Un*persönlichkeit des Arbeit-
ers" (depersonalization of the worker) in industrializing society, over the
falsity of the economy (KSA 6:316).

But beyond all these echoes, and there are many others, one strand
of thought stands out, especially since Nietzsche transvalued Schopenhauer. When ideas and metaphors are transvalued, and sometimes they
are merely adopted, aspects of what has apparently been changed are retained as the unconscious of the discourse. Nietzsche embraced what
Schopenhauer sought to escape. Images of flux abound in Brecht's
work, forming its central metaphor: from body-dissolving rivers in the
early poetry to later rivers of history. They link what some critics cate-
gorize as incompatible. This particular term, "flux of things" (Fluß der
Dinge), occurs in many places in Brecht's work. In *Me-ti* it refers to the

Marxist dialectic (GBA 18, 73 & 113). But that begs the question of its other connotations (GBA 18:73; *Über den Fluß der Dinge*). An autobiographical poem, "The Doubter" (GBA 14:376), written in dialogue with a splendid Chinese painting, which hung at the head of his bed, asks: "Are you truly in the stream of happening?" For Reinhold Grimm this implies a Nietzschean temptation to say "Yes" to the world in all its cruelty, meaning in 1937 only one thing: to accept Stalinism.[104] But this poem, as well as that painting, is about the problematics of practice. So it opposes perfect theories, political ontology, and pseudoscientific determinism. This flow of events is a critique of such "theory."[105]

Coming out of the Augsburg house Am Rain, where Brecht was born, you step onto an iron grill between door and pavement beyond. Looking down, water races past under your feet: an unforgettable image, the grid of our systems projected over a mill race. I think of Nietzsche's remark about building a cathedral of concepts on flowing water.[106] Zarathustra comments on the words of a "prophet": "'Oh, where is redemption from the flux of things and the punishment of existence?' Thus preached madness."[107]

VII.

Schopenhauer's evocation of Nirvana as *extinction* is another form of self-assertion, the only one left in a monist system of thought. In philosophical Buddhism, however, what is annihilated is not the self, but the illusion of an independent or transcendentally guaranteed self. There is no absolute, no essential self; therefore we cannot hold it in the form of perfect consciousness, but neither can we fear its loss. Nirvana is not achieved after death, but in this world by embracing samsara, by relating to all that is and helps to shape us. Everything is relational. The goal of Nirvana is therefore the road itself. In Brecht's poem about the Buddha, as in many popular stories, Buddha falls silent, refusing to describe or define Nirvana when pressed by his disciples, because his questioners seek impossible verbal abstractions and theoretical certainty instead of responding to urgent real situations: to get out of the burning house.

Adorno read *Endgame* as equating the totality invoked by Clov with nothing, and the play's negative ontology as the negation of ontology, undermining "the absolute claim of what merely is."[108] There are no more absolutes. If we speak of rehistoricizing, perhaps Beckett and

Brecht represent two sides of the problem when essentialism, no matter how metaphorized, is replaced by field theories of knowledge. What I have argued could be summarized thus: Brecht's supposed preoccupation with the rational and Beckett's with the irrational needs qualification, since the repressed of each discourse unfolds within the other. The unconscious haunts Brecht's texts from start to finish—that would be another essay—and Beckett's topic is the Schopenhauerian ghost of consciousness.

In Schopenhauer's philosophy, the Will, as blind force, realizes itself in consciousness and thereby produces its own double bind. If we rehistoricize this metaphysical trajectory, it figures the justifiable fear of an inability to control the forces, guided by a perceived and immediate but limited self-interest, that now operate through us and may well lead to our destruction. Such thoughts become possible in the early nineteenth century, as the uncontrollable monster created by Mary Shelley's Dr. Frankenstein reminds us. So we could perhaps say that an older theology of fear, unconsciously historicized by Schopenhauer, has been simultaneously dehistoricized into a metaphysic. Beckett shows us how the individual can experience this as unredeemable failure.

That vital strand in Brecht's thinking, related to Nietzsche's *flux of things,* dehistoricizes revolutionary time but then rehistoricizes it in terms of *longue durée,* because it does not abandon but rather stretches the process of change. When *das Nichts* or Nirvana is equated with acceptance of samsara, or the flux of things, identity is relationalized. Our fate, as the fate of humanity, lies outside and within us. As Gautama, the Buddha, observed: the self both exists and does not exist. Because this fate becomes an inescapable, collective responsibility, we could say that Brecht ontologizes the social.

Maybe that is why he said of his own work: "My plays and theories are applicable in bourgeois and capitalist societies, in socialist, communist and classless societies and in all subsequent social formations."[109] And maybe that is also, since problems are not solved by thinking alone, why one of his very last poems is entitled "Dauerten wir unendlich."

> If we lasted forever
> Everything would change
> But since we don't
> Many things stay the same.
>   (GBA 15:294)

NOTES

1. Martin Esslin, *Brecht: A Choice of Evils. A Critical Study of the Man, His Work, and His Opinions* (London: Eyre Spottiswoode, 1959).

2. Martin Esslin, *Mediations: Essays on Brecht, Beckett, and the Media* (London: Eyre Methuen, 1980). The chapter "The Mind as a Stage-Radio Drama" (171–87) also passes up the opportunity for comparison.

3. Samuel Beckett, *Collected Poems, 1930–1978* (London: John Calder, 1984), 9. Goethe, *Werke* (Hamburg: Christian Wegner Verlag, 1964), 1:50. The German word in Goethe and Brecht is *Geier*. This translates into English as "vulture." Beckett's use suggests he took it as eater of carrion, since his poem's last word is *offal*. But the German word was often used for any death-bringing bird of prey, and associated with hawks and eagles. I doubt there is a connection between Brecht's and Goethe's poems. For pertinent information on Goethe's *Harzreise im Winter*, see James Boyd, *Notes to Goethe's Poems* (Oxford: Blackwell, 1961), 1:134–47.

4. Esslin, *Mediations*, 113.

5. Bertolt Brecht, *Werke, Große Berliner und Frankfurter Ausgabe* (Frankfurt am Main: Suhrkamp, 1989), 1:86. This edition is hereafter cited as GBA.

6. The nuances of this passage are lost in the Methuen translation, sacrificed to an unfortunate rhyme. "Baal watches the vultures in the star-shot sky / Hovering patiently to see when Baal will die. / Sometimes Baal shams dead. The vultures swoop. / Baal, without a word, will dine on vulture soup." Bertolt Brecht, *Collected Plays*, ed. John Willett and Ralph Manheim (London: Methuen, 1970–2003), 1:4.

7. See James K. Lyon, *Bertolt Brecht in America* (Princeton: Princeton University Press, 1980), 195.

8. John Calder, *The Philosophy of Samuel Beckett* (London: Calder Publications, 2001).

9. Fredric Jameson, *Brecht and Method* (London: Verso, 1998), trans. Jürgen Pelzer as *Lust und Schrecken der unaufhörlichen Verwandlung aller Dinge: Brecht und die Zukunft* (Berlin: Argument Verlag, 1999).

10. Jameson, *Brecht and Method*, 78.

11. Jameson, *Brecht and Method*, 58.

12. On the nature of Nietzsche's "Eternal Return," see Ofelia Schutte, *Beyond Nihilism: Nietzsche without Masks* (Chicago: University of Chicago Press, 1984), 57–75.

13. Friedrich Nietzsche, *Schopenhauer als Erzieher*, in *Sämtliche Werke, Kritische Studienausgabe* (Munich: Deutscher Taschenbuch Verlag, 1988), vol. 1, especially 393–404. This edition of Nietzsche's works is hereafter cited as KSA.

14. James Knowlson, *Damned to Fame: The Life of Samuel Beckett* (New York: Simon and Schuster, 1996), 427.

15. Terry Eagleton's talk in the Abbey Theatre, Dublin, during a late celebration of Brecht's centenary in April 1999, exemplifies the first alternative, and Elizabeth Wright's *Postmodern Brecht: A Re-Presentation* (London: Routledge, 1989) the second. Neither grasps the complexities of the texts.

16. Quoted in Edith Krull, *Herbert Ihering* (Berlin: Henschelverlag, 1964), 20.

17. I am inflecting Fernand Braudel's term for the longest rhythm of time, the biogeographical, compared with individual life time and the time range of social groups, as a metaphor for the stretching of time in Brecht's "flow of things."

18. This remark is recorded in *Spectaculum* No. 6, 1963, 319. See also Knowlson, *Damned to Fame*, 427.

19. Howard Barker, *Arguments for a Theatre* (Manchester: Manchester University Press, 1997), 112. See Heiner Zimmermann, "Howard Barker's Brecht or Brecht as Whipping Boy," a paper presented at the Fifth Conference of the European Society for the Study of English (ESSE), Helsinki, 2000; also my contribution, "Ghosts in the House of Theory" in *Brecht Yearbook* 24 (1999): 1–13.

20. Written in 1940. See Werner Hecht, *Aufsätze über Brecht* (Berlin: Henschelverlag, 1970), 117.

21. Bertolt Brecht, *Über die bildenden Künste,* ed. J. Hermand (Frankfurt am Main: Suhrkamp, 1983), 213.

22. They are well described by Elizabeth Sakellaridou's "Feminist Theatre and the Brechtian Tradition: A Retrospect and a Prospect," *Brecht Yearbook* 27 (2002): 179–98.

23. Hecht, *Aufsätze über Brecht,* 123.

24. Bertolt-Brecht-Archiv, Berlin, 1061/1–52. The few emendations are made to the first act of the German edition published by Suhrkamp in 1953.

25. Heiner Müller, "Der Dramatiker und die Geschichte seiner Zeit. Ein Gespräch zwischen Horst Laube und Heiner Müller," in *Theater 1975, Sonderheft der Zeitschrift Theater Heute,* 120.

26. Though such suggestions were part of a once socially authorized discourse, I wonder about her account. She never grasped the subtleties of Brecht's *Coriolanus* adaptation. See Clas Zilliacus, "Three Times Godot: Beckett, Brecht, Bulatovic," *Comparative Drama* 4, no. 1 (1970): 8.

27. One form comes later, when Heiner Müller amalgamates Brecht's dismembering the clown in the *Badener Lehrstück* and the disappearing carafe and the prod on wheels from Beckett's *Act Without Words I* and *II* in "Nachtstück." Heiner Müller, *Germania, Tod in Berlin* (Berlin: Rotbuch Verlag, 1977), 113.

28. Adorno cites Lukács's criticism of Beckett in "Trying to Understand *Endgame,*" *New German Critique* 26 (1982): 125. Helmut Koopmann points to the animal-like anti-intellectuality of Brecht's first plays, which "reverse" the Enlightenment's human ethic mediated through the theater: "Baal is not so much the expressionist individualist, who determines his own law of life out of his animality without bothering about any alien morality, as he is the predatory animal." "Brecht-Schreiben in Gegensätzen," in *Bertolt Brecht-Aspekte seines Werkes, Spuren seiner Wirkung,* ed. Helmut Koopmann and Theo Stammen (Munich: Ernst Vögel Verlag, 1983), 9–29, esp. 16.

29. Adorno, "Trying to Understand *Endgame,*" 125.

30. Theodor W. Adorno, *Gesammelte Schriften* (Frankfurt am Main: Suhrkamp, 1974), 2:289.

31. Adorno, "Trying to Understand *Endgame,*" 125.

32. Michel Foucault, *The Order of Things: An Archaeology of the Human Sciences* (New York: Vintage, 1973), 383.

33. Brecht, *Collected Plays,* 1:42–43 (GBA 1:121–22).

34. See also W. F. Haug, *Philosophieren mit Brecht und Gramsci* (Berlin: Argument Verlag, 1996), 21–27.

35. Hans Mayer, "Beckett und Brecht. Erfahrungen und Erinnerungen. Ein Vortrag," Berliner Ensemble, Drucksache 15, 1995, 559.

36. Haug also speaks of Brecht's knowledge, "which is not for the day and must last a long time" (*Philosophieren mit Brecht und Gramsci,* 159).

37. Werner Hecht, *Brecht Chronik 1898–1956* (Frankfurt am Main: Suhrkamp, 1997), 1021. Bai Juyi, the Tang dynasty poet Brecht translated, had been physically exiled.

38. Knowlson, *Damned to Fame,* 320.

39. Siegfried Unseld, "Bis zum Äußersten," *Theater Heute,* February 2, 1990, 23.

40. Samuel Beckett, *Proust and Three Dialogues with Georges Duthuit* (London: John Calder, 1965), 113.

41. Knowlson, *Damned to Fame,* 360.

42. Bertolt Brecht, *Poems, 1913–1956,* ed. John Willett and Ralph Manheim (London: Methuen, 1976), 107; "In mir habt ihn einen, auf den könnt ihr nicht bauen" (GBA 11:120).

43. Knowlson, *Damned to Fame,* 271.

44. Brecht, *Collected Plays,* 2.2:26; "Die Liebe dauert oder dauert nicht / An dem oder jenem Ort" (GBA 2:254). Both had simultaneously to stage-manage a wife and two mistresses in Berlin.

45. Richard Kearney, "Beckett: The Demythologising Intellect," in *The Irish Mind: Exploring Intellectual Traditions,* ed. Richard Kearney (Dublin: Wolfhound Press, 1985), 286.

46. Anthony Cronin, *Samuel Beckett: The Last Modernist* (London: Flamingo, 1997), 58.

47. Knowlson, *Damned to Fame,* 112.

48. Knowlson, *Damned to Fame,* 114.

49. *Penguin Dictionary of Quotations* (London: Jonathan Cape, 1962), 106.

50. Knowlson, *Damned to Fame,* 212.

51. Knowlson, *Damned to Fame,* 536.

52. Walter Benjamin, *Versuche über Brecht* (Frankfurt am Main: Suhrkamp, 1981), 154. Conversation on July 6, 1934.

53. The actor who introduced him to Valentin, Josef Eichheim, had himself played in Brecht's *Life of Edward II.* See Knowlson, *Damned to Fame,* 241, 666.

54. Wolfgang Gersch, *Film bei Brecht* (Berlin: Henschelverlag, 1975), 23. In this short film Valentin, the barber's assistant, inadvertently cuts off a customer's head but smartly tapes it on again. In a duel shortly afterward the head falls off, to the astonishment of his opponent. The Great War had just industrialized slaughter. In this graphic deconstruction, the individual cannot command his own body. Somebody else slips up, and you lose your head. The sovereign subject is comically decapitated.

55. Beckett followed this conventional reading. David Berman argues Berkeley only ever said of "unthinking things" that "*esse* is *percipi.*" He maintained neither God nor anyone else could perceive the workings of a mind, which could only be construed analogically from observed effects. See David Berman, "Beckett and Berkeley," in *Irish University Review: A Journal of Irish Studies,* special issue, Spring 1984, 42–45.

56. Knowlson, *Damned to Fame,* 241.

57. Knowlson, *Damned to Fame,* makes these analogies.

58. See Antony Tatlow, *The Mask of Evil* (Berne: Peter Lang, 1977), 222.

59. Knowlson, *Damned to Fame,* 241. You can read Valentin, if you know German, or listen to him on recordings, if you understand Bavarian, or watch him on video.

60. Karl Valentin, *Die Raubritter von München. Szenen und Dialoge* (Munich: Deutscher Taschenbuch Verlag, 1964), 147–57.

61. "So ist jedes geschlossene System eine Selbsttäuschung, so ist die Philosophie als Selbsterkenntnis des Menschengeistes ewig unfruchtbar, und so kann Philosophie, wenn

man schon das alte Wort beibehalten will, nichts weiter sein wollen, als kritische Aufmerksamkeit auf die Sprache." Fritz Mauthner, *Beiträge zu einer Kritik der Sprache* (Stuttgart: J. G. Cotta'sche Buchhandlung Nachfolger, 1901), 1:648.

62. For Beckett, see Knowlson, *Damned to Fame*, 267 and 327; also Kearney, "Beckett," 290; for Brecht, see Tatlow, *Brechts Ost Asien* (Berlin: Parthas Verlag, 1998), 41.

63. Haug, *Philosophieren mit Brecht und Gramsci*, 103 and 10.

64. Inspectable in Tatlow, *Brechts Ost Asien*, 38.

65. "Gautama . . . said that one is mistaken in affirming that the self exists, but in affirming that it does not exist, one is no less mistaken." Samuel Beckett, *Disjecta: Miscellaneous Writings and a Dramatic Fragment*, ed. Ruby Cohn (London: Calder, 1983), 146.

66. Nietzsche, *Sämtliche Werke*, 1:337–427. Nietzsche also acknowledges this rereading of Schopenhauer in *Ecce Homo*, in *Sämtliche Werke*, 6:320.

67. Friedrich Nietzsche, *Also Sprach Zarathustra* (Stuttgart: Kröner-Verlag, 1956), 235–36, "Von alten und neuen Tafeln," no. 26. On Nietzsche and "evil," see also Schutte, *Beyond Nihilism*, 135.

68. Arthur Schopenhauer, *Parerga und Paralipomena*, in *Sämtliche Werke* (Mannheim: Brockhaus, 1988), no. 149, 6:309–10; *Essays and Aphorisms*, trans. R. J. Hollingdale (Harmondsworth: Penguin, 1970), 41–42. Both German words translate "evil," but *böse* evokes the devil, while *übel* connotes a deplorable or misbegotten state.

69. Friedrich Nietzsche, *The Birth of Tragedy*, trans. Francis Golffing (New York: Doubleday, 1956), 108; Nietzsche, *Sämtliche Werke*, 1:115. Golffing's "beguilement" translates Nietzsche's *Reizmittel*.

70. Nietzsche, *Also sprach Zarathustra*, 27; see also Schutte, *Beyond Nihilism*, 39–40.

71. See also Carl Pietzcker, "Ich kommandiere mein Herz," in *Brechts Herzneurose— ein Schlüssel zu seinem Leben und Schreiben* (Würzburg: Königshausen und Neumann, 1988).

72. Friedrich Dieckmann, "Brechts Utopia," in *Brecht 88. Anregungen zum Dialog über die Vernunft am Jahrtausendende*, ed. Wolfgang Heise (Berlin: Henschelverlag Kunst und Gesellschaft, 1987), 69–108, here 92; see also Tatlow, *Brechts Ost Asien*, 40.

73. Nietzsche, *Also sprach Zarathustra*, 154; see also Schutte, *Beyond Nihilism*, 43–44.

74. Freud once told his friend Wilhelm Fließ that he was "not at all a man of science, not an observer, not an experimenter, not a thinker. I am by temperament nothing but a conquistador—an adventurer." See *The Complete Letters of Sigmund Freud to Wilhelm Fließ, 1887–1904*, ed. Jeffrey Mason (Cambridge: Harvard University Press, 1985), 398.

75. Dale Jacquette, ed., *Schopenhauer, Philosophy, and the Arts* (Cambridge: Cambridge University Press, 1996).

76. Ulrich Pothast, *Die eigentlich metaphysische Tätigkeit. Über Schopenhauers Ästhetik und ihre Anwendung durch Samuel Beckett* (Frankfurt am Main: Suhrkamp, 1982), 24–25.

77. Pothast, *Die eigentlich metaphysische Tätigkeit*, 386. He cites Wittgenstein's diaries for 1916.

78. Beckett, *Proust*, 19.

79. Arthur Schopenhauer, *Die Welt als Wille und Vorstellung*, in *Sämtliche Werke*, no. 51, 2:300. Schopenhauer also quotes from the same passage in *The Tempest*, "We are such stuff as dreams are made on" (*Die Welt als Wille und Vorstellung*, 5:20) as *Endgame*'s "Our revels now are ended."

80. Knowlson, *Damned to Fame*, 517, 558.

81. Knowlson, *Damned to Fame*, 558.

82. Arthur Schopenhauer, *World as Will and Representation*, trans. E. F. J. Payne (New York: Dover, 1966), 1:417; *Die Welt als Wille und Vorstellung*, *Sämtliche Werke*, vol. 2, 493.

See also the preface to the first edition of *Die Welt als Wille und Vorstellung; Sämtliche Werke;* also Moira Nicholls, "The Influence of Eastern Thought on Schopenhauer's Doctrine of the Thing-in-Itself," in *The Cambridge Companion to Schopenhauer,* ed. Christopher Janaway (Cambridge: Cambridge University Press, 1999), 179.

83. Schopenhauer, *Die Welt als Wille und Vorstellung,* 1:4; see Nicholls, "Influence of Eastern Thought," 180.

84. Schopenhauer, *World as Will and Representation,* trans. Payne, vol. 2, chap. 18, 195; *Sämtliche Werke,* vol. 3, chap. 18, 218. See also Dale Jacquette, "Schopenhauer's Metaphysics of Appearance and Will in the Philosophy of Art," in Jacquette, *Schopenhauer,* 4–5.

85. Schopenhauer, *World as Will and Representation,* 1:52, 267 (modified); Schopenhauer, *Die Welt als Wille und Vorstellung, Sämtliche Werke,* vol. 1, 52, 316. See also John E. Atwell, "Art as Liberation: A Central Theme of Schopenhauer's Philosophy," in Jacquette, *Schopenhauer,* 94.

86. Schopenhauer, *World as Will and Representation,* trans. Payne, vol. 2, chap. 41, 508; *Sämtliche Werke,* vol. 3, chap. 41, 583. See also Nicholls, "Influence of Eastern Thought," 192.

87. Schopenhauer, *Essays and Aphorisms,* 61.

88. Schopenhauer, *Parerga and Paralipomena,* trans E. F. J. Payne (Oxford: Clarendon Press, 1974), 1:62.; *Sämtliche Werke,* 5:66. See also Nicholls, "Influence of Eastern Thought," 184, who misquotes.

89. Arthur Schopenhauer, *Manuscript Remains,* trans. E. F. J. Payne (Oxford: Berg, 1989), 3:376; see also Nicholls, "Influence of Eastern Thought," 193.

90. Schopenhauer, *World as Will and Representation,* vol. 1, 52.263; Schopenhauer, *Die Welt als Wille und Vorstellung,* in *Sämtliche Werke,* vol. 52, 310.

91. Schopenhauer changes Leibniz's Latin phrase. Schopenhauer, *World as Will and Representation,* vol. 1, 52, 264; Schopenhauer, *Die Welt als Wille und Vorstellung,* in *Sämtliche Werke,* vol. 52, 313. See also Lydia Goehr, "Schopenhauer and the Musicians," in Jacquette, *Schopenhauer,* 209.

92. Schopenhauer, *World as Will and Representation,* vol. 1, 52, 266; Schopenhauer, *Die Welt als Wille und Vorstellung,* in *Sämtliche Werke,* vol. 2, 52, 314, see also Jacquette, *Schopenhauer,* 209.

93. Beckett, *Proust,* 125.

94. Schopenhauer, *World as Will and Representation,* vol. 1, 52, 259; Schopenhauer, *Die Welt als Wille und Vorstellung,* in *Sämtliche Werke,* vol. 2, 52, 306ff. See also Cheryl Foster, "Ideas and Imagination: Schopenhauer on the Proper Formulation of Art," in Janaway, *Cambridge Companion to Schopenhauer,* 241.

95. Quoted in Kearney, "Beckett," 285. The divergence from Brecht's "nothing" is obvious.

96. Schopenhauer, *Die Welt als Wille und Vorstellung,* in *Sämtliche Werke,* vol. 2, 54, 327. See also Pothast, *Die eigentlich metaphysische Tätigkeit,* 366–77.

97. For Beckett's statement on the dilemma of expression, see *Proust,* 103.

98. Schopenhauer, *Die Welt als Wille und Vorstellung,* in *Sämtliche Werke,* vol. 2, 54, 327; my translation.

99. Nietzsche, *The Birth of Tragedy,* 79–80; Nietzsche, *Sämtliche Werke,* 1:85.

100. Nietzsche, *The Birth of Tragedy,* 78–79; KSA, 1:84.

101. Bertolt Brecht, *Diaries, 1920–1922,* ed. Herta Ramthun, trans. John Willett (London: Methuen, 1979), 98.

102. Friedrich Nietzsche, *The Will to Power,* trans. Walter Kaufmann and R. J.

Hollingdale (London: Weidenfeld and Nicholson, 1968), no. 1, 8; see also *Zur Genealogie der Moral,* in Nietzsche, *Sämtliche Werke,* 5:404, where "X" is equated with "Nichts" or "the void."

103. Nietzsche, *Ecce Homo,* 6:322.

104. Reinhold Grimm, *Brecht und Nietzsche oder Geständnisse eines Dichters* (Frankfurt am Main: Suhrkamp, 1979), 235. Grimm first documented Brecht's wide use of Nietzsche. "Fluß des Geschehens" is another term in Nietzsche. Here I disagree with Grimm's reading; see *Brechts Ost Asien,* 13–16.

105. Tatlow, *Brechts Ost Asien,* 13–16.

106. Nietzsche, *Sämtliche Werke,* 1:882: "Man darf hier den Menschen wohl bewundern als ein gewaltiges Baugenie, dem auf beweglichen Fundamenten und gleichsam auf fliessendem Wasser das Aufthürmen eines unendlich complicirten Begriffsdomes gelingt."

107. *Also sprach Zarathustra* II, "Von der Erlösung," 154. The soothsayer, who stands for Schopenhauer, preaches what Zarathustra rejects. This passage recalls Beckett's "holder Wahnsinn" as a description of Proustian stasis, and reminds us of Zeno's impossible heap.

108. Adorno, "Trying to Understand *Endgame,*" 148.

109. Quoted by Reinhold Grimm, "Der katholische Einstein: Brechts Dramen- und Theatertheorie," in *Brechts Dramen, Neue Interpretationen,* ed. W. Hinderer (Stuttgart: Reclam, 1984), 30.

Herbert Blau

Among the Deepening Shades: The Beckettian Moment(um) and the Brechtian Arrest

It may not be, as Nietzsche said in *The Birth of Tragedy,* that illusion as the "reflection of eternal contradiction, begetter of all things," will lead to "a radiant vision of pure delight, a rapt seeing through wide-open eyes."[1] But if, as Freud thought, illusion has a future, with civilization and its discontents, it must surely include certain illusions about illusion and the means by which it is produced—what Brecht called the "apparatus," through which society absorbs "whatever it needs to reproduce itself" and which imposes its "views as it were incognito."[2] If one may speak not only of the illusion of reality but the reality of illusion, what shadows Brecht's critique is the question that prompted Nietzsche and has always haunted the theater—synoptically there in Beckett's *Breath,* or in the "Mere eye. No mind" of the "[*Repeat play*]" of *Play*[3]—as to whether the illusion produced is a doubled over redundancy, now you see it now you don't, mere eye insufficient, whether dazzled or baffled, distracted by the gaze, in a world made out of illusion.

The canonical drama dwells on that, and despite the deconstruction that was—after the Berliner Ensemble came to Paris in 1954, shortly after the appearance of *Waiting for Godot*—a partial outgrowth of Brechtian alienation, there's a residue in our thought of the resonance of illusion: all the world's a stage, life is a dream, the insubstantial pageant fading . . . into the "precession of simulacra," as Jean Baudrillard would say, when he announced the end of the real,[4] or into the Society of the Spectacle, which, as Guy Debord had said in the wake of the sixties, "is *capital* to such a degree of accumulation that it becomes an image."[5] Nor is that any the less illusory for being thought of as commodification in a factitious economy of invisible power. In a notorious passage of his *Short Organum,* Brecht wrote scathingly of the capitulation to such power in tragic drama: to the gods who, beyond criticism, punished Oedipus, and of "Shakespeare's great solitary figures bearing on their breast the star of their fate," life becoming obscene as they collapse, "those dreamlike figures up on the stage," while the representation of their fate remains, through the "irresistible force of their futile and deadly outbursts,"[6] also beyond criticism. Despite the force of Brecht's remarks, irresistibly absorbed into an almost relentless critique of tragedy in poststructuralism, feminism, the new historicism, those dreamlike figures persist in thought, sometimes so vividly if distressingly that what we took to be illusion seems more like reality principle, with demystification itself drawn into its service.

So it was with Derrida, at the end of an essay in which he virtually identified with the ideas of Artaud, whose theater of cruelty, as the beginning of the essay insisted, "is not a *representation*. It is life itself, in the extent to which life is unrepresentable."[7] Whatever life may be or, if all the world is not a stage, however theater emerges from whatever it is, it is *not* reality. What's left of the real? What is presumably *not theater*—Derrida had to concede that "to think the closure of representation is to think the tragic: not as the representation of fate, but as the fate of representation. Its gratuitous and baseless necessity."[8] As for thinking the tragic in Beckett, or its leftover symptoms there, his solitary figures may not be great, in their futile and deadly outbursts, whether Pozzo, Hamm, or the Mouth, or without any figures at all the "recorded vagitus" of *Breath,* the two identical cries, but the gratuitousness and the baselessness he would certainly understand, with the declension of necessity into "Something is taking its course"[9] instead of a star on the breast, inside the breast "a big sore,"[10] or something dripping in the head—"A heart, a heart in my head"[11]—or, even more alarmingly, a vagrant flea in the crotch.

If such, with painful laughter, is the Beckettian fate of representation, let's go back for a moment to commodification: while the markets are described by distinguished economists as being in an essentially unstable state of "dynamic disequilibrium," controlled if at all by an "invisible hand," the spectacle is still being rehearsed in critical theory, along with the apparatus of representation, as an "economy of death," as if, Hamletically, it were ghosting itself. Preempting the ghost was, of course, the initiating prospect of Brechtian method, by strategic repetition or quotation refiguring representation, breaking down the apparatus by turning it against itself, thus producing a dynamic disequilibrium for subversive purposes, supplanting the invisible hand with a signifying body or an acutely visible sign, the *gestus,* or what Frederic Jameson calls "a properly Brechtian materialism."[12] In a curious turn of his own, Jameson sees the source of that materialism now in the Taoism of the Chinese Brecht, and he seems to be invoking another kind of ghostliness when he says of the secular and skeptical, disruptively cynical Brecht that a "hermeneutics of suspicion" is suspended "for the metaphysics that have become impossible"[13]—by which Jameson means, in his own disappointment with the future of an illusion, the metaphysics in the teleology of Marxist utopianism. It is, to be sure, the metaphysics that have become impossible which, with a dynamic of attrition in the disequilibrium, accounts for the repetitiveness in Beckett, like a pulse of dispossession or momentum of deferral that, in the permutations of absence, seems not at all strategic, or if so, vain, ill seen ill said, which is itself a kind of ghosting, of what, not sure: "No longer anywhere to be seen. Nor by the eye of flesh nor by the other. Then as suddenly there again. Long after. So on"[14]—approaching in the warped teleology of its compulsive vanity, aphasic, unutterable, nohow on, the asymptotic mirage of whatever it is, or was, "that time you went back that last time to look,"[15] even if it wasn't, "no better than shades, no worse if it wasn't,"[16] the impossible thing itself.

As to what you went back to look for, Brecht would agree with his friend Walter Benjamin that "nothing that has ever happened should be regarded as lost for history," but Benjamin would seem to encompass Beckett as well as Brecht when he says, in his "Theses on the Philosophy of History," that "the past can be seized only as an image which flashes up at the instant when it can be recognized and is never seen again." This is not a matter of recognizing, as in an older misguided historicism, "the way it really was," but rather in taking hold of "a memory as it flashes up at a moment of danger."[17] But the danger for Beckett is that whatever flashes up is in "no time gone in no time" that recurs again and again in *That Time*[18] "from the first and last that time curled up worm in slime when they lugged you out and wiped you off,"[19] without anything like the "temporal index by which," as Benjamin says in the "Theses," the past "is referred to redemption."[20] As for history, if it's not there in the "old style," as Winnie might say of the Portrait Gallery, "when was that," in *That Time,* "there before your eyes when they opened a vast oil black with age and dirt someone famous in his time," or "there in whatever thoughts you might be having whatever scenes perhaps way back in childhood or the womb worst of all or that old Chinaman long before Christ born with long white hair," then it's "just one of those things you kept making up to keep the void out just another of those old tales to keep the void from pouring in on top of you the shroud."[21] It may be that the tales, the old tales, belong to "the whore called 'Once upon a time' in historicism's bordello," as Benjamin says,[22] but the relay of voices in *That Time,* "without solution of continuity,"[23] the void pouring in, the shroud, would seem to do what he wants, and what Jameson quoting Benjamin attributes to Brecht, that is, "to blast open the continuum of history."[24] As it turns out, in a peculiar twist upon the void, nobody does that better than the shrouded Hamm—making metaphysics impossible too—when the shroud is taken off: "But what in God's name do you imagine? That the earth will awake in spring? That the rivers and seas will run with fish again? That there's manna in heaven still for imbeciles like you?"[25]

We are endowed, Benjamin says, with "a *weak* Messianic power," in a "secret agreement" with the past,[26] through which we come to the present "as the 'time of the now' . . . shot through with chips of Messianic time."[27] If there's the dying fall in Beckett that suffuses the time of the now, the vehemence, when it erupts, seems something more than weak, as when Hamm assures Clov, "*with prophetic relish,*" that he'll one day go blind too: "Infinite emptiness will be all around you, all the resurrected dead of all the ages wouldn't fill it, and there you'll be like a little bit of grit in the middle of the steppe,"[28] which may lack the luster of a Messianic chip but has its history too. And if memory flashes up, it's out of the bottomless pit of an incapacity to forget, if not history, the illusory promise of myth, and so it is in the gray chamber when Clov stares at the wall. "The wall!" rages Hamm, as if he'd conflated the Book of Daniel with the Platonic Cave, the archetypal site of illusion: "And what do you see on your wall? Mene, mene? Naked bodies." Clov: "I see my light dying."[29]

But speaking of danger and redemption in the light of that dying light, as if the secret agreement were being made, and made again, by those dreamlike figures on stage with what, recurrently, is a ghost of the past: "What, has this thing appeared again tonight?" What was asked on the ramparts of *Hamlet* (1.1.21)—and what I've written about before, the illusive substance of theater, which doesn't exist if it doesn't appear—became in the hollow of *Endgame,* "This . . . this . . . thing,"[30] while the nothing that came of nothing in pursuit of the thing itself became the Beckettian premise: "Nothing to be done."[31] As for this too, too solid flesh—for all the talk of the body as discourse, words, words, words, the words flying up, the body remaining below, naked body, libidinal body, all the bodies that matter or, with *its* repetitive acts, the body of "perfor-

mativity"[32]—if it resolves into a dew, adieu, adieu, it is born astride of a
grave, the light gleaming an instant, then gone, with maybe a forlorn
sense, as always in Beckett, that it might have been once or never—even
when parodied, all the more poignant for that—a visionary gleam:
"Look! There! All that rising corn! And there! Look! The sails of the
herring fleet! All that loveliness!"[33] Or so it was in Yeats, recalled in . . .
but the clouds . . . , "when the horizon fades . . . or a bird's sleepy cry
. . . among the deepening shades." Even in the measured countdown,
there on the video screen—"*5 seconds. Dissolve to* M. *5 seconds. Fade out
on* M. *Dark. 5 seconds*"[34]—we're still the stuff of dreams, rounded to a
sleep, though if dreams are wish fulfillment they may not feel as we wish,
no more than the begged appearance, "a begging of the mind, to her, to
appear, to me," by the voice in the "little sanctum" of the figure with
"robe and skull," and the sleep may be dubious too, begging there in
vain, "deep down into the dead of night," alienated in being, whether
awake or asleep, and—even with "break of day, to issue forth again,"[35]
voiding the little sanctum—can we be sure of that?

Meanwhile, the question of vision persists through the eternal contradiction that is—even with eyes wide open in the dispensation of the
gaze—more like a failure of the begetting in some perversion of sight.
Thus it is with the woman in *Rockabye,* "famished eyes / like hers / to
see / be seen,"[36] among the "successive fades" that have replaced the
deepening shades—"Jet sequins to glitter when rocking" and pale wood
"polished to gleam"[37]—saying to herself when being rocked, or in that
othered, recorded voice, "time she stopped / *time she stopped*"[38] till "The
day came / in the end came" and "dead one night / in the rocker" and
the rocker "rocking away"[39]—like O rocks in *Film,* cringing "away
from perceivedness"[40] but not immune to the gaze—"fuck life / stop
her eyes / rock her off / rock her off," but even through the ending
echo "coming to rest of rock,"[41] something is stirring still, what, or what
where, not sure, since it seems to escape perceivedness—and in all the
texts for nothing, by whatever number or name, it may only be an illusion but there appears no end to that.

Nor to the various ways we think about it. If illusion commingles
with faith and, to all appearances, may be thought of as fantasy too, it
may also be, as in Brecht's *Galileo,* with history taking its time, "consciousness impatient for truth," as Althusser said in an essay on the Pic-
colo Teatro and Brecht. Or it may be "The image of a consciousness of
a self living the totality of its world in the transparency of its own
myths."[42] As a function or necessity of the political, illusion may be so-

cial construction or what, without knowing it, in the ether of ideology, we've somehow come to believe. And while it is this, of course, that would seem most germane to Brecht—whose "principal aim," as stated by Althusser, "is to produce a critique of the spontaneous ideology in which men live"[43]—it is not quite where we'll see certain affinities with Beckett. That's more likely to occur with various degrees of subjectivity in the act of perception itself, despite the dramaturgical gap between a critical arrest in the service of *Verfremdung* and somatic immersion in the "science of affliction," where—as Beckett said in his essay on Proust, a proleptic definition of what infected his own thought—"The poisonous ingenuity of Time" subjects the individual to a "constant process of decantation," which leaves it "innocuous, amorphous, without character."[44]

Yet, while Brecht moved from the deobjectified characters of his early plays to those in a more gestic solid state, we have to deal in his work, as we do more egregiously in Beckett, with the perceptual status or analytics of the performative body, from Galy Gay as a human fighting machine to Dumb Kattrin's blinded eye, eye of flesh, eye of prey, to the predatory presence of the Inquisitor, alone, silent, stately, incising an empty stage, bringing to Galileo the liabilities of perceivedness, as with the swiveling light on the bodiless heads in the funeral urns of *Play*.

There are characters in Brecht who, like Anna Fierling, never miss a trick but fail to see, though we're likely to find little in Brecht that, like Beckett's body parts or absent bodies, severely abstracting or disfiguring space, not only directs but demoralizes, even stigmatizes perception, in the stigma directing it even more: Winnie, up to her diddies in the mound; a back, a bare foot, an arm, or even the "trace of a face";[45] or, with "head bowed, grey hair," the dreamer of *Nacht und Träume* and, with the dreamed self, dreamed hands, palm upward, joined, gentle, those dreamed commiserable hands, not like those in *Catastrophe,* with "fibrous degeneration,"[46] crippled to begin with and, speaking of a Brechtian *gestus,* made to look like claws. If that suggests, affect aside, or because of it, that there's a chastening semiology in Beckett, it is not quite, even in *Catastrophe* (dedicated to the imprisoned Havel), like Brecht's pointing toward the action not-done through the action that *is,* deciphering and exposing social cause. Yet it is possible to see in *Catastrophe*—its exposure of the production apparatus, the director's tyranny and the assistant's servility, what's pernicious and vitiating in the constructed mise-en-scène—a more virulent critique of the theater itself than almost anything staged in Brecht.

Meanwhile, if there's the "agony of perceivedness,"[47] there's the wanting to be seen, or in the inquisitional light of *Play* something equivocal about that: "Am I as much as . . . being seen?" With a slightest shift of accent (being *seen, being* seen) the issue of recognition passes into the notion that, however unnerving it may be, "mere eye," just the gaze, to be looked at—"Just looking. At my face. On and off"[48]—there is no being at all, nothing like identity, without being seen. Which is what Didi conveys when he advances on the Boy from Godot and says, "*(With sudden violence.)* You're sure you saw me, you won't come and tell me tomorrow that you never saw me!"[49] Here, through the stasis of the waiting, dispossession, desperate, is speaking for itself, as P in *Catastrophe* does at the end, however minimally, when he raises his head and confronts the audience with more than a trace of a face. Which is something else again than the willing anonymity of the agitators in Brecht's *The Measures Taken,* who "must not be seen," blotting out their faces on behalf of the oppressed workers of Mukden, "To win the victory / But conceal the victor."[50] This is the problematic context in which the Young Comrade, who puts "his feelings above his understanding"[51] and, taking the revolution upon himself, tears off his mask, revealing his "naked face, human, open, guileless,"[52] before capitulating to the will of the Party, accepting the measures to be taken, extreme as they are, letting himself be shot and thrown into the lime pit.

The play has been attacked as an anticipatory defense of Stalin's purge trials and, despite the animus of Brecht's critique, defended as tragic drama, and its dialectic is such that, were it to be rethought today in rehearsal, as the *Lehrstücke* were in theory meant to be, we might theorize alternatives to the Young Comrade's chilling sacrifice. This is, of course, an extremity to which Brecht himself was never quite submitted, in his more agile and cryptic dissidence in East Berlin, nor in his cautious debates with Lukács about the proprieties of socialist realism. Yet he considered the play absolutely central to what he was attempting in the theater, and it remains a temporal index of a question persisting through his work, as to how much subjectivity not only the revolution can allow, but also the epic theater, as it sublimated, say, the unappeasable appetites and narcissism of Baal, the utterly carnal version of the Canaanite fertility god, seen in cosmic scale in the opening Grand Chorale, as if he were the eroticized avatar of illusion itself. Grown in "his mother's womb so white"—and so primal, ecstatic, synesthetic, he seemed like the sky itself, "Naked, young and hugely marvelous"—Baal comes into being as something more than a subject, or less, with the voracious innocence and assurance of the modernist criminal/saint: "Baal will drag his whole sky down below,"[53] as if, incestuously, the Great Mother imaged there, he would seduce the universe itself.

When he does seduce a young woman, who drowns herself in shame, he sings a song—with another sort of detachment, not yet of the A-effect—about her slow descent: "The opal sky shone most magnificent," but as the song continues we get the nether side of Baal, who could be embraced by beauty itself, all that loveliness! and, as if longing for desecration, never leave it at that. As she floats downstream like Ophelia, there are no transfiguring garlands, no willows askant the brook, only "wrack and seaweed" clinging, with creatures and other growths, to the forlorn body that rots—as Baal's does eventually too— and he seems to relish that: "I see the world in a gentle light; it's the good Lord's excrement."[54] If that, for Yeats, is where love has pitched his mansion, it's also not far from Beckett, nor is Gougou far from Gogo, but with "a cold in the lungs," in the scene at the abysmal bar, the mordancy takes over in a tone resembling Hamm's "A slight inflammation. Nothing serious." And when Baal says of the past that it seems a strange word, Gougou ignores the notion of any secret agreement, of which, according to Benjamin, the historical materialist is aware: "Best of all is nothingness. . . . Yes, that's paradise. No more unfulfilled desires. All gone. You get over all your habits. Even the habits of desire." And when the beggar woman Maja—with a child in a crate, about as promising as the boy out the window in *Endgame*—asks, "And what happens at the end?" Gougou says, grinning, "Nothing. Nothing at all. The end never comes. Nothing lasts forever." It is here, momentarily, that Baal seems to take a position like that of the later Brecht, or a parody of him, as he rises in drunken indignation, or a mockery of it: "The worms are swelling. Crawling decomposition. The worms are glorifying themselves. . . . Bag-of-Worms, that's your name," he says to Gougou.[55]

As it happens, "crawling decomposition"—like the disjunct narrative of the man crawling on his belly in *Endgame,* and not only him, but "The place was crawling with them!"[56]—would seem to be a fair description of the momentum of Beckett's aesthetic, though the crawling accelerates from the muck in the waiting or the mud of *How It Is* to the "lifelong mess" of *That Time,*[57] with its curled up worm in slime, or the vertiginous "out" of *Not I,* not merely decomposition, "but the brain— . . . what?"[58] and the body with it, never mind desire, "whole body like gone . . . just the mouth . . . lips . . . cheeks . . .jaws . . . never- . . . what? . . . tongue?"[59] torn between screaming and silence, "crawl back in," and then through all the buzzing, "godforsaken hole . . . no love . . . spared that,"[60] until the wished-for end, "God is love . . . tender mercies," bag of worms aside, "back in the field . . . April morning . . . face in the grass . . . nothing but the larks . . . pick it up."[61] If the larks are not exactly, though "God is love," singing hymns at heaven's gate, the entreaty to pick it up may suggest the final scene of *The Good Person of Szechwan* when Shui Ta/Shen Te, who has been washed in gutter water and also known the muck, entreats the Enlightened Ones to stay, though the gods—having had enough of how it is, which is how it's going to be— fly homeward to their own nothingness, leaving the tender mercies to the audience, to whom the epilogue is addressed: "That you yourselves should ponder till you find / The ways and means and measures tending / To help good people to a happy ending."[62] Which—lips, cheeks, jaw . . . never—. . . what?—sounds like tongue in cheek.

It would certainly make Gougou laugh, or Garga of *In the Jungle of Cities,* who says, "We thought the planet would change course on our account. But what happened? Three times it rained, and one night the wind blew."[63] As for Baal, who is at the end the stinking image of crawling decomposition, Brecht apparently didn't entirely realize that almost everything about him, when the play was first done, would be seen as politically incorrect. But some years later, reviewing his early work, he took note of the criticism: "*Baal* is a play which could present all kinds of difficulties to those who have not learned to think dialectically. No doubt they will see it as a glorification of unrelieved egotism and nothing more."[64] If the dialectic seems a little devious, given the antisocial nature of Baal, he remains through Brecht's reassessment a virtual prototype of the lifestyle social protest, not unideological but at the extremity of it all, that we encountered in the sixties, when the apparently apolitical waiting for Godot could be taken as a model of passive resistance— as it was in San Francisco when I first directed the play, in 1957, the same year I staged the first American production of Brecht's *Mother Courage.* As I've pointed out before, it was *Waiting for Godot* that turned out to be, against the grain of the political Left, or—to use Benjamin's phrase from the "Theses"—"brush[ing] history against the grain,"[65] the most influential play, politically, of that period,[66] taken up then by the Left, which was ready to dismiss it as avant-garde indulgence. We didn't do *Baal,* but we should have, because—despite its apparent misogyny—it opened up ideas of sexuality that, as Sue-Ellen Case pointed out in the eighties,[67] we're still coming to terms with now. If the Young Comrade is his dialectical opposite, Baal remains a model of a polymorphous perverse spirit taking the pleasure principle to the threshold of exhaustion, where reality kicks in like the woodcutters going out, suggesting as they go a little *Verfremdung:* "Try to look at things more objectively. Tell yourself that a rat is dying. See? Just don't make a fuss. You have no teeth left." And then, as one man leans down to spit in Baal's face, another gives an additional piece of advice: "Try to schedule your stinking tomorrow."[68]

Yet, if Baal is omnivorous about his living, he is about dying as well. And if the anarchic nature of his corporeally indulgent body had to be curbed to the ideological policy of the later plays, it is not entirely extruded, for as even one of the woodcutters had to concede: "He drank like a sponge, but there's something about that pale lump of fat that makes a man think."[69] Which is about as good as you're going to get in defining the materiality of the A-effect, its arresting substance (which is what Joseph Beuys understood when he picked up the fat and used it, conceptually, in his estranging installations). One may ask: where does Baal, however surreptitiously, make his appearance in this or that play, as with the priapic figure in the garden in Galileo's meeting with the Little Monk, and when does he disappear, as Azdak does (rather like Falstaff in *Henry IV, Part II*) when a more rational order needs stabilizing toward the end of *The Caucasian Chalk Circle.* To the degree that his science is self-indulgence, an appetite, insatiable, Galileo is eventually excoriated. It's as if Baal represents, too, at another level the murky intuitive process that, as Brecht says in his essay on Chinese acting, commenting on Stanislavski, "takes place in the subconscious." This may be where it should be in what we call Method acting, but the subconscious, Brecht adds, "is not at all responsive to guidance; it has as it were a bad memory."[70]

In a sense, then, Brecht struggled throughout his career with techniques for managing or disposing of Baal, though killing him off was itself a dangerous project: "Sometimes Baal plays dead. The vultures swoop. / Baal, without a word, will dine on vulture soup."[71] If there is nothing so cunningly lethal in Beckett, his plays and short prose, as if with a failure of memory, appear to be taking place at some level of the psyche below the subconscious, though we may have to remember that the forgetting as it turns up in the *un*conscious is, as Freud remarked, the deepest form of memory. As for Brecht in the period of *Baal,* and *In the Jungle of Cities,* it may be the wrong word, but a sort of faith accompanied his cynicism, or to use President George W. Bush's phrase, a "faith-based initiative," as when Shlink urges Garga not to quit because, speaking of things below, "The forests have been cut down, the vultures are glutted, and the golden answer will be buried deep in the ground."[72] But then he may be speaking, too, in the Chicago setting of that play, of environmental depredations, corporate profits, and like President Bush today, reserves of oil in the ground.

In what would seem another definition of the Brechtian *gestus,* "a configuration pregnant with tensions" (or what Roland Barthes, writing of Brecht, calls "The pregnant moment"), Benjamin remarks that "thinking involves not only the flow of thoughts, but their arrest as well," giving the "configuration a shock, by which it crystallizes into a monad."[73] That figure is, however, in the allure of its crystallization, better suited, perhaps, to the Imagism of H. D. and Ezra Pound or, epiphanically, certain ideographic moments in the poems of T. S. Eliot. But if, as Eliot once said, as a virtual preface to the writing of Beckett (who was not at all indifferent to Eliot), words slip, slide, decay with imprecision, will not hold still, the monad is always threatened, which Brecht (whose early work, we forget, emerged into modernism with Eliot's) certainly understood. The trouble with thinking, always—to cite that dreamlike figure again, who is if anything pregnant with tensions— is that there's nothing either good or bad but thinking makes it so. If, then, the complex pedagogy of *The Measures Taken,* its painful dialectic or unbearable lesson, is characterized by the oxymoron of an ambiguous didacticism, the apparent nihilism of *Baal,* its sheer perversity, is eventually relinquished in the desire for a supportable pedagogy, which is not so much what Brecht wants us to think but rather the method by which he causes us to think.

Speaking of a certain calculated unreality, like a dead man singing, in the manifestation of a *gestus,* Brecht remarks in a footnote what we've come to expect, that this does not preclude an element of instruction, though the irrationality or even seeming lack of seriousness contributes to the gestic content that registers and defines the theatrical moment as meaning, though with the metaphysics at bay the meaning may be provisional. In Beckett, of course, with a seeming lack of seriousness the impossible and the provisional are maneuvered into a laugh: "We're not beginning to . . . to . . . mean something?" But before Hamm says *"(Vehemently.)* To think perhaps it won't all have been for nothing!" he pauses to wonder, "Imagine if a rational being came back to earth, wouldn't he be liable to get ideas into his head if he observed us long enough."[74] And whatever he says to mock it, if you didn't get ideas, a myriad of ideas—as in the circuitous, self-canceling, tortuous thinking of thought that Beckett calls the *pensum*—you must be out of your head. And the ideas, moreover, if you observed them long enough, that is, as they occur in performance, whatever the nothing done, arise from a certain ordering of perception that corresponds to an issue further defined by Brecht, still resisting illusion in the apparatus of representation. Yet, though he might put it another way, it's as if he agreed with Eliot's remark that, confronted as we are by the indeterminacies of the modern and a culture of disbelief, what we need to do is improve the quality of our illusions. Among which is the possibility entertained by Beckett, despite and by means of the derision of Clov, that we do "Mean something! You and I, mean something!"[75] As for the theater, what makes it mean something is, if by nothing more than intelligence (which was at a premium in the American theater when they first came on the scene), shared by Beckett and Brecht.

If in the culinary theater, as Brecht describes it in the *Short Organum,* the eyes wide open may signify a trance, as with the sleepers of the house who stare but do not see, the eye that observes long enough, "which looks for the *gest* in everything[,] is the moral sense."[76] Yet, if what Brecht is seeking is a moral tableau, as Diderot might have defined it (what Barthes later admired), it is not without an element of subjectivity, as when, suspended in the gaze, Galileo studies the moons of Jupiter or when, with voracious appetite and inarguable passion, he says he believes in the brain. If Beckett had any affectation it was the habit of denying its importance, but he also had quite a brain, and considerable erudition. Yet if in the elemental substance of his obsessive subjectivity—the subject seeking its subject in the regressive desperation of a never-ending quest—there is the *risus purus,* the laugh laughing at the laugh at anything like a moral sense, he is by no means without that either. And while there would seem to be a world of difference, though the actions in each instance are similarly unmomentous, between Mother Courage closing her pocketbook on the life of her son and Gogo pulling at his boot or Didi's buttoning his fly or Gogo later leaving his boots neatly at the edge of the stage, for another who may come, "just as . . . as . . . as me, but with smaller feet," he gives to that *gestus* or tableau the perhaps pathetic irony of a not unmoral sense, even through what may seem to be the burlesqued jaundice of the following exchange, about the boots being left behind:

> *Vladimir.* But you can't go barefoot.
> *Estragon.* Christ did.

Vladimir. Christ! What has Christ got to do with it? You're not
   going to compare yourself to Christ!
Estragon. All my life I've compared myself to him.
Vladimir. But where he lived it was warm, it was dry!
Estragon. Yes. And they crucified quick.

Didi, after a silence, says there's nothing more to do there of the nothing already done, and Gogo quickly replies, "Nor anywhere else,"[77]
which is not exactly promising for social change. But what could be seen
in the whole sequence about the boots is the sort of sly paradox or cun-
ning reversal you can also find in the capricious jurisprudence of Azdak
in *The Caucasian Chalk Circle* or in the water-seller Wang's opening remarks, while waiting to welcome the gods, in *The Good Person of Szechwan*. As he sizes up passersby, he says of two gentlemen, they "don't
strike me as gods, they have a brutal look, as if they were in the habit of
beating people, and gods have no need of that."[78]

One might make the case that the moral sense, in subtle and nuanced ways, suffuses the plays of Beckett, as it does through all the apparent caprice, hyperbole, and gratuitous cruelty of Hamm when he
says, at one point in his narrative about the man who crawled toward
him on his belly and wanted bread for his brat, "In the end he asked me
would I consent to take in the child as well—if he were still alive.
(Pause.) It was the moment I was waiting for. *(Pause.)* Would I consent
to take in the child . . ."[79] And the moment is suspended, with the moral
issue, as Hamm breaks off the narrative, until the end of the play, before
he puts on the stancher, when he comes back to the child, if, whoever
he is, "he could have his child with him."

It was the moment I was waiting for.
(Pause.)
You don't want to abandon him? You want him to bloom while
   you are withering? Be there to solace your last million last moments?
(Pause.)
He doesn't realize, all he knows is hunger, and cold, and death to
   crown it all. But you! You ought to know what the earth is
   like, nowadays. Oh I put him before his responsibilities!

If that's not a moral distinction, at the sticking point of thought, I
don't know what is, though it is a disturbing moral. And there is noth-

ing here like what we might see elsewhere in the almost demonic eloquence of Hamm, there at the nerve-ends, going to the quick, an extraordinary passion deflated by irony. As for the moral sense in epic theater,
it may be hard to work out the proportions of detachment and subjectivity, through an always strategic irony, but in any case, as with the
three cases distinguished by the voice of . . . *but the clouds* . . . , or the
"fourth case, or case nought,"[80] Brecht might have been making a case
for Beckett when he said, "out of mistrust of the theater" that, whatever
the case, "Theaters it all down, . . . [S]ome exercise in complex seeing is
needed." When he adds, however, that "it is perhaps more important to
be able to think above the stream than to think in the stream,"[81] it might
be hard for Beckett to imagine anything like that, for, imagination dead
imagine, the stream is all there is. And if you can't step into the same
river twice, as Heraclitus said, that's because you're always in it, even in
Come and Go. "May we not speak of the old days? [*Silence.*] Of what
came after?" But the after is more of the same and—"Holding hands . . .
that way. / Dreaming of . . . love"[82]—you can somehow never get out.

If the complex seeing occurs in other ways, Brecht nevertheless also
shares with Beckett, despite the rap about *Verfremdung* subduing emotion
by detachment, a "sensitivity to subjective differences," while there is a
similar compulsion to differentiation that, as Adorno remarks about
Beckett, "glides into ideology" too. Which doesn't, as Adorno also says,
in countering Lukács' charge that Beckett reduces humans to animality,
qualify Beckett to "testify as a key political witness . . . in the struggle
against atomic death."[83] For in Beckett's writing the terror of such death
seems to be as it always was—the dreadful thing has already happened,
"a heap, a little heap, the impossible heap"[84]—inseparable from the ordeal of being human. If Beckett is not guilty, as Lukács also charged, of
"an abstract, subjectivist ontology,"[85] his view of the subject—or at least
the subject of modernity—might have been defined by Brecht when, in
his earliest definition of epic theater, he said in no uncertain terms, "The
continuity of the ego is a myth. A man is an atom that perpetually breaks
up and forms anew. We have to show things as they are."[86] The new
purpose, for Brecht, in the era of "The petroleum complex" may have
been "paedagogics," as he says in an essay on "Form and Subject-Mat-
ter," but the fact of the matter for the subject, in things being shown as
they are, is that it can no longer appear in the drama with the old features of character, nor with the sort of motives imputed by Hebbel, Ibsen, or even Chekov. In a world where "fate is no longer a single coherent power," but dispersed into "fields of force" radiating in all

directions, actions must be shown as "pure phenomena,"[87] as they are with a motiveless specificity in *Baal* and in *In the Jungle of Cities,* more devastatingly so there than in the more rationalized epic of *Galileo* or in *Mother Courage.*

Yet, Courage pulling her wagon, after the death of Dumb Kattrin, aimlessly at the end—"infinite emptiness" all around her, as Hamm says apocalyptically in his warning to Clov, and imagination dead imagine the resurrected dead of all the ages combining with those of the ceaseless war—is an even bleaker image of a pure phenomenon than the dying Shlink asking for a cloth over his face, like Hamm, because "he doesn't want anyone to look at him,"[88] or Garga in the office of the late Shlink, saying in the final lines, "It's a good thing to be alone. The chaos is used up."[89] Or even the dying Baal, that pale lump of fat, with no teeth left, crawling on all fours like an animal to the door, for one last look at the stars. With the used-up chaos as the datum of thought, or the fields of force more entropic, this is all the more so in Beckett as he encapsulates the gratuitous and baseless necessity of the utterly negated subject, with its excruciating consciousness, or disjunctures of it, from the hollow in the wall of *Endgame* or the seeds that will never sprout to the diminishing returns or spastic brevity of the aphasic later plays.

Moreover, what we appear to encounter in Beckett—even in the plays with a more explicit political content, such as *Catastrophe,* and the clownish cycle of torture ("give him the works until he confesses") that followed in *What Where*[90]—is not merely "the nausea of satiation" or "the tedium of spirit with itself," which Adorno invoked in his essay on *Endgame,*[91] out of his own aversion to the politics of Lukács. Never mind the abstract, subjectivist ontology that Lukács charged Beckett with and Adorno rejected. Lukács may even be right, and there may be something like that there, though abstractions live in Beckett, like the pauses and silences extruded from Chekovian realism, in the lymph nodes and bloodstream of thought, where alienation is a reflex with illimitable affect that elides in the pure phenomena certain figures and gestures resembling the A-effect, as if the Brechtian arrest were in the Beckettian moment(um) the subject of thought itself. As for the subjectivist ontology, what may be most compelling or unnerving in Beckett is his response to a certain harrowing stillness in the barest rumor of being that is, all told, and told again, till the telling is intolerable, thus further dispersed in thought, as with the ceaseless stirrings of the equivocal word *still* (is it motion? or time? as endurance? or all of it under duress?), the ontological ground, if ground there be, of the subtlest, most seductive, imperceptible form of

illusion, what in the living end dying can never be seen, or seen as being, and therefore never told.

Still: "Something is taking its course." Estrange it as we will, it still
seems passing strange, only the passing certain, as in the stasis of the momentum and the plaintively quizzical moment of the waiting for Godot,
when Didi wonders, with Gogo falling asleep, and he not sure he's
awake, whether in the nothing that happened twice anything happened
at all, "That Pozzo passed, with his carrier, and that he spoke with us?
Probably. But in all that what truth will there be?"[92] It was precisely that,
the apparently impotent subjectivity of a ubiquitous indeterminacy, all
the more alluring for its teasing out of illusion—"They make a noise like
wings. / Like leaves. / Like sand. / Like leaves"[93]—which Brecht
thought he might change when he considered revising the play, linking
its oddities and incapacities to material interests and the past that's disre-
membered ("a million years ago, in the nineties"),[94] or not remembered
at all ("What were you saying when?"), surely not the beginning ("The
very beginning of WHAT?"),[95] bringing it in line with a more progressive sense of history. Yet, for all the ideological pressure of recent years
to historicize! historicize! one is occasionally tempted to say with
Gogo—who either forgets immediately or never forgets, who knows
only that "Everything oozes" and that "It's never the same pus from one
second to the next"[96]—"I'm not a historian."[97] And for the moment, arrested, still in the time of the now: the boots, the carrot, the tree, from
one second to the next, no time that time, and the waiting consigned to
illusion.

NOTES

1. Friedrich Nietzsche, *The Birth of Tragedy* (and *The Genealogy of Morals*), trans.
Francis Golffing (New York: Anchor/Doubleday, 1956), 33.

2. Bertolt Brecht, "The Modern Theater Is the Epic Theater," in *Brecht on Theater:
The Development of an Aesthetic,* ed. and trans. John Willett (New York: Hill and Wang,
1964), 34.

3. Samuel Beckett, *Play,* in *Collected Shorter Plays* (New York: Grove, 1984), 157,
160.

4. Jean Baudrillard, *Simulations,* trans. Paul Foss, Paul Patton, and Philip Betichman
(New York: Semiotext[e], 1983), 1–79.

5. Guy Debord, "Separation Perfected," in *Society of the Spectacle* (Detroit: Red and
Black, 1983) item 34, n.p.

6. *Brecht on Theater,* 189.

7. Jacques Derrida, "The Theater of Cruelty and the Closure of Representation," in
Writing and Difference, trans. Alan Bass (Chicago: University of Chicago Press, 1978), 234.

8. Derrida, "The Theater of Cruelty," 250.

9. Beckett, *Endgame* (New York: Grove Press, 1958), 13.

10. Beckett, *Endgame,* 32.

11. Beckett, *Endgame,* 18.

12. Frederic Jameson, *Brecht and Method* (London: Verso, 1998), 8.

13. Jameson, *Brecht and Method,* 12.

14. Beckett, *Ill Seen Ill Said,* in *Nohow On: Three Novels,* intro. S. E. Gontarski (New York: Grove, 1996), 56.

15. Beckett, *That Time,* in *Collected Shorter Plays,* 229.

16. Beckett, *That Time,* 231.

17. Walter Benjamin, "Theses on the Philosophy of History," in *Illuminations,* ed. Hannah Arendt, trans. Harry Zohn (New York: Harcourt, Brace and World, 1955), 256–57.

18. Beckett, *That Time,* 235.

19. Beckett, *That Time,* 230.

20. Benjamin, "Theses on the Philosophy of History," 256.

21. Beckett, *That Time,* 229–30.

22. Benjamin, "Theses on the Philosophy of History," 264.

23. Beckett, *That Time,* 227.

24. Benjamin, "Theses on the Philosophy of History," 264.

25. Beckett, *Endgame,* 53.

26. Benjamin, "Theses on the Philosophy of History," 256.

27. Benjamin, "Theses on the Philosophy of History," 265.

28. Beckett, *Endgame,* 36.

29. Beckett, *Endgame,* 12.

30. Beckett, *Endgame,* 45.

31. Beckett, *Waiting for Godot* (New York: Grove, 1954), 7.

32. See Judith Butler, *Bodies That Matter: On the Discursive Limits of Sex* (New York: Routledge, 1993), 9, 12.

33. Beckett, *Endgame,* 44.

34. Beckett, *Collected Shorter Plays,* 262.

35. Beckett, *Collected Shorter Plays,* 260–61.

36. Beckett, *Collected Shorter Plays,* 279.

37. Beckett, *Collected Shorter Plays,* 273.

38. Beckett, *Collected Shorter Plays,* 277.

39. Beckett, *Collected Shorter Plays,* 280.

40. Beckett, *Collected Shorter Plays,* 169.

41. Beckett, *Rockaby,* in *Collected Shorter Plays,* 282.

42. Louis Althusser, *For Marx,* trans. Ben Brewster (London: Verso/NLB, 1982), 144.

43. Althusser, *For Marx,* 144.

44. Beckett, *Proust* (New York: Grove, n.d.), 4–5.

45. Beckett, *Catastrophe,* in *Collected Shorter Plays,* 299.

46. Beckett, *Catastrophe,* 298.

47. Beckett, *Film,* in *Collected Shorter Plays,* 165.

48. Beckett, *Collected Shorter Plays,* 157.

49. Beckett, *Waiting for Godot,* 59.

50. Brecht, *The Measures Taken,* in *The Jewish Wife and Other Short Plays,* trans. Eric Bentley (New York: Grove Press, 1965), 81, 83.

51. Brecht, *The Measures Taken,* 87.

52. Brecht, *The Measures Taken*, 102.

53. Brecht, *Baal*, trans. William E. Smith and Ralph Manheim, *Collected Plays*, vol. 1, ed. Manheim and John Willett (New York: Vintage, 1971), 3.

54. Brecht, *Baal*, 46.

55. Brecht, *Baal*, 43–44.

56. Beckett, *Endgame*, 68.

57. Beckett, *That Time*, 230.

58. Beckett, *Collected Shorter Plays*, 217.

59. Beckett, *Collected Shorter Plays*, 220.

60. Beckett, *Collected Shorter Plays*, 222.

61. Beckett, *Collected Shorter Plays*, 222–23.

62. Brecht, *The Good Person of Szechwan*, in *Collected Plays*, vol. 6, 104.

63. Brecht, *In the Jungle of Cities*, trans. Gerhard Nellhaus, in *Collected Plays*, vol. 1, ed. Manheim and John Willett, 158.

64. Brecht, "On Looking Through My First Plays [ii]," in *Collected Plays*, vol. 1, ed. Manheim and John Willett, 345.

65. Benjamin, "Theses on the Philosophy of History," 259.

66. See, for instance, the preface to my *Sails of the Herring Fleet: Essays on Beckett* (Ann Arbor: Univ. of Michigan Press, 2000), 4–5.

67. Sue-Ellen Case, "Brecht and Women: Homosexuality and the Mother," *The Brecht Yearbook* 12 (1983): 65–74.

68. Brecht, *Baal*, 55–56.

69. Brecht, *Baal*, 56.

70. *Brecht on Theater*, 94.

71. Brecht, *Baal*, 4.

72. Brecht, *In the Jungle of Cities*, 160.

73. Benjamin, "Theses on the Philosophy of History," 264–65.

74. Beckett, *Endgame*, 32–33.

75. Beckett, *Endgame*, 33.

76. Brecht, "The Modern Theater is Epic Theater," 36n.

77. Beckett, *Waiting for Godot*, 34.

78. Brecht, *The Good Person of Szechwan: A Parable Play*, trans. Ralph Manheim, in *Collected Plays*, vol. 6, 3–4.

79. Beckett, *Endgame*, 53.

80. Beckett, *Collected Shorter Plays*, 261.

81. Brecht, "The Literarization of Theater (Notes to *The Threepenny Opera*)," in *Brecht on Theater*, 43–44.

82. Beckett, *Collected Shorter Plays*, 195.

83. Theodor W. Adorno, "Trying to Understand *Endgame*," *New German Critique* 26 (1982): 15.

84. Beckett, *Endgame*, 1.

85. Adorno, "Trying to Understand *Endgame*," 15.

86. Brecht, in an interview, "Conversation with Bert Brecht," *Brecht on Theater*, 15.

87. *Brecht on Theater*, 29–30.

88. Brecht, *In the Jungle of Cities*, 161.

89. Brecht, *In the Jungle of Cities*, 163.

90. Beckett, *Collected Shorter Plays*, 315.

91. Adorno, "Trying to Understand *Endgame*," 11.

92. Beckett, *Waiting for Godot,* 58.
93. Beckett, *Waiting for Godot,* 40.
94. Beckett, *Waiting for Godot,* 7.
95. Beckett, *Waiting for Godot,* 42.
96. Beckett, *Waiting for Godot,* 39.
97. Beckett, *Waiting for Godot,* 42.

Joseph Roach

The Great Hole of History: "Natural" Catastrophe and Liturgical Silence

That's how it is on this bitch of an earth.
—Pozzo, in *Waiting for Godot*

Jesus shall make no reply.
—Stage direction, from the Chester *Flagellation of Christ*

A particular kind of silence characterizes three plays from different places and times that also dramatize separate but related actions. These actions share memories of the modern world that elude conventional narrative. They must seek other languages for their retelling—languages of image, of gesture, of sound, and especially of silence. They seek the theater even as they resist surrendering their painful meanings to its reassuring but inhibiting conventions of time, place, and action. They seek the theater because they depend upon its fateful intersection of persons, times, and places astride the abyss of a history that disappears before it can be written and then reappears only as performance. They seek the theater because it is the last, best place, at least within the confines of European-derived forms, where the enormity of the consequences of certain unspeakable catastrophes can still be vividly enacted if not otherwise discursively voiced. They seek the theater, finally, because it is the place where deep silences can either follow significant revelations or create the emotional space into which revelation can enter. Commonly called liturgical silences, these moments carry over from devotional practices to secular performance events. They are a feature common to modern drama, but they are most famous in the theater of Samuel Beckett and still conspicuous in the works of the contemporary playwrights who self-consciously or unconsciously emulate it.

The three principal plays discussed here share liturgical silence as a medium: *Waiting for Godot* (1953), and two sequels that respond to Beckett's first and greatest drama with the sincerest form of flattery, *The Oriki of a Grasshopper* (1981) by Femi Osofisan and *The America Play* (1995) by Suzan-Lori Parks. In addition to the overlapping Atlantic-rim histories that produced them and that they in turn restage, the dramaturgical connections between these plays are not arbitrary. *The Oriki of a Grasshopper,* which premiered at the University of Ibadan at a fraught moment in West African politics in the early 1980s, depicts the ideological tensions among three Nigerians—a left-wing academic, his former student (now lover), and his longtime friend (now capitalist antagonist)—as they prepare to rehearse an amateur performance of *Waiting for Godot.* Osofisan draws heavily on Beckett's language through direct quotation and indirect allusion. He also adapts Beckett's silences. *The America Play,* which premiered as a joint production of the New York Shakespeare Festival and the Yale Repertory Theatre, is indebted to Beckett in the spareness of its language, in the density and fatality of its images, and in the cruelty of its repetitions. These include a two-act structure whereby the physical setting for each act maroons Parks's characters in predicaments that are (in a spatial contradiction perfected by Beckett's theater) at once claustrophobic and agoraphobic: "They are in a great hole. In the middle of nowhere. The hole is an exact replica of the Great Hole of History."[1]

Like a vast crater caused by the collision of the earth with an asteroid, the original Great Hole looks like the primordial work of natural history. That misleading resemblance stems from the self-evident scope of the catastrophic event that its very emptiness records. But human history, however insignificant it may be in terms of geological time, has also shown its precocious capacity to evacuate portions of the earth's surface with catastrophes of its own. Looked at from high above, say from the godlike statistical perspective of the *annalistes* (the annual production of crops, the burgeoning population; then the failure of harvests, the spiking mortality rates, the disappearance of villages or whole cultures), human history also marks its eschatological rhythms with voids and silences. They stand gaping as presumptive evidence of failed prayers. Here, where ditches once irrigated fields, is a palimpsest of sand and stone. There, where the soil was worked, on and off, for millennia, traces of the labors of generations still traverse the emptiness, worry lines fixed forever on the dead face of the earth. And here and there, their remains, dispossessed, like ruined cottages open to the sky, testify (not aloud) to the ways in which their history was and was not natural.

"That's how it is on this bitch of an earth," says Beckett's Pozzo summarily, speaking first as a witness to nature and then as her purblind victim.[2] Not a bad motto, when one thinks of it that way, to carve in

stone above the entrance doors to museums of natural history, those os-
suaries of superannuated species and the landscapes they once inhabited.
These large closets are so full of bones, to borrow the Beckettian image
of Tracy Chapman, they won't close.[3] In contrast to the more elusive allegory in *Waiting for Godot,* the historical provocation for such alienation
is clearly intimated in *Endgame* by the violent end attributed to every living creature in "Nature": "All is . . . Corpsed."[4] Theodor Adorno situates *Endgame* at human and natural history's catastrophic end. He raises
but does not exhaust the question of whether the end of history remains
within history—whether it produced the consciousness that implicates
Beckett's work in its own time, or moves outside of it, providing a position from which to contemplate with maximum disinterestedness the
terminal crisis that brought it forth. Prying partially loose the intellectual
grip of the universalizing, existentialist "theater of the absurd," Adorno
places *Endgame* in the topical company of "every aspiring drama of the
atomic age." He amends this generality with the important distinction
that as a dramatic parody—one that ironically recycles superannuated
forms "in the epoch of their impossibility"—*Endgame* stages in its vertiginous silences and demonic shtick the most appalling insight of the
postapocalyptic world: "The violence of the unutterable is mimed by
the dread of mentioning it."[5] This is a failure of language quite different
from the one plumped up by the metaphysicians of absurdity.

To insert *Waiting for Godot* into such a critical framework requires a
redirected but not wholly revised historical perspective. One bridge between the two plays appears in the two evacuated landscapes, a different
scene of desolation in each work, evoked by Beckett's actual and implied stage directions. They verge on a modernist-minimalist revival of
the pathetic fallacy. Both *Endgame* and *Godot* personify their settings as
malign by means of theatrical self-referentiality. This malignity is reciprocated by the notable peculiarity of Clov and Estragon: scenery makes
them angry. Exasperated, standing on his ladder at the porthole in
Endgame, the usually docile Clov lowers his telescope and turns to answer Hamm's annoyingly urgent query with one of his own: "What in
God's name could there be on the horizon?" (31). Already framed by an
exterior scene—"A country road. A tree. Evening"—Estragon's petu-
lant outburst in act 2 of *Godot* covers even more explicitly agoraphobic
ground: "Recognize! What is there to recognize? All my lousy life I've
crawled about in the mud! And you talk of scenery! *(Looking wildly about
him.)* Look at this muckheap! I've never stirred from it!" (39). The historical motives for topographical alienation in *Godot* are at once more

elusive and more ironic than they are in *Endgame:* "Charming spot," says Estragon, facing upstage; "Inspiring prospects," he adds, facing the auditorium; "Let's go," he concludes, cuing in Vladimir's crucial exposition about their given circumstances: "We can't. . . . We're waiting for Godot" (10).

Blurbed as "a modern morality play, on permanent themes," *Waiting for Godot* has challenged critics of every generation and intellectual camp to elucidate its tenebrous allegory. This strenuous endeavor was not made any easier by Samuel Beckett's notorious disinclination to clarify his intentions. He insisted that his words meant what they said— no more, no less. This is undoubtedly true, but the yawning gulf of the unsaid, which opens up like a gallows beneath the clever patter of the dialogue (not to mention under the ponderous weight of academic critics), threatens to leave dangling any strong reading of this play. Famously, had Beckett known the true identity of Godot, he would have said so. With the Scylla of vulgar reduction on one side and the Charybdis of mystified humanistic universality on the other, Adorno's essay on *Endgame* navigates the tricky waters of historical context. The catastrophes of which "Towards an Understanding of *Endgame*" speaks are of sufficient scope and specificity to reconcile Beckett's resistance to meaning and his engagement with the crisis of the late twentieth century, "a culture reconstructed in the shadow of Auschwitz."[6] That is as clear and as devastating as the annihilated world that Clov sees on the gray horizon. But what about the "muckheap"—the road, the tree, the low mound, the ditch, the bog—with which Estragon reproaches Vladimir? "You and your landscapes!" he fumes, "Tell me about the worms!" (39).

The landscape of *Godot* is desolate but not entirely empty. In addition to a handful of the living (Vladimir, Estragon, Lucky, Pozzo, and the boy), it is thickly populated by disembodied voices. In other words, it is haunted. From Ibsen on, modern drama has been troubled by ghosts.[7] Their ubiquity stems in part from the fact that they conveniently represent the past that is dead but that refuses final interment. The preternatural sounding of "All the dead voices" in act 2 of *Godot,* a lyrical passage as unsettling as it is dramatically inevitable, captures the intensity of this convention as poignantly as any in the canon of modern drama. It can easily be imagined as a musical number, like an operatic duet, which can be performed on its own in a concert (and separately anthologized among Beckett's greatest hits) but which acquires its fullest power only in its proper context:

Estragon. All the dead voices.
Vladimir. They make a noise like wings.
Estragon. Like leaves.
Vladimir. Like sand.
Estragon. Like leaves.
(Silence.)
Vladimir. They all speak at once.
Estragon. Each one to itself.
(Silence.)
Vladimir. Rather they whisper.
Estragon. They rustle.
Vladimir. They murmur.
Estragon. The rustle.
(Silence.)
Vladimir. What do they say?
Estragon. They talk about their lives.
Vladimir. To have lived is not enough for them.
Estragon. They have to talk about it.
Vladimir. To be dead is not enough for them.
Estragon. It is not sufficient.
(Silence.)
Vladimir. They make a noise like feathers.
Estragon. Like leaves.
Vladimir. Like ashes.
Estragon. Like leaves.
(Long silence.) (40)

As is typical among the moderns, the dead are seen as something of
an imposition. Like intrusive visitors, they speak only of themselves.
They certainly accumulate in significant numbers: "Where are all these
corpses from?" Vladimir wonders. "These skeletons," Estragon corrects
him (41), insisting on a distinction that typifies Beckett's way of marking
the passage of time by noting the progress of decay: "It's never the same
pus from one second to the next" (39). Time (one might say history)
narrows the relationship between the people and the land: "A charnel-
house! A charnel-house!" Vladimir exclaims (41), summing up the
sonorous detritus by locating the source of its macabre abundance.

Clever stage directors have found that the references to "corpses"
and "skeletons" play well when the actors insinuate that they refer in-

sultingly to the audience. This is hilarious indeed. But it can also draw in the audience as a kind of surrogate chorus, representing the dead as restless witnesses to the ineffectual efforts of the living actors to summon them into fullness of being. Like the dead, they are present in the consciousness of the quick, but they are also invisible on the horizon. Pozzo reports that after nearly a full day on the road with Lucky, he hasn't seen anyone else: "yes, six hours, that's right, six hours on end, and never a soul in sight" (16).

The poetic and dramatic tension of "All the dead voices," then, arises from the onomatopoetic reproduction of echoes that only the characters can hear in a landscape hollowed by loss. The acoustical gravity of this absence deepens cumulatively in the five excruciatingly placed silences. In an opera (or melodrama), the chorus and orchestra would enter there. But in Beckett's theater, silence mocks the speakers, threatening the finality of an evacuation that they have experienced as only partially complete: "The air is full of our cries" (58). The phantom sound plot (the rustling, the murmuring) thus supports the mise-en-scène of the skeletonized landscape. As the vibrations that make up sound diminish, they are commonly said to "die out" or "decay" (OED). As they do, the sensations of the listeners reorganize themselves into memories. Wings, leaves, and feathers may reasonably be supposed to have rustled. But these are not the only whispers in Vladimir and Estragon's evocation of "All the dead voices." It must have been the ashes that murmured.

Scholars who have written about the poet whom they call "the Irish Beckett" have noted the Irishness of the landscape in *Waiting for Godot*. They have done so in the contexts of literary influence and biographical affinity or disaffection, coming down even to the details of Beckett's sore feet on his walking tour through the countryside of Connemara in 1931.[8] What they have not pursued in detail, except by implication, is what seems most obvious in light of Adorno's "violence of the unutterable": that the landscape evoked by Beckett was created by the catastrophic actions or inactions of historical persons as well as by the workings of God or Nature. Beckett's circum-Atlantic emulators, at any rate, take him this way. In the "abode of stones" of which Lucky speaks in his thrice-repeated naming of Connemara (28–29), they seem to have found inspiration for the representation of an abyss in which violence deposits victims of mass disappearance.

The Great Hole of History and its replicas, which are implicit in

Osofisan's *Oriki of a Grasshopper,* dominate the scene of Parks's *The America Play.* Digging itself into the Hole, which is described as a theme park with parades and pageants, history competes ineffectually with simulation as a way of misappropriating the past: the role of "The Great Man," Abraham Lincoln (or his spectral image in the popular imagination) is played by "The Lesser Known," a gravedigger by trade who parlays his striking physical resemblance to the Great Man into a second career as a performance artist (or postmodern sideshow geek) under the stage name of "The Foundling Father." He takes his act on the road out "West." He finds a promising spot and digs a copy of the original hole back "East," which in its authenticating way replicates the real but unlocalized Great Hole of History. Serving as the backdrop for his performance, a specimen of roadside Americana, this tourist-trap feeds off the original theme park, which The Lesser Known first visited with his wife Lucy on their honeymoon.

With his supply of fake beards, his stovepipe hat, and his stick-on wart, The Foundling Father plays Lincoln so consummately that the public wants him to be shot. He does not disappoint. For a penny fee, thrill-seekers can play the role of John Wilkes Booth and plink at the Lincoln effigy as it sits docilely in its rocker. The Great Man mechanically laughs over and over again at the same joke from *Our American Cousin* and dies with sickening repetition—as if the Zapruder film has inspired a macabre Civil War reenactment: "*Booth shoots. Lincoln 'slumps in his chair.' Booth jumps*" (13). With each reiteration, The Foundling Father is reborn as the Founding Father at the moment of his death, an intervention in the linear protocols of genealogical succession, an inversion whereby the disavowed past reappears thinly disguised as the future:

> The Great Man lived in the past that is was an inhabitant of time immemorial and the Lesser Known out West alive a resident of the present. And the Great Mans deeds had transpired during the life of the Great Man somewhere in pastland that is somewhere "back there" and all this while the Lesser Known digging his holes bearing the burden of his resemblance all the while trying somehow to equal the Great Man in stature, word, and deed going forward in his lesser life trying somehow to follow in the Great Mans footsteps that were of course *behind* him. The Lesser Known trying somehow to *catch up* to the Great Man all this while and maybe running too fast in the wrong direction. Which is to say that maybe the Great Man had to catch him. Hhhh. Ridiculous. (17)

More sublime than ridiculous, Parks's dramatic explication of the cyclical process of forgetting reveals the attraction exerted by the future on the return of the past. To emulate, to live up to, to become like the Great Man (or even a rank-and-file ancestor) is to move in opposite directions simultaneously while apparently standing still, as if he were walking the length of a Möbius strip, searching for the other side of a one-sided surface: following in another's footsteps, ones that he has yet to leave behind, keeps him from getting back to the place he never really left. In act 2 Lucy and Brazil, her son by The Foundling Father, go west to dig up his corpse, but he returns under his own power on time for his own reburial. Parks's images of stasis or repetitive movement in place are characteristically Beckettian, as is the knife-edged memento mori that clarifies them. As the grave-digging Lincoln-impersonator puts it: "Six feet under is a long way to go" (16).

The Oriki of a Grasshopper enacts a similar scene of contradiction and stasis, and Osofisan draws his language even more directly from the dark well of Beckett's morbid circularity. For the African, the Great Hole of History is also a grave. Around it certain rituals, especially waiting, are repeated cyclically. Ostensibly a realistic play with a faculty office for its setting, The Oriki of a Grasshopper (an oriki is a praise-song; the grasshopper has to move during the dry season or die in the parched bush) actually takes on the poetic imagery and patterned language of the play its characters are rehearsing. The action of waiting for "Godot" stands in for several other exercises in waiting, in ascending order of generality: first, for a late-arriving actor (the circumstances of his nonappearance are ominous); second, for the arrival of the political police; and third, for the social revolution that will transform Nigeria, Africa, and the Third World. Osofisan tells this story through overlapping images of birth and death. Imaro, the self-hating radical professor, broods on the stillbirth of the African revolution at the very moment of his rapidly changing country's robust (and ruthlessly maldistributed) growth. Even after the rehearsal is canceled because the authorities have arrested the actor playing the role of Estragon, Imaro summarizes his predicament as an African intellectual by quoting the most famous lines from Waiting for Godot:

> How did Beckett put it? (quotes) "Astride of a grave and a difficult birth. Down in the hole, lingeringly, the grave-digger puts on the forceps. We have time to grow old. The air is full of our cries. (He listens, as in the text of Beckett's play.) But habit is a great deadener. (He looks, as if at the sleeping form of Estragon.) At me too someone is

looking, of me too someone is saying, he is sleeping, he knows nothing, let him sleep on. *(Pause)* I can't go on!"[9]

Even Osofisan's silences overlay Beckett's in a kind of aural palimpsest, gaining an added layer of ominousness by exploiting the drama of Estragon's absence from the scene. "In spite of all the metaphysical interpretations given to it in the West," Osofisan has said of *Waiting for Godot,* "the play is in fact very much a Third World play!"[10] I am not proposing to elaborate here Beckett's influence, which speaks for itself, on Osofisan and Parks, but I do want to expand on the Nigerian's claim (indeed, his exclamation) that *Godot* is a play that belongs somehow to the Third World.

Arguing for an historicized alternative to what Osofisan calls Beckett's "metaphysics," I claim that the setting of *Godot*—with its depopulated horizon of stones, bones, and stunted tree, with its harrowing imagery of food, scarcity, rot, and want, and with its haunted threnody, "All the dead voices"—evokes the greatest hole in Irish history and one of the greatest in modernity. Here as in other Great Holes of History, silence follows catastrophes that occur to the disentitled. In one sense, the history of the Great Hunger, or at least the landscape on which that history was inscribed by the evacuation of the population by emigration or death,[11] appears in Beckett's straightforward topographical descriptions, to which he adds a sinister allegorical twist. These include but are not limited to the "low mound" on which Estragon tends to his boot and Lucky's vista of a well-known point of geological interest that rises starkly among the stones that stretch like graves under the indifferent sky: "the tears the stones so blue so calm alas alas on on the skull the skull the skull the skull in Connemara" (29). In another sense, however, the deferred memory of incalculable loss appears indirectly through the acoustical insinuation of ghostly voices into an austere soundscape eroded by silence. Irish musicology records one of the eeriest consequences of "the calamities which, in 1846–7, had struck down and well nigh annihilated the Irish remnant of the great Celtic family." That was an "awful, unwonted silence," which descended during the Famine years and lingered long thereafter: "The 'Land of Song' was no longer tuneful; or, if a human sound met the traveler's ear, it was only that of the feeble and despairing wail of the dead."[12]

Other genocidal catastrophes would work as well for purposes of justifying liturgical silences: the modern dramatist has many from which to choose. The consequences of the Great Hunger, however, including the diaspora that it forced on millions, links Irish history and Beckett's landscape with the manifold hungers of the Third World as dramatized by Osofisan. Claudius, the businessman foil to the academic protagonist in *Oriki of a Grasshopper,* describes the cares that deprivation imposes even on the bureaucrats and landlords, recalling the slave driver Pozzo's self-pity for the imposition of Lucky's misery: "A hungry man, they say, is an angry man. Your workers, your children, your wife, they are all hungry" (22). Picking up on his antagonist's theme, Imaro twice compares the African situation with that of the famished character who falls on discarded scraps in the play he is rehearsing: "Like Estragon, nibbling bones . . ."[13] In both instances an ellipsis follows the borrowed stage direction (that Beckett writes for Estragon, after Pozzo throws him a sop), a sinister silence that trails behind the utterance like a long black cloak.

Beckett's active imagery of animality, death, scarcity, and his repeated use of words like *violent* in connection with hunger and food converge in the little song that opens act 2. Another bleak lyrical interlude, Vladimir's ditty heightens the perception that deprivation, violence, and punishment are the normal expectation for those whose physical needs transgress against the prevailing maldistribution:

A dog came in the kitchen
And stole a crust of bread.
Then cook up with a ladle
And beat him till he was dead . . .

Then all the dogs came running
And dug the dog a tomb
And wrote upon the tombstone
For the eyes of dogs to come:

A dog came in the kitchen
And stole a crust of bread.
(37)

And so forth, as if fighting over the last scrap were a daily ritual as efficacious as waiting for Godot. The similarly canine (and circular) impression made by Lucky's mute obedience does not end when his master throws him a bone. Of Lucky's weeping at the threat of abandonment, Pozzo says, "Old dogs have more dignity" (21), a line that occasions the master's callous rumination on the constant quantity of the world's tears: no sooner does one person begin to cry, than another stops

(22). The prevailing action of the play is one of circularity and stasis, as has often been pointed out, but it is also one of subtraction, as if the diminishing number of organs (Pozzo's eyes, Lucky's tongue) and the growing number of skeletons have some connection with the dwindling supply of carrots, radishes, and bread crusts. And why wouldn't they?

At least one certainty connects the worlds of *Waiting for Godot* and *Oriki of a Grasshopper:* the food is terrible. This is even more noticeable when it is abundant: "Funny," says Estragon, "the more you eat the worse it gets" (14). Abundance, however, is not the typical experience here. The desperation associated with food by the characters is performed through the extraordinary vaudeville business with which they acquire, exchange, share, and consume it. Estragon brings up the subject of food by "violently" announcing his deprivation: "I'm hungry!" (13). He spent the previous night in a ditch and was beaten by unidentified assailants (7). Now food preoccupies him. Vladimir, turning his pockets inside out, can offer only some turnips, which Estragon rejects, and one carrot: "Make it last," Vladimir cautions, "that's the end of them" (14). Beckett's personal selection of properties for his own stagings of *Godot* is very suggestive in this context: "the carrot was usually pitifully small, another example of diminishing resources."[14]

The final, miserable carrot does important work of dramatic exposition. In the longer arc of the action of the play, it prepares for the moment of the last of the radishes in act 2. This second pathetic offering Estragon, despite his bone hunger, has to reject, and the reason he gives evokes some of the most painful accounts of the onset of the potato blight: "It's black" (44). In the more immediate liaison of scenes in act 1, the carrot routine sets up the cruel humor of Pozzo's picnic. After Lucky unpacks the supper of a bottle of wine and chicken, Pozzo begins to eat "voraciously, throwing away the bones after having sucked them" (17), while Vladimir and Estragon distract themselves from the painful sight of watching him feast by examining Lucky's running sores. Then Estragon begs for the discarded bones after Lucky, who has first refusal as Pozzo's lackey, turns them down, which disconcerts his master: "I don't like it. I've never known him to refuse a bone before" (18). Estragon "begins to gnaw" the refuse, scandalizing Vladimir, who won't be thrown a sop, even though he too has hungrily watched while the banquet proceeded.

As in Parks, Beckett's dead won't stay dead or even play dead for long, but their intervention in the world of the living is performed in the disguise of refuse—ashes, sand, leaves, and feathers. It is also performed in the guise of echoes, repetitions that take the form of memory imperfectly deferred: "The air is full of our cries" (58). Similarly, the "Archeology" section of *The America Play* has Brazil and Lucy digging up the trash left by The Foundling Father in the Great Hole, and as they unearth the objects he left behind one by one, they listen to each for its echo, like a seashell's, hoping for a clue to the current whereabouts of their past:

> *Brazil.* This could be his!
> *Lucy.* May well be.
> *Brazil.* (*Rest.*) Whaddyahear?
> *Lucy.* Bits and pieces. (30)

The mother and child's archeological project—digging, dusting, and polishing—excavates an impressive variety of items: Washington's wooden teeth ("nibblers, lookin for uh meal"), a marble bust of Lincoln, a glass trading bead, an unspecified number of licked boots, peace treaties, bills of sale, deeds, and medals of all kinds, including one for croquet and another for "bowin and scrapin" (29–30). This inventory brings together the iconic tokens of the Founding Fathers, whose fame nominates them as representatives of each and every historical period, with the ironic memorabilia of the forgotten sojourners to the Great Hole of History, whose medals were won for heroism (or at least survival) in the conduct of humble, everyday activities, such as standing straight, standing still, and making do. Parks's "Archeology" disturbs the fragments of what the *annalistes* call "the history of events" as well as those belonging to the history of everyday life over the *longue durée*. What *The America Play* dramatizes is the way in which the former—the presidents and the assassins—arrive unbidden from the past to represent the latter in the present, imposing on them the effigies of which national memory is fabricated and honored while taking from them the stories without which they will tumble unmarked and unmourned into the Great Hole.

At this point, a magnificent Beckettian silence intervenes to enforce circumspection on the archaeologists. In answer to Brazil's question about his forebears, Lucy ends the scene with a remark that can only be followed by a moment fashioned from the monumental nonspeech of a play like *Waiting for Godot,* a liturgical silence for atheists: "Stories too horrible tuh mention" (31). Parks represents the silence following this line and others like it in *The America Play* as interactive, not absorptive: rather than featuring the individualized performance of unspoken psychological musings, the social meanings of the silence are supposed to pass back and forth between the characters onstage, and, if the actors are any good, between them and the audience. The typographical conventions of the acting edition of *The America Play* show this technique, which Parks calls a "spell," at work:

(Rest.)
Brazil.
Lucy.
Brazil.
Lucy. (31)

A spell is a place in the performance for the expression of unspoken emotion but also of transition from one feeling to another, what actors and directors in the American theater call a "beat." Brazil works as a professional mourner, and Lucy is a keeper of the secrets of the dead. In this beat or spell, they move along from the identified "bits and pieces" of the excavated past on the rim of the Great Hole of History to the losses that must remain unnameable as a condition of their passage to its yet unplumbed depths: "And how thuh nation mourns" (43).

Osofisan is even more explicit in his pantomime. From the vaudeville bit of Didi and Gogo passing back and forth the hat that Lucky has left on the stage, he has Imaro and Claudius fashion "The hat of slavery." The stage directions call for them to follow Beckett's intentions for the farce business, which had already been worn out from centuries of use when Laurel and Hardy filmed it, of two men sharing three hats so that one hat is always in motion while two rest on their heads—the simplest kind of physical comedy. But juxtaposed to the narrative that Imaro recites while he performs the business, the bit allows Osofisan to do his own kind of excavation around the edges of the Great Hole of History where the past becomes the present under the influence of a greedy future: .

> And they continue to sell our people. Once it was for mirrors, for cheap jewelry, for cowries. The rich men raided the poor, captured them, and sold them off to the slave ships. Then came the age of palm oil, of cocoa, timber, and cotton. The rich men made their slaves work on their plantations, carting off the products of their labor into the white ships. Always into the white ships. (13)

The circular action mimes a history in which the gravedigger puts on forceps. The image of "the insatiable white ships" returns several more times before the speech ends with Beckett's stage direction—Imaro throws the hat to the ground and tramples it. A long silence ensues before Claudius delivers the crushing news that he could not save the actor playing Estragon from arrest (and the unspoken possibility of torture and execution) but that he has intervened with a corrupt official to save Imaro from the same fate. If there is a liturgical silence here that taps the religious symbolism of *Waiting for Godot,* it must include an allusion to the exchange between Vladimir and Estragon about the "Two thieves, crucified at the same time as our Savior": one was saved and the other damned (9). When the business ends, no one wants to be the one left holding the hat of slavery.

Osofisan's imagery and business provide an occasion to summarize the relationship of the three plays and their dramatizations of the phenomenon that Parks calls the Great Hole of History. Beckett, Osofisan, and Parks might be seen to occupy the three points of a triangle that define the circum-Atlantic world—Europe, Africa, and America—a world that was created by the circulation of those ships, the system they sustained, and the long silence that followed. Conventional approaches to Beckett place him in the realm of what Osofisan calls "metaphysics," but there are plausible reasons for claiming *Waiting for Godot* as a social drama, even as an antislavery play, not because its conception of that cause is so moralized but because it is so dark. Beckett proffers more tangible agents of catastrophe than the abstractly malign operations of an absurd universe, while at the same time he does not, because he need not, abandon the general proposition of nihilism. In *Texts for Nothing,* the author, second-guessing himself like a well-made playwright clearing up weak motivations, asks a very suggestive question about Pozzo: "Why did Pozzo leave home, he had a castle and retainers [?]"[15] In the play, Pozzo thinks that he might have left his half-hunter back at "the manor" (31). The image of the absentee landlord, living off the sweat of his starving bondmen, preening himself over the way he indulges them, suits Pozzo, especially in the harrowing metonym of the rope that joins him to Lucky, first as chain, then as a lead. Pozzo's attitude toward his slave is specific. Harmonizing with the category of mid-nineteenth-century political economy that wrote off surplus populations of putatively inferior people as expendable, Pozzo's ideology prompts him to think of selling Lucky at the fair as leniency: "The truth is you can't drive such creatures away. The best thing would be to kill them" (21). Beckett the poet successfully evades abduction by single-issue causes, however worthy, as a condition of his austere, ironic compassion. But he does not evade history. As soon as the refugees whom Peter Hall was first to call "tramps" begin to take stock of their rotten tubers along "a country road" in an "abode of stones," history and memory come into play. They proliferate in the dramatic silences that sensitized listeners cannot but hear as choric.

In any case, that is what both Osofisan and Parks have heard in *Godot*—a manner of speaking, through excruciatingly placed silences, about things discursive historians have trouble saying out loud. Parks takes as her epigraph for *The America Play* a quotation attributed to John Locke: "In the beginning, all the world was *America*." Now that globalization seems to be returning the world to its original state, it is all the more urgent to understand, in ways that theatrical performance can best represent, the hunger at the bottom of the Great Hole of History and the silence by which it has been memorialized.

The evocation of geographical and historical specificity in *Waiting for Godot* does not foreclose more general implications. The necrology of the play explicitly includes *all* the dead voices. That the setting could be "at once Ireland and anywhere"[16] makes Adorno's contention about the natural and human historical situation of *Endgame* even more readily applicable to the earlier work: the landscape of "natural" catastrophe is an all-too-familiar one at the beginning of the twenty-first century, and there exists plenty of evidence to suggest that instead of a belated episode of premodern abjection, the cold-blooded modernity of the Great Hunger foreshadows an apocalyptic global landscape yet to come. "Sweet mother earth!" is how Estragon generalizes the prospect, voicing the apostrophe of nurture withheld as a bitter oath or ritual lament (53). This is why the chant of "All the dead voices" seems like a requiem mass—ashes to ashes, dust to dust—and why the poignantly placed silences count for so much in its performance. A liturgical silence, as in a Quaker Meeting, is an opening up of a space for God to enter, but in the play where (famously) nothing happens twice, the space remains as gnawingly empty as the bellies of the unlucky. That Vladimir and Estragon initially misrecognize Pozzo as Godot himself connects him with the elusive landlord of the larger estate. Consistent with the imagery of feudal obligations to vassals or of masters to slaves, inquiries about Godot's nature turn to his provision of food. When Vladimir interrogates the boy, he asks: "Does he give you enough to eat?" (34). The boy's reluctant and evasive answer is not reassuring. Set against the starved landscape, it is one of the expositional plantings in the play that culminate in the final nonappearance of the greatest absentee of them all.

If God can be thought of as food and if Godot can be thought of as God—and there are oft-rehearsed arguments behind both of those propositions—Godot's failure to appear not only mandates starvation but also, more terribly, appears to justify it. Godot may be nothing more than an apostrophe of nature itself, however, which, according to the preponderance of evidence in the play, could very well have died also, as God has apparently done, except for the five tiny leaves that miraculously and ironically appear on the tree during intermission. The great hole of history in Beckett's play, like so much else in the work of this most physical of playwrights, is made palpable, present to the senses as absences—a silence, a stillness, an unbroken horizon. His art mimes the "violence of the unutterable" in a place—at once remembered and prophesied—where the bounty of the earth is for the most part bestowed on the profusion of its graves.

NOTES

1. Suzan-Lori Parks, *The America Play* (New York: Dramatist's Play Service, 1995), 20.

2. Samuel Beckett, *Waiting for Godot* (New York: Grove Press, 1954), 25.

3. Cited in Peter Quinn, "Closets Full of Bones," in *Irish Hunger: Personal Reflections on the Legacy of the Famine,* ed. Tom Hayden (Boulder, Colo.: Roberts Reinhardt, 1997), 234–40.

4. Samuel Beckett, *Endgame* (New York: Grove Press, 1958), 30.

5. Theodor Adorno, "Towards an Understanding of *Endgame,*" in *Twentieth Century Interpretations of Endgame,* ed. Bell Gale Chevigny (Englewood Cliffs, N.J.: Prentice Hall, 1969), 86.

6. Adorno, "Towards an Understanding of *Endgame,*" 106.

7. For an authoritative account, see Marvin Carlson, *The Haunted Stage: The Theatre as Memory Machine* (Ann Arbor: University of Michigan Press, 2001).

8. Eoin O'Brien, *The Beckett Country* (Dublin: Black Cat Press; London: Faber and Faber, 1986), 305–7; John P. Harrington, *The Irish Beckett* (Syracuse: Syracuse University Press, 1991), 177; Mary Junker, *Beckett: The Irish Dimension* (Dublin: Wolfhound Press, 1995), 47–50; see also J. C. C. Mays, "Irish Beckett, a Borderline Instance" in *Beckett in Dublin,* ed. S. E. Wilmer (Dublin: Lilliput Press, 1992), 133–46; Rodney Sharkey, "Irish? Au Contraire! The Search for Identity in the Fictions of Samuel Beckett," *Journal of Beckett Studies* 3 (1994): 1–18; subsequent works on the subject of Beckett's Irishness cite Vivian Mercier, *Beckett/Beckett* (New York: Oxford University Press, 1977).

9. Femi Osofisan, *The Oriki of a Grasshoper and Other Plays* (Washington, D.C.: Howard University Press, 1995), 29.

10. Quoted in Sandra Richards, *Ancient Songs Set Ablaze: The Theatre of Femi Osofisan* (Washington, D.C.: Howard University Press, 1996), 31–32.

11. William Trevor, *A Writer's Ireland: Landscape in Literature* (New York: Viking Press, 1984), 95–97.

12. George Petrie, *The Ancient Music of Ireland* (Dublin: Society for the Preservation and Publication of the Melodies of Ireland, 1855), xii.

13. Osofisan, 6. Later (p. 23) it is "Estragon, munching bones . . ."

14. *The Theatrical Notebooks of Samuel Beckett,* vol. 1, *Waiting for Godot,* ed. Dougald McMillan and James Knowlson (New York: Grove Press, 1994), 109.

15. Samuel Beckett, *Texts for Nothing* (London: Calder and Boyars, 1974), 27.

16. Terry Eagleton, *Heathcliff and the Great Hunger: Studies in Irish Culture* (London: Verso, 1996), 11–26.

Section B | Beckett in Practice

S. E. Gontarski

Revising Himself: Samuel Beckett and the Art of Self-Collaboration

I should prefer the text not appear in any form before production and not
in book form until I have seen some rehearsals. . . . I can't be definitive
without actual work done in the theater.
                                                —S.B. to Barney Rosset, May 18, 1961

I have asked Faber, since correcting proofs, to hold up production of the
book. I realize I can't establish text of *Play,* especially stage directions, till I
have worked on rehearsals.
                                                —S.B. to Richard Seaver, November 29, 1963

Samuel Beckett's transformation from playwright to theatrical artist is
one of the seminal developments of late modernist theater and yet one
slighted in the critical and historical discourse. A lack of theatrical documentation may account for some of the neglect as scholars and critics
traditionally privilege print over performance, that is, the apparent sta-
bility or consistency of the literary script over its theatrical realization or
completion. The absence of Beckett's direct work on stage from the historical equation, however, distorts the arc of his creative evolution, his
emergence as an artist committed to the performance of his drama as its
full realization. Beckett was to embrace theater not just as a medium
where a preconceived work was given its accurate expression, but as *the*
means through which his theater was created. As Beckett evolved from
being an advisor on productions of his plays to taking full charge of their
staging, an apprenticeship of some fifteen years, practical theater offered
him the unique opportunity for self-collaborations through which he
rewrote himself, that is, reinvented himself as an artist, and in the process
redefined late modernist theater.

In retrospect it may seem self-evident to proclaim that the Samuel
Beckett who authored *Waiting for Godot* in 1948 and the Samuel Beckett
who staged it at the Schiller Theater, Berlin in 1978 were not one and
the same person, no less one and the same artist. Beckett provided his
own theoretical paradigm for such dialectics as early as his 1931 treatise

on Marcel Proust: "We are not merely more weary because of yesterday, we are other, no longer what we were before the calamity of yesterday."[1] The Samuel Beckett who came to *Waiting for Godot* as its director thirty years after having written it was that "other," and the conjunction of the two, the writing self of 1948 and the directing "other" of 1978 (or the reverse, the directing self of 1978 and the writing "other" of 1948), is one of the defining moments of late modernist theater. Such conjunction occurred some sixteen times on the stage and another six times in the television studio; during each of those encounters, Beckett seized directing opportunities to play both self and other: that is, to refine if not to redefine his creative vision, to continue to discover latent possibilities in his texts, and, by expunging anything he deemed extraneous, to demonstrate afresh his commitment to, if not preoccupation with, the form, the aesthetic shape of his work. Beckett's own theatrical notebooks for what was a pivotal play in his developing sensibility, *Spiel (Play),* alone contain some twenty-five separate, complex, and full outlines of the play as Beckett combed his text for visual and aural parallels, reverberations, echoes in preparation for his own staging.[2] It is Beckett's direct work in the theater, particularly between 1967 and 1985 when he directed most of his major work, that led publisher John Calder to conclude, "I have no doubt that posterity will consider him, not just a great playwright and novelist, but a theatrical director in the class of Piscator, Brecht and Felsenstein."[3] Beckett, in short, develops into a major theoretician of the theater in the process of staging and rewriting his plays.

Even before he became his own best reader, Beckett actively participated in staging his plays. From the first, he was concerned with setting what he called "a standard of fidelity" for his theater. That is, primacy, if not hegemony, was initially given at first to the playwriting self. On January 9, 1953, four days after the opening in Paris of *En attendant Godot,* the ever-vigilant Beckett wrote his French director, Roger Blin, to admonish him for a textual deviation:

> One thing which annoys me is Estragon's trousers. I naturally asked [future wife] Suzanne if they fell completely. She told me that they were held up half way. They must not, absolutely must not. . . . The spirit of the play, to the extent that it has any, is that nothing is more grotesque than the tragic, and that must be expressed until the end, and especially at the end. I have a stack of other reasons for not wanting to ruin this effect but I will spare you them. Just be good enough to restore the scene as written and performed in rehearsals,

and let the pants fall completely to his ankles. That must seem stupid to you but for me it is paramount.[4]

Despite the difficulties afforded by distance Beckett tried to maintain similar vigilance over American productions. On February 2, 1956, he wrote his American publisher, Barney Rosset, who had begun, almost by default, acting as his American theatrical agent, in order to forestall what Beckett called "unauthorized deviations" in the forthcoming Broadway production of *Godot* with new director and cast, and a producer conscious of the play's dismal failure in its Miami premiere:

> I am naturally disturbed . . . at the menace hinted at in one of your letters, of unauthorized deviations from the script. This we cannot have at any price and I am asking [London producer Donald] Albery to write [American producer Michael] Myerberg to that effect. I am not intransigent, as the [bowdlerized] Criterion production [in London] shows, about minor changes, if I feel they are necessary, but I refuse to be improved by a professional rewriter [in this case American playwright Thornton Wilder had been proposed, and Wilder had begun a draft translation of *Godot*].[5]

After completing *Krapp's Last Tape,* which as he said he "nearly entitled . . . 'Ah Well,'" Beckett wrote his American publisher on April 1, 1958, to set some guidelines for its premiere, telling Rosset, "I'd hate it to be made a balls of at the outset and that's why I question its being let out to small groups beyond our controp [*sic*] before we get it done more or less right and set a standard of fidelity at least."[6] Nine days later Beckett wrote to Rosset that he was off to London to do just that with the Royal Court Theater's production, "where I hope to get the mechanics of it right." It was this "standard of fidelity" and the degree of direct oversight entailed in getting "the mechanics of it right" that in good part finally lured Beckett to the semipublic posture of staging his own plays, and, even more important, which allowed him to move to a new phase of his creative development, that which critics usually refer to as the "late plays."

But the move to staging himself was made reluctantly, hesitantly, accomplished, as it were, in as well as on stages, as Beckett learned what theater itself had to offer him as an artist. He quickly saw that his direct involvement in productions offered opportunities beyond authorial validation and textual fidelity. By the late 1950s the physical theater became a testing ground for him, an arena for creative discovery, even self-discovery. *Krapp's Last Tape* seems to have been the watershed, as he realized that the creation of a dramatic text was not a process that could be divorced from performance, and that mounting a production brought to light recesses previously hidden, even from the author himself. In his April 1 letter to Rosset Beckett expressed the clarity of his preproduction vision of *Krapp:* "I see the whole thing so clearly (appart [*sic*] from the changes of Krapp's white face as he listens)[7] and realize now that this does not mean I have stated it clearly, though God knows I tried." Writing to Rosset six months later, on November 20, 1958, *after* the Royal Court *Krapp,* Beckett seems to have got more than "the mechanics of it right" in this production with Patrick Magee, directed by Donald McWhinnie. In fact in late 1958 Beckett began sounding very much like a director himself:

> Unerringly directed by McWhinnie[,] Magee gave a very fine performance, for me by far the most satisfactory experience in the theater up to date. I wish to goodness that Alan [Schneider] could have seen it. I can't see it being done any other way. *During rehearsal we found various pieces of business not indicated in the script and which now seem to me indispensable.* If you ever publish the work in book form I should like to incorporate them in the text. A possible solution in the meantime would be for me to see Alan again (hardly feasible) or to write to him at length on the subject and prepare for him a set of more explicit stage directions. (Emphasis added)

At fifty-two years of age, having had two major plays staged in two languages and having completed his first radio play, Samuel Beckett discovered theater. The discovery was monumental. It would transform thenceforth the way he wrote new plays, and finally force him to rethink and so rewrite his earlier work as well. By the early 1960s, then, working directly in the theater became an indispensable part of Beckett's creative process, and he wanted those direct theatrical discoveries incorporated in his published texts, before initial publication, at first, then as he began directing work already published, he assiduously revised those texts in terms of his production insights, completing them, as it were, on stage. Writing to Grove Press about *Happy Days* on May 18, 1961, Beckett said, for instance, "I should prefer the text not to appear in any form before production and not in book form until I have seen some rehearsals in London. I can't be definitive without actual work done in the theater." On November 24, 1963, he wrote to Rosset about his wife's disappointment with the German production of *Spiel (Play)*:[8]

> Suzanne went to Berlin for the opening of *Play*. She did not like the performance, but the director, Deryk Mendel, is very pleased. Well received. I realize I can't establish definitive text of *Play* without a certain number of rehearsals. These should begin with [French director Jean-Marie] Serreau next month. Alan's [Schneider's] text will certainly need correction. Not the lines but the stage directions. London rehearsals begin on March 9th [1964].

In fact, after having read an initial set of proofs for *Play* from his British publisher, Faber and Faber, Beckett panicked, and so delayed publication so that he could continue to hone the text in rehearsals. He wrote to Charles Monteith of Faber and Faber first on November 15, 1963, "I'm afraid I shall have to make some rather important changes in the stage directions of *Play*." On November 23, 1963, Beckett was even more insistent: "I suddenly see this evening, with panic, that no final text of *Play* is possible till I have had a certain number of rehearsals. These will begin here, I hope, next month [they were delayed as indicated above], and your publication should not be delayed [that is, publication should follow soon after production]. *But please regard my corrected proofs as not final*" (emphasis added). Beckett confirmed this decision to Grove Press editor Richard Seaver six days later, on November 29, 1963: "I have asked Faber, since correcting proofs, to hold up production of the book. I realize I can't establish text of *Play*, especially stage directions, till I have worked on rehearsals. I have written to Alan [Schneider] about the problems involved." Seaver confirmed in his reply of December 4 1963, "We won't do anything on the book until we hear from you." Shortly thereafter, however, Grove resumed its pressure to publish *Play* and proposed to couple it with a work by Harold Pinter. In his rejection of that project Beckett returned to his theme of the indispensability of production to his theatrical work:

> Quite frankly I am not in favour of this idea, particularly as your text of *Play* is not final and cannot be till I have had some rehearsals, i.e., not before the end of next month. It is all right for the purposes of Alan's [Schneider's] production, because I have left it open for him and he knows the problems. But not as a published work.[9]

This insistence on completing a text of his play only after "some re-hearsals" or "a certain number of rehearsals" would become, then, a central part of Beckett's method of composition from *Krapp's Last Tape* onward. Well over a decade later, Beckett sounded the same theme about the text of *Not I* in a letter to Barney Rosset of August 7, 1972: "With regard to publication, I prefer to hold it back for the sake of whatever light N. Y. & London rehearsals may shed. I have not yet sent the text to Faber." Without working on stage directly himself, Beckett seemed unsure if his late work, in this case the metonymical *Not I,* was even drama, shaken perhaps by the difficulties Alan Schneider encountered staging the world premiere (that is, setting its "standard of fidelity") with actress Jessica Tandy at New York's Lincoln Center.[10] Beckett wrote to Rosset on November 3, 1972: "Had a couple of letters from Alan. They seem to have been having a rough time. Hope smoother now. Hope to work on *Not I* in London next month and find out then if it's theater or not."

As we trace the archeology of Beckett's theater works from the 1960s onward, it becomes clear that publication was an interruption in the ongoing, often protracted process of composition. On the other hand, Beckett the author, with a long history of rejection from publishers, was unable to resist publication pressures, or even to control its pace. After publication he continued as a director to collaborate with the author of the texts, that is, himself, or, more psychoanalytically, his "other," to complete the creative process. Moreover, such self-collaboration would not be merely a "one off." Beckett very quickly found that staging a play, even directing it himself, did not necessarily produce a final text. The principle of waiting for direct work in the theater before publishing, then, did not always insure what he had variously called "corrected," "accurate," "final," or "definitive" texts in part because the process of staging as an act of textual revision, an act of creation, seems to have become for Beckett open-ended, continuous, the "definitive text," de facto, mercurial, elusive, a perpetually deferred entity. On the other hand, commercial pressures from producers in various countries were incessant after the success of *Waiting for Godot,* as were pressures from publishers. The letters from this period testify to the growing professional pressures on Samuel Beckett as an international artist (if not as an international commodity), pressures that would only intensify with the so-called "catastrophe" of the Nobel Prize in 1969. Much of this international attention forced a shift from an artisanal approach, literature as a cottage industry, say, to what seemed to be its mass production. The practical results were an inevitable diminution of quality control that took the form of a proliferation of published and produced texts. Several versions of the same text often circulated among producers, directors, and even publishers; that is, as he continued to direct, he continued to revise, and so Beckett's own creative practice, his evolving creative methodology, contributed to a proliferation of textual variants in the written record.

The text of *Play* is a case in point. As Beckett continued to revise the text through British and French productions, which were occurring simultaneously in 1964, various versions of the play circulated in typescript.[11] Working through British agent Rosica Colin, Beckett sent Charles Monteith "a revised text" of *Play* in July 1963. On November 23, 1963, Beckett sent his "panic" letter to Monteith, and requested a second set of "virgin" proofs, a request he reaffirmed on December 5: "I need a fortnight's work on *Play* in a theatre. The French production will go into rehearsals this month I hope. As soon as I have exact dates I'll let you know when to expect final proof. Could you let me have another proof (virgin)." In an internal Faber and Faber memo of December 9 1963, then, Monteith announced the delay in publishing *Play* to the staff of Faber:

> I think that *Play* will almost certainly have to be postponed until much later in the spring. Beckett won't pass his proofs for press until *Play* has been rehearsed and he decides what changes are necessary for an actual production. The latest news I have about this is that rehearsals will start in France some time this month; and he says he will need a fortnight's work on it in theatre.

Because of the scheduling delays Beckett finally acquiesced to his British publishers' pressures to publish. He wrote to Montieth on "January 9, 1963" [*recte* 1964], "I shall. . . re-correct your proofs of *Play*. Rehearsals here [i.e., in Paris] are delayed and I don't want to hold you up any longer, especially as Grove Press seem set on publishing this play in the near future." Beckett then sent Monteith the second set of corrected proofs on January 17, 1964, before rehearsals began in either country, and Faber and Faber published the work on March 27, 1964, in order to have a text available for the play's London opening. But between Beckett's correcting the second set of proofs on January 17 and the play's opening on April 7, 1964, Beckett revised the text yet again. Working uneasily in Paris with French director Jean-Marie Serreau on staging the

French text, *Comédie,* before the London rehearsals had begun, it became clear to Beckett that additional revisions were not only desirable
but necessary, and he wrote to British director George Devine on March
9, 1964, less than one month before the scheduled opening and while
the Faber text was in final production, to warn him of necessary revisions, this just as the published version of the play was about to appear in
Britain:

> The last rehearsals with Serreau have led us to a view of the *da capo*
> which I think you should know about. According to the text it is
> rigorously identical with the first statement. We now think it would
> be dramatically more effective to have it express a slight weakening,
> both of question and of response, by means of less and perhaps
> slower light and correspondingly less volume and speed of voice.[12]

Before those rehearsals, however, Beckett believed that he had got
things right in the second set of galleys he revised for Faber, and writing
to Grove Press on August 17, 1964, that is, after British and French productions (in which, as he wrote to Monteith on the same day, "I was
happy with production and actors and think we got pretty close to it")
regarding a Swedish translation, Beckett at first confirmed the Faber
text: "As to your MS text, it is less likely to be accurate than the Faber
published text for which I corrected proofs" [i.e., at least twice]. But the
same letter suggested the need for further revisions, another version that
would reflect more of the theater work (as well as an uncharacteristically
cavalier attitude about his text in Swedish translation): "[Grove editor
Fred] Jordan suggested publishing in *Evergreen Review* the text *in extenso*
[i.e., at full length] (as played in London and Paris), i.e., giving changed
order of speeches in the repeat and indicating vocal levels. This is quite
a job to prepare and I suggest we reserve this presentation for Grove and
let translations follow the existing text, simply correcting 'Repeat play
exactly' to 'Repeat play.'" When Barney Rosset's personal assistant, Judith Schmidt, compared the Faber text of *Play* to the Grove Press typescript, she wrote to Beckett on August 26, "I can see that there are a
good many changes." Jordan, then wrote to Beckett on the same day,
"We are using the Faber and Faber text in the next issue of *Evergreen Review,* but I believe you asked to have one word changed [i.e., the dele-
tion of "exactly," as above]. Could you indicate what the change is, giving me page and line number, assuming we both work from the same
edition." If we wonder at the complexities of the textual (and so perfor-

mance) history of Beckett's work, here is a case in point: two editors of
the same firm writing their major author on the same day each proposing to publish a different version of the same work. Beckett solved some
of this confusion, but only some of it, on August 28 by fully revising the
text yet again, "Herewith corrections to Faber text of *Play*," which text
then became the basis of the *Evergreen Review* version. The *Evergreen Review* text of 1964 (hereafter *ER*) then was the text of *Play* in extenso, the
one for which Beckett made his final revisions, but it is a text wholly ig-
nored by Beckett's English-language publishers and producers. The revisions were never fully incorporated into any Faber text, and inexplic-
ably it was not its own text in extenso that Grove Press published in
book form in 1968.[13]

The American book publication was taken some four years later not
from Grove's own fully "corrected" *ER* text but from the penultimately
revised Faber edition. The *ER* text, for instance, was the first to include
Beckett's major postproduction revision, the note on "Repeat" (the
Cascando edition of 1968, four years after Beckett made the revision,
does not include this note at all but it does delete the word "exactly"
from the phrase in the *first* Faber edition, "Repeat play exactly"). The
ER edition, moreover, is the first printing in which the opening instructions on lighting were emended by deleting "not quite" from the
original Faber version, "The response to light is not quite immediate."
The Grove book edition, subsequently, retained "not quite" even after
it was cut from its own *ER* text. But the *ER* text has its own corruption;
the sentence subsequent to the revision was illogically retained, as it is
today in both Faber and Grove standard editions (but not in the collected editions, *Collected Shorter Plays* (Grove Press and Faber and Faber,
1984) and *Complete Dramatic Works* (Faber and Faber only, 1986, revised
and corrected paperback edition 1990) in which the problem was reme-
died): "At every solicitation a pause of about one second before utterance is achieved, except where a longer delay is indicated." Logically,
the response to the light must be either "immediate" or delayed, not
both, and so the retention of the phrase "of about one second" in the
ER version seems clearly to have been a major oversight.[14]

Such a revision may at first seem minor, little more than a technical
adjustment, instructions to the lighting designer. But in the delicate balance of verbal and visual images that constitutes Beckettian theater, such
changes are fundamental, thematically potent, especially since light can
function as a character in Beckett's theater. This is the case with *Play* in
particular. If a delay exists between light's command and the response,

then a certain amount of deliberation is possible among the subjects. The situation of the urn-encrusted characters is thus humanized. In Beckett's revision, the final vestiges of humanity (and humanism) are drained from an inquisitorial process, which Beckett ironically calls *Play*.

The textual history of the dramaticule (Beckett's coinage) *Come and Go* is here illustrative as well since it combines the three dominant problems affecting Beckett's dramatic texts: a proliferation of versions on initial publication, adjustments made in translation, and revisions Beckett made for production, in this case well after the work's initial publication. An uncertain publication history plagued the initial publication of *Come and Go* in 1978 even though Beckett read proofs for the first edition. The opening four lines of the parallel English and German text Beckett reviewed as he prepared to direct *Kommen und Gehen (Come and Go)* in 1978 were as follows:

> *Vi*. Ru.
> *Ru*. Yes.
> *Vi*. Flo.
> *Flo*. Yes.

These lines were not, however, included in the first edition published by Calder and Boyars in 1967. When Beckett read proofs for Calder's edition he suggested in a letter of December 7, 1966, that something was amiss: "Here are the *Texts for Nothing*. I return to Paris tomorrow and shall send you the other proofs corrected, including *Come and Go,* which at first glance doesn't look right." Whatever didn't "look right" to Beckett, his review of the proofs did not result in the inclusion of the opening four lines in the Calder edition. The opening lines did appear, however, in the first American edition, *Cascando and Other Short Dramatic Pieces* published by Grove Press the following year, and in all translations, particularly the French and German. More important they were also part of the final English text that Beckett reviewed carefully and revised for the Schiller Theater production in 1978 (which, although Beckett prepared to direct, was finally directed by Walter Asmus). Subsequent English texts by Faber and Faber were then based on the Calder and Boyars text of 1967 and not the Grove Press text of 1968 that included the four fugitive lines. Since both the *Collected Dramatic Works* and *Collected Shorter Plays* were projects initiated by Faber and photo-offset by Grove Press, they reprint the incomplete Calder and Boyars edition, and so no major English text other than the first American edition contains Beckett's opening lines.[15]

In addition the French and German texts include revisions introduced by Beckett after the publication of the English and American editions. FLO invokes the names of the two other characters before her final, "I can feel the rings." This final incantation then echoes the opening recitation of names, but it appears in no English language text. Finally, Beckett made a significant textual revision for his 1978 production which changed the speaker for two speeches: Ru's first speech was given to Flo, and Flo's "Dreaming of. . . love" was given to Vi. Although Beckett finally did not direct *Kommen und Gehen (Come and Go)*, he reviewed both English and German texts in anticipation of production, and so clearly established the English version of the text. Had he directed the production himself, he may have made further discoveries and so made additional revisions, but he did not. To date, then, no English language text includes Beckett's final revisions.

With *Footfalls* Beckett also revised the published English text at various times for various stages. He directed three productions of the play in three languages: with Billie Whitelaw at the Royal Court Theater in London in 1976; shortly thereafter with Hildegard Schmahl, on the bill with *Damals (That Time)* also in 1976; and finally with Delphine Seyrig at the Théâtre d'Orsay in 1978. Beckett revised the English script in detail, changing, for example, the number of May's pacing steps from seven to nine. Most, but not all, of those revisions were incorporated into subsequent revised English texts, *Ends and Odds*[16] at first, and then in both the *Collected Dramatic Works* and *Collected Shorter Plays* both published by Faber and Faber but only the latter by Grove Press. But Beckett also made significant lighting changes that he never incorporated directly into any English text, changes that were central to and consistent in all three of his productions. For each of his stagings, for instance, he introduced a "Dim spot on face during halts at R [right] and L [left]" so that May's face would be visible during her monologues. In addition, he introduced a vertical ray of light that seemed to be coming through a door barely ajar, this to counterpoint the horizontal beam on the floor along which May paces. These lighting changes were not only part of all three of Beckett's productions, they were incorporated into the French translation, and certainly should be part of any English text or production. Without these final revisions, the only accurate text of *Footfalls*, that closest to Beckett's final conception of the work, is the French text, *Pas*.

II.

The textual problems outlined here were the result, then, of Beckett's continued work in the theater and his desire to have his published texts reflect his most recent theatrical insights, discoveries that could only have been made in rehearsals. It was Beckett's at least tacit acknowledgment that theater is its performance; the theater space, as Peter Brook has insisted for years, is an arena for creative discovery. At first such revisions as those with *Play* were restricted to works not yet in print. But much of Beckett's most intense and concentrated theatrical work with his texts occurred well after their original publication when as a director he turned to them afresh. Staging himself even well after initial publication would mean revising himself and would allow him to move forward by returning to the past, to implement, refine, and extend his creative vision to work published before he became his own best interpreter. In retrospect such self-collaboration seemed inevitable since Beckett's theatrical vision was often at odds with those of even his most sympathetic directors. "He had ideas about [*Fin de partie*]," recalled Roger Blin, his first French director, "that made it a little difficult to act. At first, he looked on his play as a kind of musical score. When a word occurred or was repeated, when Hamm called Clov, Clov should always come in the same way every time, like a musical phrase coming from the same instrument with the same volume."[17] Ten years after writing *Fin de partie* (*Endgame*) Beckett would score the play to his satisfaction in his own Berlin production. "The play is full of echoes," he told his German cast, "they all answer each other." And he revised his texts accordingly. His final revisions to the texts of *Play, Come and Go,* and *Footfalls* reflect just such musical preoccupations.

During his nineteen-year directing career, from 1967 to 1986, Beckett staged (or videotaped) over twenty productions of his plays in three languages, English, French, and German. Each time he came to reread a script to prepare its staging, he usually found it wordy, encumbered, and incompletely conceived for the stage, and so he set about "correcting" it, the word he used most often for the process of theater, the continued development and refinement of his work that directing afforded. Such a commitment protracted the creative process. For Beckett composition, that is, the act of creation, did not end with publication, and certainly not with initial production, even those on which he had worked closely, but was continuous, subject to constant refinement if not on occasion redefinition: "from the 1967 *Endspiel* [*Endgame*], Beckett used directorial opportunities to continue the creative process, cutting, revising, tightening his original script. Once Beckett took full control, directing was not a process separate from the generation of a text but its continuation if not its culmination. Writing, translating and directing were of a piece, part of a continuous creative process."[18]

It was this direct work in the theater, this extension of the creative process, Beckett's reintervention into his own established canon, into texts that were not only already in print but often well established in critical discourse as well, that has forced to the fore unique questions not only about Beckett's individual texts but about the relationship of theatrical performance to its published record and so about the nature, the quality, the validity of the theatrical experience itself. The sheer complexity of Beckett's creative vision, however, has forced some analysts into critical denial. Michael Worton, for one, has argued that Beckett's direct work in the theater should simply be dismissed as irrelevant. Worton is bent on devaluing the performing arts by dismissing Beckett's work as a director, work Worton considers more impulsive than deliberative: "we should focus on the text itself and not seek to make our interpretations fit with what the dramatist may have said at any particular moment."[19] "Any particular moment" presumably refers to the twenty years Beckett spent as a theatrical director, which Worton would simply dismiss as irrelevant to textual production. Worton seems confused about what constitutes "text" in the theater and so takes it to mean simply script. What Beckett began to understand about theater, however, was that text *is* performance, which is why he was always so fastidious not about interpretation per se but about his stage directions. As we continue to evaluate that relationship, the literary text to its performative realization, and the playwright's relationship to both, the case of Samuel Beckett's acting simultaneously as theater artist staging a play and author revising it, an almost unique instance of self-collaboration in the modern (and modernist) theater, may force us to reevaluate the centrality of performance to the literary field of drama.[20] For Beckett's drama, performance would become his principal text. The results of that direct theatrical process, that fastidious attention to the aesthetic details of the artwork, a salient characteristic of late modernism, need to enter our critical and performative equations if we are not to underestimate and so distort Samuel Beckett's creative vision, and his own theoretical contributions to the modernist theater.

That's the theory. The practice, that is, the actual accommodation of performance into a written record, is not always easily achieved. As he began increasingly to work directly on stage, to trust his direct work in theater, Beckett did not, unfortunately, always record those insights or revise his texts accordingly. For some productions Beckett simply never got around to making the full and complete revisions to his English text, that is, never committed his revisions to paper, revisions that were clearly part of his developing conception of the play, but let the production stand as the final text. The most obvious and stunning example is the ballet (or mime) called *Quad* in English. Beckett's final version of the work, the production for German television, broadcast on October 8, 1981, is called *Quadrat I & II,* a title that suggests at least two acts, if not two plays. Near the end of the taping, Beckett created what amounted to an unplanned second act for the play. When he saw the color production of *Quad* rebroadcast on a black-and-white monitor, he decided instantly to create *Quad II.* Beckett's printed text (in any language) was, however, never revised to acknowledge this remarkable revision of the work's fundamental structure. No printed version of the play bears the title of the production, and so no accurate version, one that includes Beckett's revisions, exists in print. Beckett's own videotaped German production, then, remains the only "final" text for *Quad.*

Finally, for his own television version of his stage play *Was Wo (What Where),* Beckett again revised the German text extensively, but he never fully revised the stage directions of the original. This omission was due in part to Beckett's continued work on the central visual imagery of the play through rehearsals up to the final taping. By this stage of his directing career in 1985, he had developed enough confidence and trust in the collaborations that theater entails, indeed that it necessitates, that he was creating his theater work almost wholly in rehearsals, directly on the stage (or in this case, in the studio), although he kept a theatrical notebook for the production as well. As his longtime cameraman and technical assistant, Jim Lewis, recalled:

> If you want to compare this production [of *Was Wo*] with the others for television, there's one major difference. And that is his concept was not set. He changed and changed and changed. . . . I've never experienced that with him before. You know how concrete he is, how precise he is. Other times we could usually follow through on that with minor, minor changes; but this time there were several basic changes and he still wasn't sure.[21]

Lewis's observation suggests the single most significant element in Beckett's evolution from playwright to theater artist, from writer to director: his commitment to the idea of performance. In practical and literary terms such a commitment meant that nothing like a "final script" for his theatrical work could be established before he worked with it and reworked it directly on stage. What he insisted to his American publisher about *Play* he reiterated at the same time to his principal American director, Alan Schneider, in response to Schneider's queries. Beckett expressed what had become obvious and axiomatic to him: "I realize that no final script is possible until I work on rehearsals."[22] With *Play* Beckett's emphasis on performance had been necessitated by his revision of the work between its English publication and its French and English performances, and it was such demanding technical difficulties as *Play* presented that finally prompted Beckett to take full charge of directing his work.[23] With *What Where*, however, Beckett went on to revise French and English stage versions of his play after he had adapted and taped the German television production, but again without revising the opening stage directions. A clear diagram and a paragraph describing the revised stage set, however, were part of his theatrical notebook for *Was Wo (What Where)*, and so those passages could be adopted for a revised text by simply substituting Beckett's exact words for the original.[24]

One can, however, easily overstate Beckett's attraction to theater, even romanticize it. While the process of working on stage was fruitful and grew finally indispensable to his theatrical art, it did not always proceed smoothly. And at times Beckett seemed exasperated by the whole process of theater. With the success of *Godot,* the demands for new work, for advice on productions and translations of his work, from all over the world, became almost suffocating. Much in his expanded semipublic role as director did not sit comfortably with him, in particular the practical demands of differing theaters, the constraints of deadlines, and the inevitable intercourse with an intrusive broader public; reporters with cameras managed to insinuate themselves into rehearsals all too often, and Beckett periodically announced his abandonment of theater. On March 23, 1975, for instance, he wrote to his longtime friend and sometime literary agent, George Reavey: "rehearsing French *Not I* with M. Renaud, with yet another *Krapp* to eke it out, opening April 8. Then farewell to theater." On April 14, he reaffirmed his retirement, "*Pas Moi* off to a goodish start. Vast relief at thought of no more theater."[25] But a year later, in April 1976, he was in London directing Billie Whitelaw in

Footfalls at the Royal Court Theater, to which he returned three years later to stage what was perhaps his English-language directorial master-work, Billie Whitelaw's tour de force performance of *Happy Days,* which premiered in June 1979. In 1977, two years after his supposed re-tirement, Beckett only began his long directorial relationship with the San Quentin Drama Workshop, directing its founder Rick Cluchey in *Krapp's Last Tape* at the Akademie der Künst in Berlin in 1977, and *Endgame* with the company in May 1980 at the Riverside Studios in London. In July 1983 Beckett announced the end of his directorial ca-reer yet again: "Omitted to mention in my last, in reply to your evoca-tion of the Riverside rehearsals [for the San Quentin *Endgame*], that I have done with directing, or it with me. Never again."[26] But as he wrote to his American publisher and theatrical agent in 1959, "the call of the theater is strong," and it remained so through most of the 1980s. By Feb-ruary 1984 Beckett was back in London at least supervising Walter As-mus's re-creation of Beckett's own 1978 Berlin staging of *Godot,* now with the San Quentin Drama Workshop. In the course of what was in-tended as simple supervision of the 1978 staging, Beckett again revised, refined, corrected his earlier staging significantly.[27] By early 1984 he had also already accepted an offer to adapt and direct his stage play *What Where* for German television in Stuttgart, although the work was delayed until June 1985.

But as useful as working directly in the concrete space of theater turned out to be, it did not always resolve all creative and textual ques-tions. Having worked closely with Anthony Page on the Royal Court Theater production of *Not I* in January 1975, for instance, and having di-rected it himself at the Théâtre d'Orsay later that year (April 1975) and again in April 1978, Beckett remained uncertain, hesitant, and ambiva-lent about several fundamental details of the play: even how many char-acters it should contain, for example. The best advice he could offer a pair of young American directors in 1986 was "simply to omit the Au-ditor. He is very difficult to stage (light? position) and may well be of more harm than good. For me the play needs him but I can do without him. *I have never seen him function effectively.*"[28] Beckett's assessment of Auditor's ineffectiveness presumably includes the 1973 Royal Court production with Billie Whitelaw that he supervised and that was even-tually taped for broadcast by the BBC. For the videotape Auditor was, of course, dropped in favor of a tight close-up of actress Billie Whitelaw's bespittled lips. And for his own 1978 French production (his second) with Madeleine Renaud, he omitted Auditor entirely.

To call even those texts that include all of Beckett's theatrical revisions "definitive," however, as Beckett occasionally did (if offhandedly), is not only to evoke the discourse of another era but to shift the emphasis away from the process of textual evolution that they represent. The revised texts are "final" only in the sense that Samuel Beckett's physical life is now final, that is, over. It is quite clear to those who worked with him in the theater that had he directed any of his plays again, he would have generated more refinements, additional corrections, another revised text. The revised texts do, however, come closer to being finished than those originally published, in the sense that Maurice Blanchot used the term in his 1955 work, *L'Espace littéraire:* "A work is finished, not when it is completed, but when he who labors at it from within can just as well finish it from without."[29] If these revised and corrected plays are "finished" it is because Beckett has approached them from "without," as another, as a reader and *metteur-en-scène.* Like any good reader, Beckett saw more in his texts at each reading, and directing offered him the opportunity of intense rereading.

What the revised and corrected texts represent, finally, is Beckett's physical work in the theater, a period of self-collaboration and so self-revision that all but dominated the final two decades of his life. They emphasize that his direct work with actors and technicians, while not always tranquil, was always productive and of no less importance, of no less value than the work he did in the seclusion of his study to produce and translate the first versions of his play scripts. Beckett's theatrical texts, however, were created not in his study but in the theater, and as such they stand as testimony to Beckett's creative vitality into the eighth decade of his life and to his faith in the living theater as a vital, creative force in the waning days of the twentieth century.

NOTES

1. Samuel Beckett, *Proust* (New York: Grove Press, 1957), 3.

2. These notebooks are on deposit at the University of Reading's Samuel Beckett Archive and are published in facsimile and transcription in *The Theatrical Notebooks of Samuel Beckett,* vol. 4, *The Shorter Plays,* ed. S. E. Gontarski (London: Faber and Faber; New York: Grove Press, 1999).

3. John Calder, "Editorial and Theater Diary," *Gambit: International Theater Review* 7 (1976): 3.

4. The French transcript of this letter appears in the introduction to *The Theatrical Notebooks of Samuel Beckett,* vol. 2, *Endgame,* ed. S. E. Gontarski (New York: Grove Press, 1993), xiv. The author has taken the opportunity of republication to simplify his translation of Beckett's original French.

5. Unless otherwise stipulated, letters are in the respective publishers' archives, Grove Press, Faber and Faber, and John Calder Ltd., and are used with permission of the publishers and Samuel Beckett.

6. It would, of course, be Alan Schneider who set the "standard of fidelity" for the American *Krapp's Last Tape.*

7. This problem was finally solved when Beckett directed his own production and eliminated Krapp's white face. See *The Theatrical Notebooks of Samuel Beckett,* vol. 3, *Krapp's Last Tape,* ed. by James Knowlson (London: Faber and Faber; New York: Grove Press, 1992).

8. This would be Deryk Mendel's world premiere production, *Spiel* at the Ulmer Theater, Ulm-Donau, June 14, 1963.

9. Beckett had apparently given up on Schneider's production of *Play.* His instructions to Alan Schneider were that "*Play* was to be played through twice without interruption and at a very fast pace, each time taking no longer than nine minutes," that is, eighteen minutes overall. The producers, Richard Barr, Clinton Wilder, and, of all people, Edward Albee, threatened to drop the play from the program if Schneider followed Beckett's instructions. Schneider, unlike Devine, capitulated, and wrote to Beckett for permission to slow the pace and eliminate the *da capo:* "For the first and last time in my long relationship with Sam, I did something I despised myself for doing. I wrote to him, asking if we could try having his text spoken only once, more slowly. Instead of telling me to blast off, Sam offered us his reluctant permission." See Alan Schneider, *Entrances: An American Director's Journey* (New York: Viking Press, 1986), 342. The exchange to which Schneider alludes may have been verbal since it does not appear in *No Author Better Served: The Correspondence of Samuel Beckett and Alan Schneider,* ed. by Maurice Harmon (Cambridge: Harvard University Press, 1998).

10. When actress Jessica Tandy complained that the play's suggested running time of twenty-three minutes rendered the work unintelligible to audiences, Beckett telegraphed back his now famous (but oft misinterpreted) injunction, "I'm not unduly concerned with intelligibility. I hope the piece may work on the nerves of the audience, not its intellect." For a discussion of Tandy's performance see Enoch Brater, "The 'I' in Beckett's *Not I,*" *Twentieth Century Literature* 20 (1974): 200.

11. For details on the production of *Play* see "De-theatricalizing Theater: The Post-*Play* Plays," in Beckett, *Theatrical Notebooks,* 4:xv–xxix.

12. The letter is published in facsimile in *New Theatre Magazine: Samuel Beckett Issue* 11 (1971): 16–17.

13. *Cascando and Other Short Dramatic Pieces* (New York: Grove Press, 1968), 45–63.

14. Beckett sent another set of revisions to Richard Seaver at Grove Press on June 20, 1968, in anticipation of the book publication of *Play.* Except for the reduction of "Pardon" to "-don" (p. 20, l. 10), these same revisions were *not* included in the Faber revised text of 1968, *Play and Two Short Pieces for Radio* (originally published 1964), nor in subsequent Faber reprints. They were dutifully incorporated into Grove's *Cascando and Other Short Dramatic Pieces,* 1968. For *The Collected Shorter Plays* (1984) and *Complete Dramatic Works* (1986) the changes were made save the requested cut of the paragraph in the section entitled "Urns," that is paragraph 2, from "Should traps" to "Should conform."

15. They do appear in the text that critic Breon Mitchell edited and published in the journal *Modern Drama* in 1976, but that text introduces additional and unnecessary variants. See Breon Mitchell, "Art in Microcosm: The Manuscript Stages of Beckett's *Come and Go,*" *Modern Drama* 19 (1976): 245–60.

16. For additional details on the texts of *Footfalls* see "Texts and Pre-texts in Samuel Beckett's *Footfalls*," *Papers of the Bibliographical Society of America* 77 (1983): 191–95.

17. "Blin on Beckett," in *On Beckett: Essays and Criticism,* ed. S. E. Gontarski (New York: Grove Press, 1986), 233.

18. Beckett, *Theatrical Notebooks,* 2:xiii.

19. Michael Worton, "*Waiting for Godot* and *Endgame:* Theater as Text," in *The Cambridge Companion to Beckett,* ed. John Pilling (Cambridge: Cambridge University Press), 68. Worton is not, of course, alone in his resistance to Beckett's theatrical work. For Colin Duckworth, for instance, the very fact that Beckett's revisions were made in response to the exigencies of production essentially disqualifies them. That is, Duckworth has attacked the most compelling reasons for revisions at all—most particularly those for *Waiting for Godot,* but by extension for all of Beckett's work. While he admits that with those revisions, "we can now have a clear insight into [Beckett's] own view of his most famous play a third of a century after he wrote it" (175), he finally recoils from that view, concluding, "It is difficult to explain this textual vandalism, perpetrated on some of the most magical moments of the play" (190). "It makes one wonder," he continues, "whether authors should be let loose on their plays thirty-odd years later" (191). Colin Duckworth, "Beckett's New *Godot,*" in *Beckett's Later Fiction and Drama,* ed. James Acheson and Kateryna Arthur (Basingstoke: Macmillan, 1987), 175–92.

20. For some tentative explorations of these problems see Philip Gaskell's work on Tom Stoppard in "Stoppard, *Travesties,* 1974," in *From Writer to Reader: Studies in Editorial Method* (Oxford: Oxford University Press, 1978), 245–62; and "*Night and Day:* Development of a Play Text," *Textual Criticism and Literary Interpretation,* ed. Jerome J. McGann (Chicago: University of Chicago Press, 1985), 162–79. Although Gaskell deals with the idea of a "performance text" and the "reading text" that follows it, revised on the basis of the performance in which the author was an active collaborator with his director (in this case Tom Stoppard and Peter Wood), the situation is the opposite with Beckett's self-collaborations where the "reading text" was often established by publication well before Beckett intervened through his direction to create a "performance text." In Beckett's case the problems of accurate texts is complicated by the author's continued revision of even his "reading text."

21. Martha Fehsenfeld, "Beckett's Reshaping of *What Where* for Television," *Modern Drama* 29 (1986): 236.

22. Alec Reid makes something of the same point in the posthumous "Impact and Parable in Beckett: A First Encounter with *Not I,*" published in a tribute issue of *Hermathena* 141 (1986), ed. Terence Brown and Nicholas Grene: Beckett "will speak of the first run-through with actors as the 'realization' of the play and when it has been performed publicly, he will say that it has been 'created'" (12). Delivering the first Annenberg Lecture at the University of Reading's Beckett Archive in May 1993, Billie Whitelaw made the following observation of *Not I:* "I very much had the feeling that it was a work in progress."

23. For details see "De-theatricalizing Theater," xx.

24. For a fuller discussion of these revisions see my "What Where II: Revision as Recreation," *Review of Contemporary Fiction* 7 (1987): 120–23, as well as the *What Where* portion of the *Theatrical Notebooks,* vol. 4, and Martha Fehsenfeld, "Beckett's Reshaping of *What Where* for Television," *Modern Drama* 29 (1986): 236. See also "*What Where:* The Revised Text," ed. and with Textual Notes by S. E. Gontarski, *Journal of Beckett Studies,* (New Series) 2 (1992): 1–25.

25. Carlton Lake, ed., *No Symbols Where None Intended: A Catalogue of Books, Manuscripts, and Other Material Relating to Samuel Beckett in the Collections of the Humanities Research Center* (Austin, Tex.: Humanities Research Center, 1984), 155.

26. Samuel Beckett, letter to S. E. Gontarski, July 24, 1983.

27. See *Theatrical Notebooks of Samuel Beckett,* vol. 1, *Waiting for Godot,* ed. James Knowlson and Dougald McMillan (London: Faber and Faber; New York: Grove Press, 1994).

28. Samuel Beckett, letter to David Hunsberger and Linda Kendall dated November 16, 1986; emphasis added. A copy is in possession of the author.

29. Maurice Blanchot, *The Space of Literature,* trans. Ann Smock (Lincoln: University of Nebraska Press, 1982), 54.

Barry McGovern

"They want to be entertained":
Performing Beckett

Bertolt Brecht, toward the end of his life, wanted to adapt *Waiting for Godot* for his Berliner Ensemble. He had two principal ideas for this adaptation. One involved numerous cuts and textual revisions to make the dialogue more colloquial, and specified "social" roles for the characters. Vladimir was to be "an intellectual"; Estragon "a proletarian" (and Brecht used the word *prolet,* which was a contemptuous term for this); Pozzo—now called von Pozzo to give him a sort of aristocratic status— "a big landowner"; and Lucky, "a donkey or policeman." The second bright idea divided the action into scenes where Vladimir and Estragon wait for Godot while music plays, and films are projected behind them depicting revolutionary movements in the Soviet Union, China, other parts of Asia, and Africa. Brecht did not live long enough to see these plans through, although in 1971 a production in Stuttgart influenced by his ideas was put on by one of his students.[1]

One can only begin to imagine what Beckett would have made of all this. But it is interesting that Brecht, one of the giants of twentieth-century theater, should want to do something with *Waiting for Godot,* the most famous play (at that time the only published play) of another of the giants of twentieth-century theater, even though they stand, in many ways, as polar opposites in the theatrical scheme of things. Brecht was intrigued enough to want to perform Beckett.

One of the questions I'm most frequently asked when talking to students about Beckett is, "Is playing in Beckett different from playing in other playwrights' work?" And my answer is invariably no. And yes. No, because I try always to approach each play as a new script, whether it's by Sophocles or Beckett. Yes, because each playwright, indeed each play, requires an approach that ultimately is going to be different from that which we would use for another playwright or play. But finding this approach comes via the usual avenues of reading, preparation, and, ultimately, the rehearsal process. So I don't say to myself, I'm going to do a Beckett play; I've got to get into "Beckett mode." No more than I try to get into a Shakespeare mode or a Synge mode. No, the play's the thing and I play with that thing; trying, ultimately, to get to the heart of the play—the character, the words, the movement, the light (or indeed the darkness) at that heart. "The lamp is more important than the lamp-lighter."[2]

But because Beckett is a poet who uses words so meticulously and for whom the shape of things was paramount, we have to be careful. With the exception of *Waiting for Godot* Beckett's plays are very circumscribed in their movements. The drama is in the words (except the mimes, of course), and what movement there is, is in the shape of the piece. In other words, in the music. And here is the crux of the matter. Beckett is "music, *music,* MUSIC."[3] A Beckett play is like a musical score. The notes are there—how, then, to play them properly? How do we find the right instruments, the right sounds, the right voice? So many Beckett plays have characters that are called, or could be called, "voice." What is the right voice? Or *a* right voice, for there is no *one* right voice. But Beckett's "scores" are not merely music. They are ballets. They need the right choreography. Or *a* right choreography, for there is no *one* right choreography. Anyone who has seen Beckett's own production of *Waiting for Godot* in German or a good production of *Footfalls* or *Quad* or *Come and Go* will know what I mean. "It's the shape that matters."[4] As with music, Beckett had a great love and knowledge of painting. His plays are suffused with vivid visual imagery. "Here form *is* content, content *is* form."[5] So playing in Beckett requires meticulousness with regard to words and movement in a way that is different from that which is necessary for, shall we say, more prosaic plays or plays that are structured more on a grand scale than in miniature. Of course there are exceptions: plays by Pinter, for example, another exquisite wordsmith; or Yeats, whose theater is shamefully underrated and misunderstood and all too infrequently performed.

Having said all this, the object, the play, must be taken as such and carefully read and prepared and rehearsed just like any other play. The journey of discovery will lead us down many roads unique to that play, but we must never lose sight of the fact that the objective is to entertain. And I mean entertain in the full sense of that word—to hold together—to occupy the attention and time of those in attendance. To keep up; maintain a process. In other words to keep going; going on. To hold an audience—to interest them and change them in some way. Because if an audience is not held or entertained, the exercise is doomed. Beckett famously once replied to a complaint by the actress Billie Whitelaw that if she did it Beckett's way the audience would be bored. "Bore them to death," he said. "Bore the pants off them!"[6] With great respect to Beckett and presuming that he said it with tongue firmly in cheek, an audience must never be bored.

When I say that a Beckett play is like a piece of music, I mean the following: A musical score is a series of symbols, a series of many thousands or hundreds of thousands of notes. Each note can be different in pitch, in length, in dynamics—loudness or softness. Many of these notes are sounded together; many are sounded while others are held from an earlier moment, or are held while other notes cease or change to different notes; just as in speech we overlap and use different pitches and length of tones, and so forth. But whereas some plays in so-called realistic or naturalistic styles aim to simulate so-called real life, real speech, or real manners, Beckett's plays are poems: tone poems. They have an element of ritual and are sculpted. While not stinking of artifice, they are, nonetheless, artificial constructs, and this must be borne in mind in order to give them full value.

Before dealing with what I think should be a director's or an actor's approach to the works of Beckett, let me first consider some of the myths about Beckett and his plays. There is a perception abroad that you mustn't change a single comma; that every dot, pause, silence, must be honored scrupulously; that Beckett himself was punctilious about every word, every gesture. Well, when Beckett directed his own plays, which he did from time to time from 1966 to the mid-1980s, he proved to be a very practical man of the theater and was amenable to changing things when necessary, whether they be words, gestures, pauses, or movements. He also made cuts, some quite considerable, of well-known passages, much to the chagrin of certain well-known commentators who liked the received standard version rather than the revised one. When he was rehearsing *Krapp's Last Tape* with Rick Cluchey of the San Quentin Drama Workshop in 1977, Cluchey, reputedly, could not easily pronounce the word "Connaught," so Beckett changed it to "Kerry."[7] In 1967 he eliminated the very red faces of Hamm and Clov and the very white faces of Nagg and Nell in his Schiller-Theater Werkstatt production of *Endgame* in Berlin. He said it was "trop recherché." (He later reinstated Nagg's and Nell's white faces.) He also cut the bloodstains on Hamm's handkerchief but later allowed a "faint trace of blood." He simplified the opening mime of Clov. He cut the business of Clov turning the telescope on the audience and saying "I see a multitude in transports of joy. That's what I call a magnifier."[8] In *Happy Days* he cut portions of the text and changed some of the stage directions. Even short plays like *Footfalls* and *Come and Go* have variations in different editions; and his final play *What Where* was radically altered in the light of his experience of directing a television version for Süddeutscher Rundfunk in Stuttgart in 1986. Of particular interest were the radical changes he made to his most famous play, *Waiting for Godot,* when he directed it at the Schiller-Theater in Berlin in 1975. As well as changing lines and moves and making small cuts here and there, he made two substantial cuts, one in act 1 shortly before Lucky's speech, and a longer one in act 2 when Vladimir and Estragon are holding up Pozzo. To many who knew and revered this play as a modern classic it was like cutting away part of a limb. And many an Estragon in this version has lamented the loss of the line, "My left lung is very weak! . . . But my right lung is as sound as a bell!" But Beckett stuck to his guns. He felt the passage in question dragged a bit (like the passage in act 2), and so it did. Even the most famous refrain in the play, "Let's go. We can't. Why not? We're waiting for Godot. Ah!" now ended with "Ah yes!" because Beckett liked the two syllables that ended the refrain in French, "C'est vrai," and in German, "Ach ja."[9]

These are a few examples of Beckett's practicality as a man of the theater that, I hope, will debunk the myth that he was absolutely intolerant of changes in his plays. Beckett was more than happy to agree that there are many ways to achieve a production of a play and each way will be different according to the talents and vision of the director and actors and designers.

So let's assume you are a director and you want to direct a Beckett play. Apart from the usual niceties of having a theater in which to perform it, and having the rights cleared and so on, where do you start? Obviously, you acquire a text of the play (if you don't have one already) and you read and reread it and familiarize yourself with it as much as you can. Just as you would with any other play. But here is the first of many potential pitfalls. Which edition do you use? A British edition published by Faber and Faber or an American edition published by Grove Press? And which Faber edition? "There are differences?" You may well ask— just as Beckett did once of Everett Frost, who was directing the radio play *Embers*. Frost wanted to know about the final all-important sound effect "Sea," which was, and still is, absent from the *Complete Dramatic Works* and later the *Collected Shorter Plays*. Misprints creep in all over the place; and not only misprints. In the first edition of the *Complete Dra-*

matic Works published by Faber and Faber in 1986, the version of *Waiting for Godot* printed is the 1956 expurgated version and not the 1965 standard version. (When I pointed this out to Beckett he was horrified.) Up to the late 1960s all plays put on in England had to be sent to the Lord Chamberlain's office for approval, and he—and it was invariably a he—would send back a letter saying you must change this or that, or cut such and such a line or passage. For example, Estragon's line "You might button it all the same," referring to Vladamir's open fly, was cut. The line following Estragon's question "What about hanging ourselves?"— "Hmm, it would give us an erection"—was cut, making nonsense of Estragon's reply, "Let's hang ourselves immediately." The mother of the Gozzo family did not have the clap, she had warts; and Pozzo, instead of talking of kicking Lucky out on his "arse," must make do with his "backside." The real fun and games begin in Lucky's speech where in reference to the Deity the pronoun "who" has to be capitalized (though, obviously, this is for the reader only) and "Fartov and Belcher" becomes "Popov and Belcher." In act 2 "you piss better" becomes "you do it better"; "bolloxed" becomes "banjaxed" (foreign scholars would have a field day with that one); "who farted" becomes "who belched" and despite the ban on male tumescence in act 1, we find a line not in the standard edition when Vladimir says of Pozzo, "He must get used to being erect again." Beckett trying to get a rise out of someone, no doubt.

These are some of the problems a director faces when trying to decide which edition to use. Fortunately the standard Faber edition of 1965 has been around long enough to remain just that. But in 1993 Faber published (at seventy-five pounds sterling) *The Theatrical Notebooks of Samuel Beckett,* volume 1, *Waiting for Godot.* (The fact that volumes 3 and 2, in that order, had already been published, in true Wattian sequence, is neither here nor there.) Here was a new text—another new text—based on Beckett's own production in German in 1975, and changed in the light of that production. This text, with cuts and additions—some from the original French that never before had been in any English version—was said to be Samuel Beckett's very last word on the matter. But you'll note that the date of publication was 1993 (it actually came out in 1994), some four years after Beckett's death. So we have only the editors' word for this. Much of the information gathered by the editors, Dougald McMillan and James Knowlson, came from people like Walter Asmus (assistant director to Beckett on the 1975 Berlin *Godot* who directed an English-language production at the Brooklyn Academy of Music in 1978 that tried to replicate Beckett's Berlin production) and members of the San Quentin Drama Workshop, who, in 1984, performed *Godot* in a production by Asmus, overseen by Beckett. There are variations, as shown in McMillan and Knowlson's notes, of word and phrase in the new bits of text, and no uniformity with regard to certain cuts. In the 1988 Dublin Gate Theatre production—also directed by Asmus—certain bits of business and certain lines that were cut in Berlin were restored. Though this production, so far as I know, had no bearing on the so-called revised text, it is interesting to note that a sort of Chinese whispers seemed to obtain with regard to each new English-language production of the revised text.

So where does that leave us? It seems to me that like Stravinsky's *Petrushka,* Bruckner's Third Symphony, or Copland's *Appalachian Spring,* we have two versions to choose from if we are contemplating a production of *Waiting for Godot.* My advice to anyone who is about to direct *Godot* would be to read the introduction to the revised text edition and then make up your own mind. With regard to other plays, there are revised text editions of *Endgame, Krapp's Last Tape, Happy Days* in a different format—published in 1985—and *The Shorter Plays,* which includes revised text versions of *Come and Go, Footfalls,* and *What Where,* and facsimiles of Beckett's production notebooks for these and *Play, Eh Joe, That Time,* and *Not I.* But if one wishes to stick to the original text, one should compare editions for errors, as there are quite a few; and in the case of the American Grove Press texts, variations with regard to certain words or phrases. For example, *Come and Go* has a different beginning. As Beckett himself once said to me, "My texts are a mess."[10]

So let's assume we have settled on a text. Where now?

It's stating the obvious to recommend a thorough reading of the text, many times, having perhaps, a pencil to hand and marking the script as a conductor would a score—perhaps with different colored pencils. Beckett himself in his preparation of plays he directed divided each play (at least each longer play) into sections, A 1–6 and B 1–5 in the case of each of the acts of *Godot,* 1–16 in the case of *Endgame* and A 1–8 and B 1–4 in the case of the two-act *Happy Days.* Even the one-act *Krapp's Last Tape* was divided into six sections, each further divided into two, three, or four subsections. These divisions I find very useful, but a director may want to find his or her own divisions. What is of great importance is the architecture of the play—how a section builds or how a certain stillness is created to give the right context for certain passages. The main thing for a director is to get an overall feel for the piece—to understand not *what* the play means but *how* it means. How to play the notes. And here we come to the crucial part—the actors. Casting is always crucial, nowhere more so than in Beckett. I have seen fine actors murder Beckett and unlikely actors play him superbly. There ought to exist a certain empathy with the material. It needn't be understanding. Billie Whitelaw, famously, has said, "I always understood the *feelings* he wanted to convey, even when I·didn't understand the *words*."[11] To my mind an actor will only succeed in Beckett if he or she is willing to serve the work and not use the work as a vehicle for the actor's own ego. Actors who come from a Stanislavskian or Method background often have difficulty with Beckett. ("Not for me these Grotowskis and Methods," Beckett once said.)[12] Actors who come from this system may want to know who Hamm and Clov really are, where they come from, the background to their characters, what they had for breakfast, and so on. As Beckett once stated in a letter to Alan Schneider in December 1957:

> My work is a matter of fundamental sounds (no joke intended), made as fully as possible, and I accept responsibility for nothing else. If people want to have headaches among the overtones, let them. And provide their own aspirin. Hamm as stated and Clov as stated, *nec tecum nec sine te,* in such a place, and in such a world, that's all I can manage, more than I could.[13]

And to Barney Rosset, his American publisher, he wrote in October 1954:

> I stopped off in London . . . and had a highly unsatisfactory interview with SIR Ralph Richardson who wanted the low-down on Pozzo, his home address and curriculum vitae, and seemed to make the forthcoming of this and similar information the condition of his condescending to illustrate the part of Vladimir. Too tired to give satisfaction I told him that all I knew about Pozzo was in the text, that if I had known more I would have put it in the text, and that this was true also of the other character which I trust puts an end to that star . . . I also told Richardson that if by Godot I had meant God I would say God, and not Godot. This seemed to disappoint him greatly.[14]

So, we have the text and the world of the text and the information in the text. On page 1 of *Godot* we read, "A country road. A tree. Evening" (or in the revised text, "A country road. A tree. A stone.

Evening"). Following that we have the text and stage directions. *Waiting for Godot* is an exception in Beckett's canon because it is freer in its stage directions than any other play of Beckett. Let us leave *Godot* for a moment and discuss the other plays with regard to stage directions.

In the other longer plays, *Endgame* and *Happy Days,* the characters are fairly circumscribed by their physical circumstances. In *Endgame* Hamm is in an armchair in the center of a bare room. Nagg and Nell are in ashbins at the front of the stage on the left. (That is, audience left. Beckett's stage directions left and right refer to audience left and right, not stage left and right from the actors' perspective.) Clov is the only character who moves, and he comes and goes from a door on the right or moves about the room as indicated by the text and stage directions. While Clov's moves are not set in stone, most of them are fairly circumscribed by the text. In *Happy Days* Winnie has little possibility of movement other than with her head, upper torso and arms in act 1, and none, except with her head and face, in act 2. Willie's moves are so detailed that it would be perverse to change them. In *Krapp's Last Tape* there is a small amount of movement—the opening mime, the journeys to and from Krapp's cubbyhole (or darkness upstage) and his own movements seated at the table with the tape recorder. But when we look at the shorter plays, the ones after *Happy Days,* there is little movement, and what movement there is is minimal and carefully detailed. Some plays have virtually no movement at all: *Play, Not I, That Time, A Piece of Monologue,* and *Rockaby.* Some are almost balletic in their prescribed movements, like *Come and Go, Footfalls, Ohio Impromptu, Catastrophe, What Where* and especially the television play *Quad.* Even earlier plays like the two *Roughs* are carefully choreographed, and the movement in the two mimes is described in detail.

So apart from *Waiting for Godot* there is very little one can do with regard to movement in the plays without being perverse. This hasn't stopped people doing their own thing and finding all sorts of movement in the plays. But I have often encountered directors who tried "something else," found it didn't work, went back to what Beckett wrote, and found that that *did* work. Frequently theater directors try to do something perversely original or new with a script—try to put their stamp on a production; to change something, often for the sake of change. There are plays you can do that with, provided the changes or innovations serve the play. But Beckett's plays in my experience are not that sort of material.

This doesn't mean slavishly following every stage direction. But if we're going to perform a play by one of the acknowledged masters of drama of the twentieth century who also happens to be a very poetic and punctilious writer, and a man who had considerable practical experience of the theater, then I think we deviate from his words and directions at our peril. This does *not* mean that every production will be the same. Different directors, different actors, different stage or costume designers, different lighting designers will all bring something new and fresh to each production. From my own personal experience (and speaking to other actors who have worked on Beckett plays) I feel a great sense of freedom when confronted with a Beckett text. I don't feel at all strait-jacketed or regimented. I try to find my way of playing that score just as a soloist in musical terms would. Each performance of a violin sonata or a piano concerto is very different even though the same notes are being played. In the case of *Waiting for Godot* there is much freedom. This was Beckett's first published play, in 1952. It was written between October 1948 and January 1949. Beckett had had only a limited experience of theater at this stage apart from that of a playgoer. He had played Don Diègue in a parody of Corneille's *Le Cid* entitled *Le Kid,* which was performed at the Peacock Theatre in 1931 as the annual presentation of the Trinity College Dublin Modern Languages Society. This "Cornelian Nightmare," as it was described in the program, was written by Beckett's friend from Paris Georges Pelorson with, perhaps, some assistance from Beckett. And by 1940 Beckett had written a scene of an unfinished play about Dr. Johnson called "Human Wishes." He also had written, in 1947, a play called *Eleutheria* with seventeen characters and three sets. Roger Blin, Beckett's first director, having to choose between *Eleutheria* and *Waiting for Godot,* naturally chose *Godot:* five characters and one set. A lot cheaper. Also a much better play. *Eleutheria* is to *Godot* is what *Dream of Fair to Middling Women* is to *Molloy.* No comparison, no comparison.

Let's assume then that we have a director, cast, designer, lighting designer, and so on who are committed and eager to put on a production of *Waiting for Godot.* Where to start? What are the danger areas to avoid and what qualities will make it memorable? Simplicity, for a start. As Beckett himself said, "Keep it simple."[15] The design—the total look of the piece; set, costumes, lighting—should all be integrated. Beckett loved painting—indeed one of the original impetuses for *Waiting for Godot* was Casper David Friedrich's paintings *Man and Woman Contemplating the Moon* and *Two Men Contemplating the Moon.* For Beckett it was the shape that mattered. Estragon—earthy, of the earth, concerned with his feet, his boots. Vladimir—airy, of the air, concerned with his head, his hat. Estragon—given up on most things. Vladimir—optimistic about most things, at least for a while. Pozzo—absurd, slightly brutish, dominant on the surface, weak underneath. Lucky—abject, debased, enslaved, reconciled, but in a strange way, strong underneath, though obviously cowed by his treatment over a period of time. Beckett was once asked by Colin Duckworth, "Is Lucky so named because he has found his Godot?" Beckett's reply was, "I suppose he is Lucky to have no more expectations."[16] But an audience has expectations—two hours of them; and even the most skeptical will be won over if the shape or ballet of the play is carefully worked and played out. Didi and Gogo are yin and yang, but at times their roles are reversed. There are moments when Vladimir gets depressed and Estragon becomes the one who encourages. In act 2, Lucky puts the whip and rope tenderly into the hands of his now blind master, Pozzo; there is an equivalent tenderness to the moments when Vladimir covers the sleeping Estragon with his coat or when Estragon positions the downbeat Vladimir near the wings and tells him to watch out for Godot. The director and actors must manage carefully these moments that echo other moments in the play if the shape of the piece is to emerge. The language too has passages of quite fast delivery that culminate in silences. It is the manipulation of these words and silences that will give the required shape to the piece. The two scenes with the boy—similar in some ways but very different in mood, need to echo each other. Likewise, the effect of night falling suddenly and the rising of the moon. Again, musicality is the key to these scenes. The big explosive moment in the play is Lucky's speech in act 1 (echoed in a poignant way by Pozzo's wonderful valedictory speech in act 2). It is interesting to note that when Beckett directed the play, he began by working on Lucky's speech. It is central to the play and a good or bad performance of it can, to some extent, alter the shape of the play.

I would like to consider the other three of Beckett's longer plays, namely *Endgame, Krapp's Last Tape,* and *Happy Days.*

Endgame was Beckett's own favorite among his plays and it has always been my favorite too. I think *Endgame* is one of the great plays of the twentieth century. It says more about the emptiness and savagery of the most horrific century in man's history, and says it better, than any other I know. It is the *King Lear* of our time—a beautiful, terrible, impossible play. Beckett once described it to Georges Pelorson as a "cantata for two voices"[17] (meaning Hamm and Clov). The wonderful scene between Nagg and Nell is a kind of subcantata within the play. As Beckett said, "The play is full of echoes; they all answer each other."[18] Why this play is so often gilded with otherness, when its starkness and integrity are what make it so powerful, is beyond me. Here, again, the execution of the play should be musical. The "maximum hate," as Beckett called it, between Hamm and Clov in certain passages is contrasted by the fierce black humor in the exchanges, Hamm is a king, and emperor, monarch of all he surveys. But he is also a chess player, a bad chess player who knows he can't win but refuses to give up. He, like Clov, is waiting for the end. Clov has decided to leave. The late Jack MacGowan once rightly said that if *Godot* is "the anguish of waiting, *Endgame* is the anguish of going."[19] "I'll leave you" is an even more frequent refrain in *Endgame* than "We're waiting for Godot" is in the earlier play. Hamm is also a ham actor, one who over does the business of performing; and perform he does, like Pozzo in *Godot*. "Stories, stories, years and years of stories . . ." says Henry in the radio play *Embers*. Just as many of the characters in Beckett's prose works are obsessed with the need to *say,* the need to *tell,* so Hamm in *Endgame* is a compulsive storyteller. His "chronicle," which remains unfinished, is at the heart of his big monologue that is the centerpoint of the play. This speech is very difficult to bring off properly. It requires the voice of a great tragedian (the old style) and the timing of a good comedian. Hamm's cruelty is interspersed with light comedy with Clov. This contrast in playing is of utmost importance. Clov's first word, "finished," which is also the first word in the play, signifies the end. This is going to be the last day that Clov will serve Hamm. (What do you stick in ham to spice it?—cloves. And the character's name *is* pronounced "clove": I had it from the horse's mouth.) Clov is no longer afraid. He has made his decision. He will leave. But will he? This is the tension of the play. And at the end, Clov is standing at the door "dressed for the road." When the play ends he is still there. He has not yet gone. He is about to leave. That's all we know—or should know—or need to know. Beckett once said to Pat Magee, "Hamm is the kind of man who likes things coming to an end but doesn't want them to end just yet."[20]

In *Endgame,* four is a very significant number. There are four characters, Beckett divided the play into sixteen sections, four groups of four. There are four very definite sounds at the opening of the play: the opening of each curtain at the windows and the shutting of each ashbin. When I played Clov in Antoni Libera's Gate Theatre production in 1991 I made Clov's laughter into a four-syllable cackle. I took four steps from the door of the kitchen to the place beside Hamm. Nagg knocked four times on Nell's bin-lid. These were, I hope, not made too obviously, too technically, but they help to underline subconsciously a pattern or shape in the design that, hopefully, enriches the whole fabric.

One of the things Beckett liked to do was, when a phrase or word recurred a number of times in a play, to emphasize it or speak it in an unusual manner so that each time it recurs we are aware of its significance. Something like a leitmotif in Wagner, perhaps; though in Wagner, the recurrence of leitmotifs often finds them transmuted in some way—something music can do more easily than words. Beckett does indeed transmute certain words or phrases. In *Godot* the famous refrain "We're waiting for Godot" sometimes appears as "I'm waiting for Godot" or "to wait for Godot." Or in *Endgame,* Clov says, "I'll leave you" eleven times but on three occasions he adds, "I have things to do," which also appears on another occasion after a different line. On eight occasions Hamm says, "Go and get" or "go and see" followed by whatever. On seven occasions Clov says, "I'll go and get the . . ." whatever it is, or "I'll go and see." Again on four occasions Clov says, "I'm back again with the . . ." whatever—biscuit, glass, steps, insecticide. This repetition is fundamental to the play and must be spoken in such a way that some sort of recognition of these motifs is imported to the audience. But what must be guarded against is something too artificial, which, unfortunately, some actors who try to be faithful to Beckett's wishes have achieved. It is important to be aware of the power these repetitions and the necessity to play them, but there is a thin line between something memorable and something awkward and artificial. Each actor must find his or her own way of playing these motifs in ways that ring true for them. In *Happy Days* an example of this is the phrase "the old style" or "to speak in the old style, the sweet old style" (playing on Dante's "dolce stil nuovo,"[21] or sweet new style); or "that is what I find so wonderful" or "great mercies" or "here all is strange" or "such wilderness." These phrases recur throughout the play, and if they are phrased in such a way as to echo in the memory each time they are heard, the musicality of the performance will be greatly enhanced, giving a far better apprehension of the play to an audience.

In *Krapp's Last Tape* the two words "Ah well" are spoken four times, three times on the first "listen" of Krapp to the tape and later when the present-day Krapp (so to speak) says wearily, "Ah well, maybe he was right." The actor should give a shading to these words, a nuance that is picked up in each subsequent utterance of them. There is summation in these words, given their context, of everything that is in Krapp's mind and soul. All the might-have-beens. At one stage Beckett considered calling the play "Ah Well." I'm glad he didn't, but it shows how important these words were to him. *Krapp's Last Tape* is an example of a play that can vary so much in performance and still remain faithful to Beckett. I have seen many productions over the years, and each time I come away having seen something new. *Krapp's Last Tape* is the most autobiographical of Beckett's plays, although Krapp is not Beckett. Jean Martin, who played Krapp in 1970 directed by Beckett, had this to say: "He told me very precisely about the genesis of the play, the personal links between himself and Krapp. . . . He worked hard on removing all sentimentality from the play. That was something he insisted on rather a lot. Above all, he stressed that it should be played without too much emotion or regret. I remember, in fact, more or less what he said at the time: 'Krapp is an old fool, who is rather less of a fool as a very old man than he was, as he listens to the recording of his stupidity of thirty years earlier.'"[22] Which rather gives the lie to the story about Cyril Cusack, another actor who played Krapp, who, it is alleged, said to Beckett one day, "Sam, it seems to me that *Krapp's Last Tape* is just a piece of Irish Protestant sentimentality." To which Beckett replied tartly, "That's what it's supposed to be."

Happy Days is a very difficult play to perform. It requires a towering performance from an actress and a line in the architecture of the play that is operatic. It will be very tedious if it is not performed and directed with great skill. The sweep of the play is of utmost importance. It is a very difficult play to read because of all the pauses and stage directions. But each of these has been worked out with meticulous care. Rehearsing this play is a fascinating experience. I had the good fortune to play Willie to Rosaleen Linehan's Winnie in the late Karel Reisz's Gate Theatre production in 1996. I learned so much by just being there. Perhaps more than any other Beckett play, it is built up brick by brick, section by section, until these sections eventually join together. This is a tale of Everywoman. When Billie Whitelaw first read the play prior to playing it at the Royal Court Theatre in London under Beckett's direction in 1979 she said, "I was immediately struck by the thought: how on earth could this man have written the story of my life so long before he knew me?"[23] It is also a phenomenally difficult play to learn. Whitelaw at one point rang Brenda Bruce, the original London Winnie, and asked her how on earth did she ever learn the part; and added, "I supposed once you've learned *Happy Days* you can learn anything." To her shock and amazement Bruce replied, "No, no; after *Happy Days* I felt I could do *nothing*. I never recovered. Even after all these years."[24] But, like anything else, with hard work it is possible. And I know many actresses who have done it and remain sane and healthy. Mind you, later in rehearsals Whitelaw felt she was going to pieces. As she says herself, "I rang Peggy Ashcroft" (who had played Winnie four years earlier). 'I'm going mad.' I told her. 'I don't know what to do.' 'You've got to ask him to leave, dear,' she said, 'He's impossible. Throw him out.' I said, 'I can't do that.' She said simply, 'Well, you'll have to.'"[25]

Beckett said the play was a sonata for voice and movement—back to music again. The rhythm of the play is so important. There are passages that race along and there are passages that are very soft and slow—just as in music. And there are moods—outgoing, bright, optimistic; and introspective, sad, melancholic. One day in rehearsal Billie Whitelaw said to Beckett, "Sam, I want to ask you a technical question. Where shall I look on this next page?" He said, "Inward." She replied, "Of course, inward."[26] Now few actresses would work like that—Whitelaw had an unusual working relationship with Beckett—but it does illustrate something important when performing Beckett. Beckett has done a lot of the work an actor usually does. If actors and directors *trusted* Beckett more, there would be less trouble with his plays. His stage and acting directions are almost invariably right. Compare the plays of another playwright who could hardly be further apart in style and technique than Beckett—Alan Ayckbourn. If you do not stick to Ayckbourn's stage directions you will come to grief. Some of his plays, technically, can't be done and will fall apart unless you follow them to the letter. It's like assembling one of those build-it-yourself wardrobes. If you follow the step-by-step instructions you will have a wardrobe. Likewise with Beckett. It might sound crass but Beckett, as well as being an exquisite poet of the theater, was also a great technician. His notebooks are full of doodles—many of them mathematical in construct. He works things out. It is only after the technical aspect of things has been accomplished that the art, the poetry, the music of the piece will emerge. But all the clever direction and wonderful acting in the world won't save a Beckett play unless the groundwork has been prepared and the foundations laid. Theater is mainly technical. The technique should not be apparent, but unless it's there the artistry will flounder.

I would like to turn briefly to the shorter plays. These are pieces of theatrical chamber music: intimate, resonant, to be played and experienced in small spaces. If anything these plays are more difficult to pull off than the so-called full-length plays. (All Beckett's plays are full-length: many are short but that's their full length.) Some like *Play* and *Not I* are virtuoso pieces needing technical vocal skill of the highest caliber. Others like *Ohio Impromptu* and *Come and Go* are delicate traceries needing the refinement of a slow movement in a Beethoven quartet. Some, like the mimes, need expert movement to make them work, while others like *Rockaby, That Time,* and *A Piece of Monologue* need damn good acting to prevent them boring the pants off an audience. But perhaps the most difficult of all of them is *Footfalls.* I have, on a few occasions, been asked by actresses who are about to play May, "What is *Footfalls* about?" The problem is not the answer, it's the question. As a very young Beckett said in 1929 about Joyce, with regard to *Finnegans Wake,* "His writing is not *about* something; *it is that something itself.*"[27] To say what *Footfalls* is about, or, indeed, what some other Beckett plays are about, is almost impossible. They are vignettes of experience. For an actor approaching, say, the role of May in *Footfalls,* one need only compare the preparation of two actresses who have played the role, Billie Whitelaw and Hildegard Schmahl, as recounted by Jonathan Kalb. Whitelaw has said, "I am not interested in what the plays are about, to be absolutely honest, that's an academic's job. I get a bit nervous when people get too reverent about Beckett's work. . . . When I work with Sam, we don't analyze the plays at all."[28] Though she did ask Beckett while rehearsing *Footfalls,* "Am I dead?" To which he replied, after a second's thought, "Well, let's just say you're not quite there."[29] "My first task," Whitelaw went on, "is to find the music of it. . . . Beckett blows the notes. I want them to come out of me and create feeling in whoever's sitting out front."[30] On the other hand, with regard to Hildegard Schmahl's approach to *Footfalls,* we find something very different. As Walter Asmus says in his rehearsal diary for the production in German, "In Berlin, Beckett was confronted with an actress . . . whose work in the theatre is based on the search for realistic concrete motivations and who is not willing or not able automatically to work in an intuitively structural way." When Schmahl announced that she did not "understand the play," she received a response from Beckett to the effect that she should emphasize her footsteps. "But," she would say, "I can't do it mechanically. I must understand it first and then think."[31] Apparently she struggled heroically to fulfill Beckett's wishes and even at one point visited a psychiatric clinic to consult a doctor about female patients with obsessions. But Beckett continued to stress the importance of physicalization—he said, "The position of the body will help to find the right voice."[32] Schmahl persevered and after relinquishing all changes of finding May through active, conscious means, she eventually decided (a great leap of faith for her) to make the primary basis for her performance physical and not psychic. As Beckett told her, the process of understanding cannot be forced—(echoes of Hamm here "no forcing, no forcing, it's fatal"). Beckett said to her, "You are acting in too healthy a way. . . . Try gradually, while you speak the words, to see the whole inwardly. It has a visionary character . . . it is an image which develops gradually."[33] As Asmus said in his rehearsal diary, once she relinquished the attempt to "produce the images from the inside," all the "more or less unconscious movements of the body, especially of the head" that inevitably accompanied her physical intentions, disappeared. She was able to hold her body stiffly, avoid all uncalculated movement, and that new tautness in turn affected her articulation. Asmus concludes, "May stands independent of her footsteps as a concentrated bundle on the strip of light. No superfluous movement distracts, the tension communicates itself to the observer, one is drawn into the undertow of her story—the concentration is passed on and challenges the observer to an absolute concentration. Beckett is satisfied with the result. 'You have found the trick' is his comment."[34]

I think this is a good example of how preconceived ideas about acting are redundant when it comes to performing Beckett. There is no background, in a conventional sense, to his characters. They exist in the time and space of the play. Just as music or painting has no background—it simply *is*—so Beckett's plays simply *are*.

And they are *plays* and their players must go on playing. In *Godot*, Vladimir, trying to keep Estragon from leaving, says, in desperation, "Will you not play?" In *Play*, Man says, "I know now, all that was just . . . play. And all this, when will all this have been . . . just play?" And in *Endgame* there is a terrifying moment when Clov imploringly says, "Let's stop playing," and Hamm thunders back, "Never!" Play they must; we all must. As the narrator of *The Unnamable* says, "It's the old story, they want to be entertained."[35]

NOTES

1. Jonathan Kalb, *Beckett in Performance* (Cambridge: Cambridge University Press, 1989), 73–74.

2. Samuel Beckett, "Dante . . . Bruno. Vico.. Joyce," in *Disjecta: Miscellaneous Writings and a Dramatic Fragment,* ed. Ruby Cohn (London: Calder, 1983), 22.

3. Samuel Beckett, *Murphy* (New York: Grove Press, 1957), 236.

4. Harold Hobson, "Samuel Beckett, Dramatist of the Year," *International Theatre Annual* 1 (1956): 153.

5. Beckett, "Dante . . . Bruno," 27.

6. Billie Whitelaw, *Billie Whitelaw . . . Who He?* (New York: St Martin's Press, 1995), 145.

7. *The Theatrical Notebooks of Samuel Beckett,* vol. 3, *Krapp's Last Tape,* ed. James Knowlson (London: Faber and Faber; New York: Grove Press, 1992), 23–24.

8. *The Theatrical Notebooks of Samuel Beckett,* vol. 2: *Endgame,* ed. S. E. Gontarski (London: Faber and Faber; New York: Grove Press, 1993), 17.

9. *The Theatrical Notebooks of Samuel Beckett,* vol. 1, *Waiting for Godot,* ed. Dougald McMillan and James Knowlson (New York: Grove Press, 1994), 101.

10. Personal communication, 1986.

11. Billie Whitelaw interviewed in the film, *The Making of Rockaby,* directed by D. A. Pennebaker for the BBC's *Arena* program, 1982.

12. Enoch Brater, *Why Beckett* (London: Thames and Hudson, 1989), 110.

13. Alec Reid, *All I Can Manage, More Than I Could* (Dublin: Dolmen, 1968), 33.

14. Samuel Beckett to Barney Rosset, October 18, 1954, *Review of Contemporary Fiction* 10, no. 3 (1990): 70.

15. Dougald McMillan and Martha Fehsenfeld, *Beckett in the Theatre: The Author as Practical Playwright and Director* (London: John Calder, 1988), 204.

16. *En attendant Godot,* ed. Colin Duckworth (London: Harrap, 1966), lxiii.

17. McMillan and Fehsenfeld, *Beckett in the Theatre,* 163.

18. McMillan and Fehsenfeld, *Beckett in the Theatre,* 208.

19. Reid, *All I Can Manage,* 71.

20. McMillan and Fehsenfeld, *Beckett in the Theater,* 177.

21. Dante Alighieri, *Divina Commedia,* "Purgatorio," canto 24, line 57.

22. Samuel Beckett, *Krapp's Last Tape: Theatre Workbook 1,* ed. James Knowlson (London: Brutus Books, 1980), 81.

23. Whitelaw, *Billie Whitelaw,* 148.

24. Whitelaw, *Billie Whitelaw,* 150.

25. Whitelaw, *Billie Whitelaw,* 152.

26. Whitelaw, *Billie Whitelaw,* 152.

27. Beckett, "Dante . . . Bruno," 27.

28. Kalb, *Beckett in Performance,* 17.

29. Whitelaw, *Billie Whitelaw,* 143.

30. Kalb, *Beckett in Performance,* 17, 19.

31. Kalb, *Beckett in Performance,* 62.

32. Kalb, *Beckett in Performance,* 64.

33. Kalb, *Beckett in Performance,* 64.

34. Kalb, *Beckett in Performance,* 64.

35. Samuel Beckett, *Three Novels: Molloy/Malone Dies/The Unnamable* (New York: Grove Press, 1977), 372.

Enoch Brater

Beckett's "Beckett": So Many Words for Silence

I.

This essay begins by urging the reader to observe with its author a full moment of silence, as follows:

. . . .
. . . .
. . . .
. . . .
. . . .
. . . .
. . . .
. . . .
. . . .
. . . .

"Something," as Beckett might say—and in fact did say—"is taking its course." But what, exactly? *Silence once broken will never again be whole.*[1]

Now, any number of things might have happened to interrupt the moment of silence this essay has just tried to manufacture for you. Who knows? You may have laughed, or sighed, or burped, even cried out in dismay. A stomach may have grumbled. That is what live, warm bodies do: throats clear, mouths cough, there's sneezing and—who knows?—perhaps (the matter's delicate) even a Beckettian "fart fraught with meaning."[2]

A pager may have rung. A beeper might have gone off. A battery in a hearing aid might have suddenly set off an alarm. Then there's the omnipresent cell phone. The clock ticks. A foot taps. A pencil falls to the ground, or a paper clip, a coin, a slim piece of paper. Is there music in the background? A door slams. Is the American reader chewing gum or—worse still—is "lip lipping lip"?[3] And so on. Such a busy world!

This reading space in which you sit or stand or lie, too, is hardly invio-
late: sounds from a hallway and a street life beyond may have already
fouled this lame and scripted session of sweet silent thought. Above all,
literally, there's the treacherous white noise of electric lights. Proust
would be very dismayed. And, to top it off, framing "it all,"[4] there may
even be the spectacle of you, reading aloud.

As a celebrated European writer of fiction, poetry, and drama (including in this case the plays written for both the live stage and the mechanical media), Beckett is of course well known for the liberties he has
taken with such strange texts of silence. He is by no means the first to
have done so. The contentious modernist tradition, from Lamartine to
Mallarmé, from Proust to Joyce to Pound, from Schoenberg to John
Cage and Giorgio Morandi,[5] has been from the start hell-bent on cau-
terizing stillness in word and image and sound: *so* many words for silence, so *many* words for silence. But perhaps more so than any other
writer of his generation, Beckett structures an absence that is fraught
with consequence, yielding (when it works) a resonant blank, full of ges-
tural vigor and pungency:

> Past midnight. Never knew such silence. The earth might be un-
> inhabited.[6]

The lone figure in the single-act *Krapp's Last Tape* is only one of
many lost ones we will encounter in Beckett's enigmatic repertory of
solitary searchers. "Silence and darkness were all I craved," cries his simulacrum in *Play,* this time planted—buried really—in an urn. "Well, I
get a certain amount of both. They being one."[7] "Now the day is over,
/ Night is drawing nigh-igh," intones Krapp as he stares into stage nothingness near the end of his dubious recording session, his performance
richly ironizing the lines of a Protestant hymn he can barely remember
from his long ago youth: "Shadows—*(coughing, then almost inaudible)*—of
the evening / Steal across the sky." The rest—and Beckett will show it
to be the much greater part—is silence.

An Irish writer of the mid–twentieth century, Beckett inherits a tradition of the half-light, the gloaming, a liminal world that is always on
the verge of being recovered in some unspecified elsewhere halfway between perceived silence and arrested speech—"relieved," as Didi says in
Waiting for Godot, but at the same timed "appalled."[8] His early writings,
in English and in prose, like to intellectualize *vacuum* and theorize
plenum, as though further Celtic twilights, all passion spent, might be put

on some indefinite hold, not quite gone but definitely on Death Row.[9] His novel *Murphy,* published in London by Routledge in 1938, opens with a real "stinger": "The sun shone, having no alternative, on the nothing new." So far so good. But before long the eponymous hero, whose "fourth highest attribute" is said to be silence, is bound naked to a rocking chair, contemplating in his own time and in his own garret space the dizzying vastness of a "superfine chaos" most readers would be tempted to call the void:

> Now the silence above was a different silence, no longer strangled. The silence not of vacuum, but of plenum.[10]

Beckett's imaginative world will not take fire, however, until he agrees to let the silence in, *both* the vacuum *and* the plenum, not making it—whatever "it" is—into something else, "the screaming silence," for example, "of no's knife in yes's wound."[11] And that's what this critic calls, following Hamm's lead in *Endgame,* a real magnifier:

> Who may tell the tale
> of the old man?
> weigh absence in a scale?
> mete want with a span?
> the sum assess
> of the world's woes?
> nothingness
> in words enclose?[12]

Beckett's cautionary lyric from the Addenda to *Watt,* the novel he was writing in English during the period he was trying to elude the Gestapo by hiding out in the south of France, already thematizes the creative dilemma of not-quite-being-there that will shadow Beckett's work over the next four decades. Even earlier than *Watt,* in the famous letter he wrote to his German friend Axel Kaun on July 9, 1937, he begins to speculate on a highly problematic "literature of the unword" that may finally let silence have its authoritative and persuasive say:

> As we cannot eliminate language all at once, we should at least leave nothing undone that might contribute to its falling into disrepute. To bore one hole after another in it, until what lurks behind it—be it something or nothing—begins to seep through; I cannot imagine

a higher goal for a writer today. Or is literature alone to remain behind in the old lazy ways that have so long ago been abandoned by music and painting? Is there something paralysingly holy in the vicious nature of the word that is not found in the elements of the other arts? Is there any reason why that terrible materiality of the word surface should not be capable of being dissolved, like for example the sound surface, torn by enormous pauses, of Beethoven's seventh Symphony, so that through whole pages we can perceive nothing but a path of sounds suspended in giddy heights, linking unfathomable abysses of silence? An answer is requested.[13]

Building silence into words will become for Beckett a real "teaser," always a question in his "case nought" of vision rather than technique, though the formidable techniques he develops to do so will be everywhere immaculate and precise.[14] In these post-poststructuralist days terms like *vision* and *technique* seem to have fallen into hard times, if not downright disrepute, but they are nonetheless the terms Beckett uses to frame Beckett's "Beckett." These are, moreover, the same congratulatory notes he will sound to negotiate a space for his writing in-between a constructed "said" and the ever-elusive "unsaid," then—*mirabile dictu*—in the even wilder territory that separates the "unsaid" from a previously uncharted "ununsaid." So much for the "Art and Con."[15] Erasure has rarely been subjected to the firm pressure of such an arch and heavy and equally deceptive hand. A term like *overdetermined* now seems like some giddy understatement. The same, of course, might be said of Dante.[16]

Beckett's maturity as a writer's writer comes with the composition of *Molloy, Malone Dies,* and *The Unnamable,* the three novels he started writing in French in the late 1940s, then translated fairly quickly into English (though it did not seem so at the time). With virtually simultaneous publication on both sides of the Atlantic, the trilogy, as it became known, soon established his credentials as *the* fifties writer, the most remarked-upon practitioner of all that was fractious and hilarious and nouveau in the *nouveau roman.*

In these books Beckett literally writes himself into the void as his heroes, talkers really, rush pell-mell into silence, every story's final destination. Molloy ends up in a ditch, while the tables fatally turn on his could-be clone, aka Jacques Moran, the Frenchified Irishman; Malone dies, or at the very least suffers a cataclysmic novelistic knockout; and what we may have taken for the Unnamable's endless tirade, despite all protests to the contrary, famously stops dead, all gimmicks gone:

. . . you must go on, I can't go on, you must go on, I'll go on, you must say words, as long as there are any, until they find me, until they say me, strange pain, strange sin, you must go on, perhaps it's done already, perhaps they have said me already, perhaps they have carried me to the threshold of my story, before the door that opens on my story, that would surprise me, if it opens, it will be I, it will be the silence, where I am, I don't know, I'll never know, in the silence you don't know, you must go on, I can't go on, I'll go on.[17]

End stop. So many, many words, only to arrive at silence, which was always already there, waiting for Beckett, at the beginning of his tri-part tale. "After all," as Murphy says, after all is said and done and spoken and written down, "there is nothing like dead silence." Quite. Murphy's words ring true. The novel has proven to be a clumsy vehicle indeed for letting silence speak its text into this lame unwording of the transparent word. There must be other stratagems.

II.

In the interval between the completion of *Malone Dies* and beginning work on *The Unnamable,* Beckett had the idea of writing a play, mostly, as he told Colin Duckworth, "as a relaxation, to get away from the awful prose I was writing at the time." "I wrote *Godot,*" he noted in 1985, "to come into the light. I needed a habitable space, and I found it on the stage."[18] The shift in genre will have enormous practical consequences; they bear not so much on the metaphoric representation of silence as on its actual evolution into a highly choreographed performance space. In the theater Beckett will make silence toe the line. Stage directions like *pause, brief tableau,* and *Waiting for Godot*'s unforgettable terminus ad quem, *"They do not move,"* will freeze the action, letting silence hold the stage with authority, sometimes even poignancy. Ellipsis, as in Winnie's bravura exploitation of this device in *Happy Days,* allows silence, now palpable and theatrically real, to punctuate, formalize, advance, even dictate the direction of the multiple resonances built through nuance into her richly intercalated monologue. Here, too, an embedded *pause* will quite literally allow silence to perform itself, reversing our normal expectations for the conventional relationship between text and subtext. Expanding the moment and arresting the action, silence chastens and conditions dialogue until, beaten into something like submission, it reappears in a rhythm of return, tail, so to speak, between its legs. Mime, as in Clov's spectacular "opener" in *Endgame,* extends the moment even further. Now playing a duet with the lead, silence musicalizes Clov's physical action, clarifying and elevating the complicity of movement in the communication of all stage meaning. Silence, *so to speak,* has suddenly upstaged the provenance of the word.

That is not to say that Beckett's trilogy fiction, so far as silence is concerned, is not without its considerable charms. Although the dual struggle to *be* silent and to let silence *be* is always getting caught in its own delirious traps—and particularly memorable are the ones it sets now deliberately, now inadvertently for itself (as in the humdinger, "I am obliged to speak. I shall never be silent. Never.")—such "idle talk" is nevertheless heard, as fiction generally is, in silence (unless we assume that this outlaw fiction is designed to be read fully and completely out loud, as the actor Barry McGovern has done, a point to consider later in this essay). In *Watt* Beckett tried to describe this phenomenon as something like "a disquieting sound, that of soliloquy, under dictation."[19] But such a mechanism, clever though it is, will not hold still. The very act of saying "silence" makes it far from "absolute," as all three texts in the trilogy are quick to acknowledge. This unnamable subject that both spurns and desires a name sure runs into problems here *(celui-ci)*—as well as there *(celui-là).* The speaker speaking this speech before long finds himself, in spite of himself, narrativizing and thematizing like crazy. And yet "the real silence" is supposed to—and for once in a way let's agree to split the infinitive—only and elegantly *be.*

What a lot of words this trilogy will use to talk instead *around* the subject, if indeed there is (only) one. The so-called silence is at various times alleged to be "little," then "tiny," then "unbroken," then "black," then "immaculate," then "grey," then "perfect," then "comparative" (there's a good one), then "outside," then "inside," then "long," "true," "the same," "murmurous," "short," "absolute," "profound," "different," and "strangled" (my list is not complete).[20] In this ruinous catalog every word is "very rightly wrong," both "ill seen" and "ill said."[21] And each is fated to be equally metonymic, for each can only render up a small part of some unobtainable (w)hole. Undaunted, the emerging word-horde (in various places referenced as "wordshit")[22] holds out the hope of a miraculous "dream silence" and—get this—a "silent silence." Can it be that fiction itself is running out of adjectives—or rather that it "dare not be silent for long, the whole fabrication might collapse"? The inscripted silence that cannot be described is also "prohibited"; on the one hand the text is "condemned to silence," but then on the other hand it has a so-said "right" to it. On "the brink of silence" there are, suggestively,

1. "confines of silence"
2. "drops of silence"
3. "an instant of silence"
4. "a second of silence"

Though "not one person in a hundred knows how to be silent," *things*—and in Beckett there is nothing like things—will be rumored to be mysteriously silent: the dust, various objects, the grave, "my last abode." "To restore silence" is in fact "the role of objects." At times such equivocal silence can only be captured in metaphor or simile, as in "the faint sound of aerial surf." Beckett's narrator "yelp[s]" against such flights of fancy "in vain," for, as he says, "that's the worst, to speak of silence." He longs to "enter living into silence," but then again he has to admit that there's "something gone wrong" with it; "it can never be known." So many words bring the speaker and this speech (not to mention every reader of the trilogy) "not a syllable nearer silence." The fundamentalist taxonomy has been a fraud, a complete waste of time. So, finally, "to hell with silence."

But then, again, when and where the reader least expects to find it, "silence falls with rhetorical intent." There is at long last at the conclusion of this trilogy the blissful finitude of a signature ellipsis, that silent place where the *what* and the *where* of any fiction must end: ". . . . ."

That is all.

Make sense who may.

I switch off.[23]

III.

Beckett's formalist concern—for that is how it is—with the evocation of silence will get a new lease on life once he turns his attention to the stage—and in ways that may have surprised even himself. For in the theater Beckett will be free to explore the mediation of *silence, pause,* and *pacing* as economical and efficient grace notes, attenuated time signatures establishing both movement and meaning. When the poor player struts and frets his hour upon Beckett's stage, as on any other, this certainly can signify a whole lot more than nothing. Let us think for a moment of Shakespeare, always a reliable but problematic repertory when it comes to figuring out just where silence is supposed to fall. Shakespeare's script will be hard to quantify here. But that should not indicate that in performance the text must necessarily surrender itself to a director's sometimes heavy hand. When, for example (and as Malone says, "there is nothing like examples"), Othello is about to kill Desdemona in V.ii.7, Shakespeare gives him a curiously suspended line:

Put out the light, and then put out the light . . .

What is this line supposed to mean? Punctuation, in this case a marked caesura, calls the reader's attention to a pause that must break the line. What the caesura tells us is that we must not in any case recite the line, staccato, like this:

Put-out-the-light-and-then-put-out-the-light . . .

In this line the caesura is, among other things, the guarantor of metaphor: without silence there will be no meaning here. As always in textual studies of Shakespeare, meaning determines sound; but from the line's point of view it is really the other way around.[24] Just how long does this silence want itself to *be*? And of course there can be no pause here unless it is surrounded and shaped by the sound of Shakespeare's language, a rich "farrago" indeed "of silence and words."[25]

This "pell-mell babel of silence and words"[26] presents us in *Macbeth* with still other problems. In this play an even shorter line can speak volumes, as when Lady Macbeth responds to her husband's hesitation at executing the bloody regicide at hand. "If we should fail?" he cries out in I.vii.59. She completes the broken pentameter line with two well-chosen words:

We fail?

What roles does silence want to play here in establishing the dynamics of potential meaning in the line? Is it, among other possibilities, *We? Fail?* or is it, rather, the upended shrug of *We fail!* Caesura will not be of the slightest use to us in this instance; and that punctuating question mark has proven to be a deceptive tool before, as in Hamlet's

> . . . O my prophetic soul!
> My uncle?
>
>   (I.v.40–41)

Could it be that these lines yearn to achieve, for strictly characterologi-
cal reasons, quite a different sound, as follows:

> . . . O my prophetic soul!
> My uncle!

In *Othello* (I.i.118) even an unmarked caesura can authorize the value of
silence in advancing the "speaking" of the line. When Brabantio calls
Iago a "villain" in the first act of the play, the supersubtle Venetian
quickly reacts by giving Desdemona's father his appropriate honorific.
Their heated conversation is poised to go something like this, as Iago
permutes Brabantio's angry and patrician "thou" to the icy civility of a
class-conscious "you." Consider for a moment the very particular inter-
polation below:

> *Brabantio.* Thou art a villain.
> *Iago.* You are [. . . *(pause)* . . .] a senator.

Beckett's dramaturgy will be highly informed by interventions like
these. For as his repertory develops and matures, so do his framing devices for the playing of silence. In the theater, as in music, there will be
no silence unless it finds a place for itself in the parenthesis that exists between the sound of other sounds. Lines recited on stage are in this respect both violators and interpreters of silence; in their delay and in their
hesitation, in their absence as much as in their presence, they mark silence, ironically, as acutely "real." On stage, as Beckett has shown, following the path of master playwrights like Strindberg, Maeterlinck, and
especially Chekhov, silence becomes a highly accomplished ventrilo-
quist, capable of "speaking" for itself in many different tongues. It need
no longer rely on a steady stream of questionable adjectives only to say
that it is really something else. Words, Beckett's words, "enough to ex-
terminate a regiment of dragoons," have been everywhere calculated on
"the Board" to make silence dramatically happen.[27]
  Beckett's increasing sensitivity to their volubility can be traced not
only in the printed directions for their delivery, an annotation that

deepens and expands as the actor moves from *Godot* to *Endgame* to *Happy Days* to *Not I* and beyond, but even more so in the production notebooks the playwright, serving as his own director, kept for the stagings he supervised in London, Stuttgart, and Berlin.[28] This option simply does not exist in the case of Shakespeare (though it does exist to a certain extent in staging Brecht). Words in set repertory with silence and pause, as we have already seen in *Endgame* and *Happy Days,* will not be the only vehicles through which the sound of Beckett's "Beckett" discovers its weight and volume, making itself heard. In the plays he wrote in the 1970s and 1980s, dialogue in the form of soliloquy and monologue will often be overwhelmed by the steady reliance on a far more comprehensive theatrical soundscape, revealing an unexpected urgency where time becomes negotiable in terms of stage space. Here technology, most particularly in the form of the modulation accomplished through sophisticated electronic amplification, will be called upon to play its reciprocal part: chimes, heavy breathing, footfalls, the rocking of a chair, the knocking of a hand on a plain deal table, the closing of a book, or the notation a pencil makes on a notepad will establish and sustain the tonal quality appropriate for each new mise-en-scène. It will be lighting, however, rather than sound, surprisingly, that clarifies mood and atmosphere in this late style, even and especially when the space reveals, as it does in *Rockaby,* a seated figure whose few words— "More"—play a stunning duet with an offstage voice previously recorded on tape, now broadcast as from some unspecified elsewhere.[29] In these short, complex plays, "that MINE,"[30] Beckett's image-making is at full stretch, tacitly admitting the enigma of light as it slowly fades to isolate, diminish, marginalize, fix, and conceal. Such silence is well-spoken indeed.

IV.

In the mechanical media Beckett's staging of silence will become ever more mathematical and precise, sometimes calibrated to the micromillisecond and "every mute micromillisyllable."[31] Here the coefficients can be splendidly timed but also anecdotal, as in the twenty-one-minute "comic and unreal" *Film,* directed by Alan Schneider, where the close-up on a woman's "sssh!" as her finger crosses her lips simultaneously repudiates and intensifies the palpable sound of this black-and-white movie's otherwise silent soundtrack.[32] With the playwright's move to television, the drama in the machine stylizes technology one step further, offering the viewer uninterrupted access to the details of its own heady composition. In plays like *Ghost Trio, . . . but the clouds . . .*, and *Nacht und Träume*, Beckett finds a new vocabulary for silence, one primarily designed to suspend the moment for the digitally oriented. Structuring silence and letting it play in black and white and "shades of the colour grey,"[33] Beckett fictionalizes its enterprise and makes us wonder what happens to it as it crosses electronic borders. Recorded music fills in the gaps, surrounding and shaping words but also lending silence body, texture, and, above all, volume. Silence never "acted" quite like this before, Schubert and Beethoven notwithstanding. In *. . . but the clouds . . .* Beckett even makes us hear in silence as the transparency of a woman's face is deftly edited into the frame; when she lingers there in close-up soft focus, she mouths but does not speak the haunting closing lines of Yeats's "The Tower," which we (and then the male voice-over) start to complete for her:

> *W's lips move, uttering inaudibly:* ". . . clouds . . . but the clouds . . . of the sky . . . ," V *murmuring, synchronous with lips:* ". . . but the clouds . . ." *Lips cease. 5 seconds.*[34]

Mallarmé would be pleased; for it was, as he said, only in silence that music might finally achieve its ideal fulfillment.[35]

No one who reads Beckett closely and sympathetically will fail to notice the details of his radiophonic sensibility. His is a full and complete grammar of listening. In his work for the BBC Radio Drama Division with Martin Esslin and Barbara Bray,[36] he ponders the aesthetics of the medium at the same time that he exploits it for practical advantage. In this electronic medium of pure sound, Beckett's vocabulary can become truly bizarre:

> Do you find anything . . . bizarre about my way of speaking? *(Pause.)* I do not mean the voice. *(Pause.)* No, I mean the words. *(Pause. More to herself.)* I use none but the simplest words, I hope, and yet I sometimes find my way of speaking very . . . bizarre. *(Pause.)*[37]

So sounds Maddy Rooney née Donne, the "big pale blur," a formidable woman who must "sound" fat just as her husband Dan must "sound"

blind. She quivers like a "blanc mange" and wonders whether her "cre-
tonne" is so unbecoming that she "merge[s] into the masonry." She is
also the first of Beckett's destabilizers whose speech intrudes upon the
organized presence of radiophonic white noise. On these soundtracks,
silence will be both purposeful and percussive as it shapes into being the
beat and tempo of an imagined world that insists on getting itself heard.
"I open . . . And I close," intones a disembodied voice in the well-
named *Cascando;* and "I have come to listen," says a shadowy character
named She in *Rough for Radio I*.[38] Rather than hold it at bay, each voice
distorts, vitalizes, and animates silence, rendering it whole, giving it
body and texture, making us hear the sound of *sound* as if for the first and
only time—and for the last time, too, before it fades once more into the
void. "Joyce was a synthesizer," Beckett shrewdly observed. "I am an
analyzer."[39]

V.

Beckett's groundbreaking late fiction introduces us to the verbal equivalent of solitude, a mysterious atmosphere everywhere empowered by
the new lines for "recited" silence previously authorized in the dramas
written for the mechanical media where, as he has shown, it knows full
well how to pull the pin from the grenade. Especially in the first two
volumes of a second trilogy comprising *Company, Ill Seen Ill Said,* and
Worstward Ho, "silence" and "stillness" demand to be read aloud, since
much of their emotional resonance lodges in their tonality. In these lyrical works, as in the three-part *Stirrings Still,* the imperatives of silence,
literally crying out loud, seek the sound of a human voice, a "helping
hand,"[40] in order to formalize and elucidate the stubborn stillness of the
universe. Now hear this:

> From where she lies she sees Venus rise. On. From where she lies
> when the skies are clear she sees Venus rise followed by the sun.
> Then she rails at the source of all life. On. At evening when the
> skies are clear she savours its star's revenge. At the other window.
> Rigid upright on her old chair she watches for the radiant one.
> Her old deal spindlebacked kitchen chair. It emerges from out the
> last rays and sinking ever brighter is engulfed in its turn. On. She
> sits on erect and rigid in the deepening gloom. Such helplessness
> to move she cannot help.[41]

VI.

Wordsworth was lucky. When, in book 1 of *The Prelude,* in a celebrated autobiographical passage, the young poet fixes his "view / Upon the summit of a craggy ridge" and sees the mountain looming beyond, to the very "horizon's utmost boundary," he opens his imagination and his canon to the power and the wonder, the mystery and the silence all around him.[42] Beckett's triumph over stillness (if indeed it is one) will be far "less Wordsworthy."[43] But it will be no less vexed, no less tentative, no less suspect, no less "real," no less intuitive and no less seductive. A contemplative for sure, Beckett is, in this respect, like one of his own early bums, something of a "dud mystic," though he is far from being a full-fledged romantic: no "mystique raté," he just wants to find his text's final word.[44] "Got it at last, my legend." And *what is the word?*[45] Let us listen to it again:

. . . .
. . . .
. . . .
. . . .
. . . .
. . . .
. . . .
. . . .
. . . .
. . . .

After Beckett's "Beckett" and his so *many* words for silence, "so many words for silence" will never sound

. . . .

quite the same again.

NOTES

1. Samuel Beckett, *Endgame* (New York: Grove Press, 1958), 32; and *The Unnamable* (New York: Grove Press, 1958), 110.

2. Samuel Beckett, *How It Is* (New York: Grove Press, 1964), 26.

3. Samuel Beckett, *A Piece of Monologue,* in *The Collected Shorter Plays of Samuel Beckett* (New York: Grove Press, 1984), 268.

4. Samuel Beckett, *Footfalls,* in *Collected Shorter Plays,* 240–43.

5. See Richard Begam, *Samuel Beckett and the End of Modernity* (Stanford: Stanford University Press, 1996); and H. Porter Abbott, "Late Modernism: Samuel Beckett and the Art of the Oeuvre," in *Around the Absurd: Essays on Modern and Postmodern Drama,* ed. Enoch Brater and Ruby Cohn (Ann Arbor: University of Michigan Press, 1990),

73–96. See also John Cage, *Silence: Lectures and Writings* (Middletown, Conn.: Wesleyan University Press, 1961).

6. Samuel Beckett, *Krapp's Last Tape,* in *Collected Shorter Plays,* 63.

7. Samuel Beckett, *Play,* in *Collected Shorter Plays,* 156.

8. Samuel Beckett, *Waiting for Godot* (New York: Grove Press, 1954), 8.

9. See John Banville, *The Sea* (London: Picador, 2005), 129.

10. Samuel Beckett, *Murphy* (New York: Grove Press, 1957), 148.

11. Samuel Beckett, *Stories and Texts for Nothing* (New York: Grove Press, 1967), 139.

12. Samuel Beckett, *Watt* (New York: Grove Press, 1959), 247.

13. See Samuel Beckett, *Disjecta: Miscellaneous Writings and a Dramatic Fragment,* ed. Ruby Cohn (London: John Calder, 1983), 51–54, 170–73.

14. Samuel Beckett, *. . .but the clouds . . .,* in *Collected Shorter Plays,* 261; and *Watt,* 147.

15. For the "unsaid" and the "ununsaid," see in particular Samuel Beckett, *Ill Seen Ill Said* (New York: Grove Press, 1981); and *Worstward Ho* (New York: Grove Press, 1983). See also *Watt,* 101.

16. See Daniela Caselli, *Beckett's Dantes: Intertextuality in the Fiction and Criticism* (Manchester: Manchester University Press, 2005).

17. *The Unnamable,* 179.

18. See Enoch Brater, *The Essential Samuel Beckett* (London: Thames and Hudson, 2003), 55.

19. *Watt,* 237. *Molloy, Malone Dies* and *The Unnamable,* read by Barry McGovern, were recorded in their entirety and produced for RTE Radio in 2006 by Tim Lehane at The Base, Dublin.

20. For the numerous adjectives modifying *silence* in the trilogy, see *A KWIC Concordance to Samuel Beckett's Trilogy: "Molloy," "Malone Dies," and "The Unnamable,"* vol. 2, ed. Michèle Aina Barale and Rubin Rabinovitz (New York: Garland, 1988), 830–33.

21. Samuel Beckett, *Molloy* (New York: Grove Press, 1955), 41; and *Ill Seen Ill Said,* for example, 48.

22. *Stories and Texts for Nothing,* 118.

23. Samuel Beckett, *What Where,* in *Collected Shorter Plays,* 316.

24. See Cicely Berry, *The Actor and His Text* (London: Harrap, 1973).

25. *Stories and Texts for Nothing,* 10.

26. *Stories and Texts for Nothing,* 10.

27. *The Unnamable,* 20; *Waiting for Godot,* 55b.

28. See *The Theatrical Notebooks of Samuel Beckett,* vols. 1–4, ed. James Knowlson (London: Faber and Faber, 1993–99). See also Knowlson's *'Happy Days': Samuel Beckett's Production Notebook* (New York: Grove Press, 1985).

29. Samuel Beckett, *Rockaby,* in *Collected Shorter Plays,* 275–80.

30. *. . .but the clouds. . .,* 261.

31. *Stories and Texts for Nothing,* 139.

32. Samuel Beckett, *Film,* in *Collected Shorter Plays,* 163, 165.

33. Samuel Beckett, *Ghost Trio,* in *Collected Shorter Plays,* 248.

34. *. . .but the clouds. . .,* 261.

35. See Enoch Brater, *Beyond Minimalism: Beckett's Late Style in the Theater* (New York: Oxford University Press, 1987), 93.

36. See James Knowlson, *Damned to Fame: The Life of Samuel Beckett* (New York: Simon and Schuster, 1996), 385–87, 421, 442–43; and Martin Esslin, *Mediations: Essays on Brecht, Beckett, and the Media* (Baton Rouge: Louisiana State University Press, 1980), 125–54. See also Bernard Beckerman, "Beckett and the Act of Listening," in *Beckett at*

80/Beckett in Context, ed. Enoch Brater (New York: Oxford University Press, 1986), 149–67.

37. Samuel Beckett, *All That Fall,* in *Collected Shorter Plays,* 13.

38. Samuel Beckett, *Cascando* and *Rough for Radio I,* in *Collected Shorter Plays,* 107, 137.

39. Quoted by Brater, *Beyond Minimalism,* 5.

40. See *Stories and Texts for Nothing,* 55; and *All That Fall,* 23. For a discussion of this point, see Enoch Brater, *The Drama in the Text: Beckett's Late Fiction* (New York: Oxford University Press, 1994).

41. *Ill Seen Ill Said,* 7.

42. William Wordsworth, *The Prelude,* book 1, ll. 369–71; see *English Romantic Writers,* ed. David Perkins (New York: Harcourt, Brace and World, 1967), 217.

43. *Murphy,* 106.

44. A "dud mystic" is the term Belacqua uses to announce the presence of a fictional "Mr. Beckett." He "meant mystique raté, but shrank always from the mot juste." See Samuel Beckett, *Dream of Fair to Middling Women* (Dublin: Black Cat Press, 1992), 186.

45. Samuel Beckett, *Malone Dies* (New York: Grove Press, 1956), 51; and *As the Story Was Told* (London: John Calder, 1990), 131–34.

Ruby Cohn

Beckett's Trinities

Samuel Beckett always spoke with deep affection of Trinity College, his alma mater, even though in 1931 he followed the resolution of Saint Augustine "gently to withdraw the service of [his] tongue from the marts of lip-labour,"[1] which in plain English means that he withdrew from lecturing at Trinity College. For my own lip-labor I want to consider that name, since trinities, triads, trios, and triptychs figure so prominently in Beckett's work. In a review of Jack Yeats's *Amaranthers* Beckett himself wrote somewhat disapprovingly of the "rule of three"[2] wherein two elements always relate to a third. Nonetheless he himself repeated many forms of trinity, only sometimes obeying that rule of three. And in spite of my trinitarian title, my own rule of three will be rather unruly. But it's hardly coincidental that I divide my lip-labor into nine scenes, three threes, culled from my half century of involvement with Samuel Beckett.

Scene 1. *Waiting for Godot* was the occasion of my first encounter with Samuel Beckett. In January 1953, that play existed only as *En attendant Godot.* As a student of comparative literature at the Sorbonne, and an addict of theater everywhere, I lived only a few Paris streets away from the Théâtre de Babylone on the Boulevard Raspail, and I must echo Beckett there—"No symbols where none intended."[3] Passing the theater one winter day, I noticed a poster about the premiere of a new play by "un compagnon de James Joyce, l'irlandais Samuel Beckett." I went to see *En attendant Godot,* and I've never recovered from its grip.

It's a long while since that production, but I can still recall my fascination and at the same time my consternation. I knew I didn't understand the play, whatever understand may mean in the theater. My French was pretty fair, and I thought I grasped the individual *words,* except for sections of Lucky's spastic monologue. Overall I absorbed the short sentences, with their proliferation of interrogatives and negatives, but the whole didn't jell. Of course, I didn't know then, as I know now, that it wasn't supposed to jell. And I couldn't possibly know then as I know now, that you go as a student to a fresh new play, and before you know it half a century speeds by, and you yourself become "like something out of Beckett." Or, in the words of another poet—"Sans teeth, sans eyes, sans taste, sans everything"[4]—well, perhaps not *quite* "sans everything."

In 1953 it never occurred to me to seek out the author of *En attendant Godot*. Although I read no reviews, I did hear vaguely about a radio broadcast of excerpts from *Godot*, undertaken at the initiative of a twenty-year-old producer, Michel Polac. Years later I learned that that young man asked Beckett to write a radio introduction to his strange new play, and the playwright surprisingly obliged. Beckett's radio introduction to *Godot* has surfaced only recently, and I quote from it,[5] for it includes the first of my trinities, which I do intend symbolically—three repetitions of "je ne sais pas"—French for "I don't know." This is a translation of Beckett's introduction:

> I don't know who Godot is. I don't even know if he exists. And I don't know if they believe in him or not—the two who are waiting for him. The other two who pass by toward the end of each of the two acts, that must be to break the monotony. Everything that I knew I showed. It's not much, but it's enough for me, by a wide margin. I'll even say that I would have been satisfied with less. As for wanting to find in all that a broader, loftier meaning to take away after the performance, along with the program and the Eskimo pie, I don't see the point of it. But it must be possible. I'm no longer part of all that and never again will be. Estragon, Vladimir, Pozzo, Lucky, their time and their space, I was able to know them a little, only at a great distance from the need to understand. Maybe they owe you explanations. Let them supply it. Without me. They and I are through with each other.[6]

The concluding sentence was wishful thinking on Beckett's part. Since *Godot* remains Beckett's best-known work, and a part of our culture, he was never to be quite through with it.

Scene 2 shifts to my study in California. Between scenes 1 and 2, I embarked on a doctoral dissertation on Beckett's comic techniques.[7] During my research I made a list of what seemed to me errors in the Grove Press editions of Beckett's novels, but after reading *Watt* I became uncertain that these were printing errors, rather than authorial subversions. I sent Grove Press a list of eight errors in *Watt*, fourteen in *Molloy*, and four in *Malone Dies*. Grove Press consulted Mr. Beckett, who soon replied that four items—alas, not three but four—were intentional, but the others were indeed errors. Only after I made Mr. Beckett's acquaintance did I learn how punctilious he was about reading proof, and perhaps I made Mr. Beckett's acquaintance *because* I had punctiliously noted those printing errors. Still in my study, having received this indirect communication from Beckett, I wrote him care of his French publisher, Les Editions de Minuit: I would be in Paris during summer, 1962, and although I knew he never granted interviews, it would be a privilege to meet him. Some intuition made me promise not to talk about his work, but I nevertheless wondered whether he would reply at all. In what I later learned to recognize as Beckett's company handwriting came an invitation to have dinner together, if I was free. He would be at my hotel at 8:00 p.m. on June 23.

Scene 3. I was unscholarly enough not to save Beckett's invitation, but I remember that my hotel was on the rue Casimir-Delavigne in the Fifth Arrondissement of Paris. At eight o'clock I was waiting for Beckett in the hotel lobby, for there was no telephone in my frugal room. At 8:15 I was still waiting for Beckett. By 8:30 I wondered whether he had had third thoughts about meeting a stranger, for by then I had heard about his shyness. It was nearly nine o'clock when Beckett rushed in. I recognized him at once from his published photographs, and I introduced myself—in English. Also in English he muttered that he had mistakenly driven to rue Casimir-Perrier in the Seventh Arrondissement, instead of rue Casimir-Delavigne in the Fifth. Only later did I learn how prompt he usually was, and how rarely he found himself in the wrong place. From that evening in 1962, which began in anxiety, I date my friendship with Samuel Beckett. Thereafter we met at least once a year including 1989, the year of his death. I think Beckett felt at ease in my company, and I managed to suppress my awe of him. Since we met all too seldom—in my view at least—we kept in touch by writing, Beckett usually complaining to me about rehearsal or translation. He sent me each book as Les Editions de Minuit published it, always inscribed with *three* lines in English: "For Ruby / with love / from Sam." By the 1970s he sometimes sent me photocopies of his final typescripts, and only once he sent me a photocopy of a work in progress, which he subsequently revised radically; it happens to have a three-word title in French, *Pour en finir*. Beckett's English is wordier—*For to end yet again*. Over the years I more or less kept to my promise not to discuss Beckett's work with him, but I learned which questions were permissible. For instance, when I read the phrase "the great Cham" in one of his letters, I asked who that was. Surprised by my ignorance, he explained that it was Dr. Samuel Johnson, who had obsessed him for years.

Scene 4. On April 23, 1966, while I was away from my Paris hotel, I returned to find a package. I recognized Beckett's handwriting on the thick manila envelope, which I took to my room to open. I found three notebooks of notes about Dr. Johnson and his circle. What interested me more than the notes were Beckett's plans for a play about the relationship between Dr. Johnson and Mrs. Thrale. Even after a rapid glance, I knew that such a treasure should not be in my possession. I rushed to a post office to telephone Beckett; in the 1960s he could still be reached by telephone. I protested: "Sam, I shouldn't have this; it should go to a library." Beckett snapped back: "I don't want it in a library. If you don't want it, return it to me." I changed my tune: "I want it, and I'll cherish it." Beckett added: "I'd rather you didn't say anything about it." I did not say anything about it for a few years, but when I was writing *Back to Beckett* in the 1970s, I asked Beckett whether I might mention the Johnson material, and he replied: "Yes, of course, why not?" I don't think I answered that question. Then, in 1980, working on my *third* Beckett book[8] I asked him whether I could publish his Johnson scene, which was entitled "Human Wishes." He consented readily, without even rereading the material, and I subsequently republished it when I edited *Disjecta*.[9] With Beckett's permission, I later brought the Johnson material to the Beckett Archive at the University of Reading.

Since "Human Wishes" does not appear either in the *Complete Dramatic Works* or the *Complete Short Plays*—which are patently incomplete—I'll take just a moment to summarize it. The scene is a sustained trinity in that the speaking characters are three historical members of Dr. Johnson's household—Mrs. Desmoulins, Miss Carmichael, and blind Mrs. Williams. The trio are waiting for Dr. Johnson, and while they wait, they converse—rhythmically, abrasively, and with occasional repetitions. Although Beckett's Johnson research was probably done in the late 1930s, the scene may date from 1940, when Beckett was already living in France, and daily expecting war to explode, with its concomitant suffering and deaths. Of the female trio, however, who resemble an eighteenth-century version of the three fates, only blind Mrs. Williams touches on death. Beckett's fragmentary scene breaks off on a mellifluous quotation from Jeremy Taylor's *The Rule and Exercises of Holy Dying*. I recommend the scene for exercises in wholly acting.

Scene 5 is saturated with trinities. Some time during 1974 Beckett sent me a photocopy of his typescript of *That Time;* he was uncertain as to whether it actually was a play. That typescript is quite close to the published version, with a few notable exceptions. In that play the stage is in darkness, except for a white-haired head high in the air. The face is immobile, except for three gestures—opening the eyes when the words stop, closing the eyes when they start, and finally smiling. Beckett's scenic direction instructs us: "Voices A B C are his own coming to him from both sides and above."[10] Beckett actually wrote the individual A, B, and C voices consecutively, but he then sliced those continuities into thirty-six paragraphs, which are spoken in groups of twelve. Although the story is already present in the photocopy Beckett sent me, replete with phrasal triads, it was not yet orchestrated in the final strict order: ACB in the first part, CBA in the second, and BAC in the third, with some variation in the final triad, but never ABC. The A-voice tells of a search for a childhood haunt, the B-voice describes scenes where love-vows are exchanged, and the C-voice follows the trajectory of a derelict old man. Each strand describes three places: the A-voice moves its protagonist from a ferry to a disaffected railway station to a doorstep; the B-voice situates vows of love of a couple in a wheatfield, on a canal tow-path, and on a sandy beach; the C-voice traces its protagonist's escapes from winter in public buildings—a portrait gallery, a post office, and a library. All three voices address their owner in the second person—you, and all three protagonists sit on stone at some time. All the scenes are re-fracted through memory. In the final thirty-sixth paragraph, dust is named three times, inevitably recalling the verse of Genesis: "From dust thou art, and unto dust shalt thou return." At the end of Beckett's *That Time* an "it" speaks to the ancient C-voice; it may be the dust, saying: "what was it it said come and gone was that it something like that come and gone come and gone no one come and gone in no time gone in no time."[11] That time eventuates in no time, in both senses—immeasurably swift and immeasurably timeless. Isolating triads in this way may make *That Time* sound mechanical, but it is brimful of emotion, and of impatience with that emotion.

Between my photocopy and Beckett's final version, he made some dozen word changes—"shufflers" for "pantofles," for example, or "shades" for "figments"—that enhance the mood of *That Time.* However, in his nineteenth paragraph there was a phrase that seemed to me to spoil the mood. The A-voice is speaking: "not a curse for the old scenes the old names the passers pausing to gape at you like something out of Beckett quick gape then pass on by on the other side."[12] I had the temerity to implore Beckett—by letter—to omit "something out of Beckett." He never spoke to me of my letter, but the published text lacks the coy phrase, and I have no regrets.

My scene 6 also abounds in trinities, although the dominant pattern of *Warten auf Godot* is binary. In February 1975, Beckett invited me to rehearsals of his first attempt to direct his most celebrated play—in German. Not only did I daily watch him in action, but we often walked about Berlin together after rehearsals at the Schiller Theater. To me, who had only school German, Beckett's command of the language seemed impressive, and I asked him: "Is your Italian as good as your German?" "*Much* better," he replied. It's the only time I ever heard him boast.

Before my arrival in Berlin, I read the text of *Godot* in German, and I was quite sure I hadn't read a phrase that I heard in rehearsal near the end of the play. Vladimir asks the boy: "Tragt er einen Bart, Herr Godot?" ("Has he a beard, Mr Godot?")[13] The boy answers in the affirmative, and Vladimir persists: "Blond oder . . . *er zögert* . . . schwarz . . . *er zögert* . . . oder rot?" The "oder rot" (or red) was new. Walking away from the theater later, Beckett asked me merrily: "Did you notice the red beard? To balance the three colors of the whores' hair in Estragon's brothel joke."

Beckett volunteered the information about Godot's beard, so I asked him about a phrase that puzzled me when Pozzo mocks Lucky: "Atlas, son of Jupiter!" "Why did you make Atlas the son of Jupiter?" The reply was another question: "Isn't he the son of Jupiter?" Pedantically, like the academic I was, I informed Beckett that in Greek mythology Atlas and Zeus were cousins who fought on opposite sides in the War of the Titans. When *Warten auf Godot* was next rehearsed, Pozzo accurately designated Atlas as the son of Iapetus, with no loss of scorn for Lucky.

Perhaps the most striking stage trinity of *Warten auf Godot* was Lucky's tirade. Instead of the frantic rant of most productions, the actor Klaus Herm delivered a reasoned harangue, divided into three parts: "Given the existence as uttered forth . . . and considering what is more . . . and considering what is more much more grave."[14] In Beckett's words the first part presented an indifferent heaven, the second focused on dwindling man, and in the third part earth wound down to an abode of stones. Pozzo reacts in three movements to his menial's recitation; he first puts his fingers in his ears, then his coat over his head, and finally his stool over his coat as he sinks helplessly to his knees. In counterpoint to this Pozzo-Lucky act 1 trinity is the Didi-Gogo act 2 farcical trinity, the juggling of three hats.

In each act of *Godot* three light changes bathe the set. Props are also triadic. At the end of act 1 two splayed shoes and a hat form a triangle; in act 2 the tree had three leaves. Vladimir and Estragon examine their respective hat and shoe in three steps: (1) After removal of the object, each of them looks into it and shakes it; (2) after removal, each looks into it, feels around in it, taps it, shakes it, and looks again; (3) after removal, each looks into it, feels around in it, blows air into it, taps it, shakes it, and looks again. In what was already being called Beckett's choreography, he often had the friends move in three steps across the stage. Thus, Estragon undermines Vladimir's faith in their appointment in three insidious steps, Vladimir wakes Estragon in three panicky steps, Estragon makes up with Vladimir in three conciliatory steps, Vladimir and Estragon approach Lucky in three curious steps. In act 2 each man falls to the ground in three stylized movements. Such triads are quickly summarized, but it was lovely to watch them being introduced and gradually mastered in rehearsal.

My scene 7 has the same setting—Berlin in February 1975, but I will cite trinities of other Beckett works, even while *Warten auf Godot* was in rehearsal. In spite of the weather, I did a good deal of walking with Beckett, and every once in a while he would stop and listen; in a museum he called my attention to footsteps. He did not tell me he was creating *Footfalls,* a short play intended for the English actress Billie Whitelaw, which he would complete later that year. However, I mention it here because I was unknowingly present at its birth in Beckett's ear, and because its trinities are so different from those of *That Time,* or indeed of *Godot. Footfalls* is divided into four scenes, but human agents are present in only three.

In those three human scenes a woman paces nine steps back and forth on a strip of board. In the first scene that woman, M in the text, tries to alleviate the suffering of her invisible but audible mother. In the second scene the invisible mother flashes back to an account of her daughter May's pacing back and forth. In the third scene M tells three disjunctive stories; the first two are titled "Sequel" and "Semblance." M's third and longest narrative is untitled. In *Footfalls* three mother-daughter scenes both progress and repeat. On the one hand, they move from an actual dialogue about the mother's suffering, to a mother's monologue in a biographical flashback, to a daughter's monologue that seeks to fictionalize "how it was." On the other hand, all three scenes repeat how it is when mothers and daughters are interlocked in suffering. Implicit is the realization that mothers give birth to daughters who give birth to daughters, who give birth to human beings who begin to die as soon as they are born. Moreover, there is a fourth scene in *Footfalls,* where the wooden strip is empty. In performance that bare strip is haunted by the ghost of the visible faint tangle of pale gray tatters who is said to walk on the transept of a locked church and who is said to utter an amen to a prayer, even when she is absent from Vespers. Although we see only one woman in *Footfalls,* and hear only two women, a ghostly female trinity is hinted through absences.

Still in my scene 7 I happened on another Beckett work in progress in Berlin. On his desk I saw sheets of music and teased him about wanting to be a composer. He smiled enigmatically: "Beautiful, Beethoven's *Ghost Trio.*" Beckett did not tell me that he was enfolding that music into a television play. The title of Beckett's *Ghost Trio* was changed at the last moment from *Tryst,* thus emphasizing the triadic nature of the piece, but the instruments are less obvious than those of Beethoven. The playwright's adoption of the unofficial title of Beethoven's Piano Trio no. 5 in D minor seems to me to designate three elements—Beethoven's Largo, a woman's voice, and a camera eye.

Beckett's *Ghost Trio* is divided into three parts—"Pre-action," "Action," and "Re-action." Those are Beckett's titles in print, but they are not heard on television. In the "Pre-action" a woman's voice presents her own voice and "the [so-called] familiar chamber"[15] to the television viewer—window, door, wall, floor, and pallet-bed in spartan surroundings. However, the chamber is not familiar in itself, but a composite of the almost bare chambers in some of Beckett's works; one might term that room "something out of Beckett." At the voice's bidding, the camera closes in on three rectangle-specimens of the elements mentioned, and this enables Beckett to reduce the room's contents in a kind of cubism that might be called rectanglism. The woman's voice does not mention three other rectangles that we see—a mirror, a stool, and a cassette. Finally, the voice announces: "Sole sign of life a seated figure" (409), but the figure shows no sign of life, bent as he is, motionless over his cassette. His signs of life begin in the part 2 "Action" when the female voice announces: "He will now think he hears her" (410). The figure lifts his head from his seated position; then he goes first to the door and then to the window, to look out, but no one is there. When the voice reiterates: "Now to door," he returns to his stool, and bends again over his cassette. Attentive again to the voice's instructions, he returns to the door. Again no one is there. Back on his stool, he listens to the music, which stops on the order of the female voice. Its last command is "Repeat," but so little is this obeyed that the voice is not heard again in Beckett's *Ghost Trio*.

Part 3 is titled "Re-action," and Beckett hyphenates the word, I think to emphasize its meaning as both repetition and opposition. In part 1 the camera moved, but the man was immobile; in part 2 the man moved, but the camera was virtually immobile. In part 3 they both move, and the woman's voice is absent, but Beckett's piece remains a trio because her voice is replaced by bruitage. Now when the man opens and closes the door and the window, they creak. The open window admits the sound of rain outside. When the man returns to his cassette, he and we hear footsteps, then a knock on the door. The man opens the door to reveal a small boy "*in black oilskin with hood glistening with rain*" (413). Like Mr. Godot's Boy, this one delivers a negative message, but he does so without words. He shakes his head twice; then he turns and goes into darkness, and we hear his receding steps. The man returns to his cassette and listens to the end of Beethoven's Largo, whereupon he reveals his face to us, and the camera backs off to a fadeout.

After I saw *Ghost Trio* on television in 1977, I reminded Beckett that I had been present at its birth, when I discovered him studying the Beethoven score. However, he told me that the initial inspiration had come not from Beethoven, but from the notion of a calm image that would reveal an inner storm as the camera moved closer. "But the figure resisted me," Beckett mused, "and he remained outwardly calm throughout. So I resorted to rectangles." That "so" sounds like a non sequitur, but I think I've come to understand it. As the many repetitions of "that time" pulverized time in *That Time,* I think the several rectangles of *Ghost Trio* pulverize boundaries and objects of space, while retaining a pattern for the viewer of the teleplay. What strikes me in retrospect is how often Beckett used trinities during his seventieth year: introducing them into the performance of the German *Godot* over and beyond the text, creating two stage plays predicated on that structure— *That Time* and *Footfalls,* and enfolding three instruments of sorts into the teleplays *Ghost Trio* and . . . *but the clouds*. . . .

Scene 8. Through Beckett I met famous theater people like Alan Schneider and Billie Whitelaw; and less famous people who were scholars like myself. One of these, James Acheson of Christchurch College in New Zealand, complained to me that it was impossible, far from large libraries, to read Beckett's early critical journalism, and he requested that

I request Beckett to permit their republication. He even supplied me with much of the list of what later was included in *Disjecta*. Knowing how Beckett disliked his early work, I photocopied the material and brought it with me, when making my request of him, face to face in 1982. Beckett somewhat reluctantly agreed to peruse the material and give me his reaction in a few days time, when we would meet at La Coupole at 7:00 p.m. What followed was a near-repetition of my scene 3, our very first meeting. Seven o'clock came and no Beckett; seven-thirty and no Beckett; eight o'clock and no Beckett. By this time I knew how prompt he was, so I guessed that he was so dismayed at his early writing that he never wanted to see it or me again. Moreover, after the Nobel Prize in 1969 it was impossible to telephone Beckett. At nine o'clock I despondently returned to my Paris hotel. It was just short of midnight when the telephone rang with an apologetic Beckett: "I don't know what happened, Ruby, but I fell asleep and woke up only now. Can we meet tomorrow at 11:00 a.m.?" Embarrassed at the missed appointment, Beckett arrived promptly the next morning, laden with gifts, including permission to publish the as yet unnamed *Disjecta*. However, my original table of contents contained four parts: (1) "Essays at Esthetics"; (2) "Words about Writers"; (3) "Words about Painters"; and (4) "Previously Published Interviews." Beckett disallowed the interviews, so I can point to the remaining three parts as the last trinity in this essay. It was Beckett who later titled the collection *Disjecta,* from Horace's *disjecti membra poetae*—scattered remains of a poet.

Despite my title, my scene 9 will lack a trinity. This would seem to be the point to try to make the various trinities cohere, but I will refrain from doing so. I think there has been too much drive to discover Beckett's fundamental coherence, including at times his own. What I cherish in Beckett's work are so many unique and uniquely moving fragments, with his signature on each one. I've tried to touch on his ternary rhythms in staging, his triptychs in writing, his triplication of phrases, his instrumental trios, his character trios, his triple props, lighting effects, gestures; his triadic phases of memory. You can probably add other trinities—his trilogy of novels, mid- and late in his writing life, his three-character play with a three-word title *Come and Go,* his three-act play *Eleutheria,* his *Three Dialogues with Georges Duthuit,* and so forth.

So I move on to my nontriadic scene 9, which, however, I triangulate between Reading, Paris, and San Francisco. In 1988 Beckett suffered a stroke, and he lived thereafter in a nursing home. He accepted visits from friends and even confessed to me that he had never had so much

Irish whiskey, since each visitor brought him a bottle. Over Irish whiskey he entrusted me with materials to carry to the Beckett Archive, which Jim Knowlson had founded at the University of Reading. With Beckett's permission, I read the material before delivering it—various drafts of a poem finally entitled "Comment dire"—how to say. That title might summarize Beckett's whole canon, a quest *comment dire*. As often with Beckett, he began the work in a concrete situation—that of paralysis after his stroke, and then the slow, strenuous reacquisition of speech.

"Comment dire" still seems to me the most moving lyric Beckett has written. From the moment I read it, I connected that staccato poem with the actor-director Joe Chaikin (1935–2003). At the age of five Joe had rheumatic fever, and his heart so misbehaved thereafter that death seemed imminent several times. But Joe fooled his heart by his fierce determination to live, and to live creatively. In 1985, after Joe's third open heart surgery, he suffered a stroke that left him aphasic. I thought that "Comment dire" would have a special significance for Joe, but he knew no French. So, visiting Beckett early in 1989, I asked whether he would translate it for Joe, whom he had met and liked. Beckett could not remember the poem. I laughed and said that it was fortunately in the Beckett Archive at Reading, and not a fantasy on my part. "Well," said Beckett dubiously, "send it to me, and I'll see." I mailed Beckett a copy of "Comment dire"—on St. Patrick's Day, as it happens. In April 1989, Joe Chaikin in New York City and I in San Francisco simultaneously received copies of "What is the Word." Who but Beckett would translate "Comment dire" as "What is the word?" My copy was accompanied by one of Beckett's white cards: "Here it is done in the eye into English (?) Have sent a copy to Joe. Hope he can use it. Love, Sam."

I'll conclude with the last words of Beckett's last creation:

folly for to need to seem to glimpse afaint afar away over there
what—
what—
what is the word—

what is the word

NOTES

1. *The Confessions of St. Augustine,* book 9 (New York: Airmont, 1969), 145.
2. Samuel Beckett, *Disjecta: Miscellaneous Writings and a Dramatic Fragment,* ed. Ruby Cohn (London: Calder, 1983), 90.

3. Samuel Beckett, *Watt* (London: Calder, 1976), 255.

4. Last line of Jacques's ages-of-man speech, Shakespeare, *As You Like It*.

5. Published in French with English translation in Angela Moorjani, "*En Attendant Godot* on Michel Polac's Entrée des auteurs," in Marius Buning, Danielle de Ruyter, Matthijs Engelberts and Sjef Houppermans, eds., *Samuel Beckett Today/Aujourd'hui* 7 (1998): 47–56.

6. Moorjani, "Polac's Entrée des auteurs," 54.

7. Published as *Samuel Beckett: The Comic Gamut* (New Brunswick, N.J.: Rutgers University Press, 1962).

8. Ruby Cohn, *Just Play: Beckett's Theater* (Princeton: Princeton University Press, 1980).

9. Beckett, *Disjecta*.

10. Samuel Beckett, *The Complete Dramatic Works* (London: Faber and Faber, 1990), 388.

11. Beckett, *Complete Dramatic Works,* 395.

12. Beckett, *Complete Dramatic Works,* 392.

13. Beckett, *Complete Dramatic Works,* 85.

14. Beckett, *Complete Dramatic Works,* 42–43.

15. Beckett, *Complete Dramatic Works,* 408.

Select Bibliography

Abbott, H. Porter. "Late Modernism: Samuel Beckett and the Art of the Oeuvre." In *Around the Absurd: Essays on Modern and Postmodern Drama,* ed. Enoch Brater and Ruby Cohn. Ann Arbor: University of Michigan Press, 1990.

Adams, Stephen L., and George Mills Harper. "The Manuscript of Leo Africanus." *Yeats Annual* 1 (1982): 3–47.

Adorno, Theodor W. *Gesammelte Schriften.* Frankfurt am Main: Suhrkamp, 1974.

Adorno, Theodor W. "Towards an Understanding of *Endgame.*" In *Twentieth Century Interpretations of Endgame,* ed. Bell Gale Chevigny. Englewood Cliffs, N.J.: Prentice Hall, 1969.

Adorno, Theodor W. "Trying to Understand *Endgame.*" *New German Critique* 26 (1982):119–50.

Alighieri, Dante. *The Divine Comedy.* 3 vols. Trans. and ed. John D. Sinclair. London: Bodley Head, 1958.

Althusser, Louis. *For Marx.* Trans. Ben Brewster. London: Verso/NLB, 1982.

Anzieu, Didieu. "Beckett and Bion." *International Journal of Psycho-Analysis* 16 (1989): 193–99.

Atik, Anne. *How It Is: A Memoir of Samuel Beckett.* London: Faber and Faber, 2001.

Atwell, John E. "Art as Liberation: A Central Theme of Schopenhauer's Philosophy." In *Schopenhauer, Philosophy, and the Arts,* ed. Dale Jacquette. Cambridge: Cambridge University Press, 1996.

Augustine. *The Confessions of St Augustine.* New York: Airmont, 1969.

Bair, Deirdre. *Samuel Beckett: A Biography.* New York: Harcourt Brace, 1978.

Banville, John. *The Sea.* London: Picador, 2005.

Barale, Michèle Aina, and Rubin Rabinovitz, eds. *A KWIC Concordance to Samuel Beckett's Trilogy: "Molloy," "Malone Dies," and "The Unnamable."* Vol. 2. New York: Garland, 1988.

Barker, Francis. *The Tremulous Private Body.* London: Methuen, 1984, 1995.

Barker, Howard. *Arguments for a Theatre.* Manchester: Manchester University Press, 1997.

Bate, W. Jackson. *Samuel Johnson.* New York: Harcourt Brace, 1977.

Baudelaire, Charles. "Morale du joujou." In *Oeuvres complètes,* ed. Marcel A. Ruff. Paris: Éditions du Seuil, 1968.

Baudrillard, Jean. *Simulations.* Trans. Paul Foss, Paul Patton, and Philip Betichman. New York: Semiotext[e], 1983.

Beckerman, Bernard. "Beckett and the Act of Listening." In *Beckett at 80/Beckett in Context,* ed. Enoch Brater. New York: Oxford University Press, 1986.

Beckett, Samuel. *As the Story Was Told.* London: Calder, 1990.

Beckett, Samuel. *Cascando and Other Short Dramatic Pieces.* New York: Grove Press, 1968.

Beckett, Samuel. *Collected Poems, 1930–1978.* London: Calder, 1984.

Beckett, Samuel. *The Collected Shorter Plays.* New York: Grove Weidenfeld, 1984.

Beckett, Samuel. *Company.* New York: Grove Press, 1980.

Beckett, Samuel. *The Complete Dramatic Works.* London: Faber and Faber, 1990.

Beckett, Samuel. *Complete Short Prose, 1929–1989.* Ed. S. E. Gontarski. New York: Grove Press, 1995.

Beckett, Samuel. "Dante . . . Bruno. Vico. . Joyce." In *Our Exagmination Round His Factification for Incamination of Work in Progress.* London: Faber and Faber, 1972.

Beckett, Samuel. *Disjecta: Miscellaneous Writings and a Dramatic Fragment.* Ed. Ruby Cohn. London: Calder, 1983.

Beckett, Samuel. *Dream of Fair to Middling Women.* Ed. Eoin O'Brien and Edith Fournier. New York: Arcade; Dublin: Black Cat Press, 1992.

Beckett, Samuel. *En attendant Godot.* Ed. Colin Duckworth. London: Harrap, 1984.

Beckett, Samuel. *Endgame.* New York: Grove Press; London: Faber and Faber, 1958.

Beckett, Samuel. *Film: Complete Scenario, Illustrations, Production Shots, with an Essay "On Directing 'Film'"* by Alan Schneider. London: Faber and Faber, 1972.

Beckett, Samuel. *Fin de Partie.* Paris: Les Éditions de Minuit, 1961.

Beckett, Samuel. *First Love and Other Shorts.* New York: Grove Press, 1974.

Beckett, Samuel. *Happy Days.* London: Faber and Faber, 1976.

Beckett, Samuel. *"Happy Days": Samuel Beckett's Production Notebook.* Ed. James Knowlson. New York: Grove Press, 1985.

Beckett, Samuel. *How It Is.* New York: Grove Press, 1964.

Beckett, Samuel. "Human Wishes." In *Just Play: Beckett's Theater.* Ed. Ruby Cohn. Princeton: Princeton University Press, 1980.

Beckett, Samuel. *Ill Seen Ill Said.* New York: Grove Press, 1981.

Beckett, Samuel. *Ill Seen Ill Said.* In *Nohow On: Three Novels.* New York: Grove Press, 1996.

Beckett, Samuel. *Krapp's Last Tape: Theatre Workbook 1.* Ed. James Knowlson. London: Brutus Books, 1980.

Beckett, Samuel. "Letter to Axel Kaun." In *Disjecta: Miscellaneous Writings and a Dramatic Fragment.* Ed. Ruby Cohn. London: Calder, 1983.

Beckett, Samuel. *Malone Dies.* New York: Grove Press, 1956; Harmondsworth: Penguin, 1965.

Beckett, Samuel. *Molloy.* New York: Grove Press, 1955.

Beckett, Samuel. *More Pricks Than Kicks.* New York: Grove Press, 1972.

Beckett, Samuel. *Murphy.* New York: Grove Press, 1957.

Beckett, Samuel. *Poems, 1930–1989.* London: Calder, 1978.

Beckett, Samuel. *Poems in English.* London: Calder, 1961.

Beckett, Samuel. *Proust.* New York: Grove Press, 1931, 1957.

Beckett, Samuel. *Proust and Three Dialogues with Georges Duthuit.* London: Calder, 1965.

Beckett, Samuel. *Stories and Texts for Nothing.* New York: Grove Press, 1967.

Beckett, Samuel. *Texts for Nothing.* London: Calder and Boyars, 1974.

Beckett, Samuel. *The Theatrical Notebooks of Samuel Beckett.* Vol. 1, *Waiting for Godot.* Ed. Dougald McMillan and James Knowlson. New York: Grove Press, 1994. Vol. 2, *Endgame.* Ed. S. E. Gontarski. London: Faber and Faber; New York: Grove Press, 1993. Vol. 3, *Krapp's Last Tape.* Ed. James Knowlson. London: Faber and Faber; New

York: Grove Press, 1992. Vol. 4, *The Shorter Plays*. Ed. S. E. Gontarski. London: Faber and Faber; New York: Grove Press, 1999.

Beckett, Samuel. "Three Dialogues." In *Samuel Beckett: A Collection of Critical Essays*, ed. Martin Esslin. Englewood Cliffs, N.J.: Prentice-Hall, 1965.

Beckett, Samuel. *Three Novels: Molloy/Malone Dies/The Unnamable*. New York: Grove Press, 1977.

Beckett, Samuel. *The Unnamable*. New York: Grove Press, 1958.

Beckett, Samuel. *Waiting for Godot*. New York: Grove Press, 1954; London: Faber and Faber, 1956.

Beckett, Samuel. *Watt*. New York: Grove Press, 1959; London: Calder, 1976.

Beckett, Samuel. *Worstward Ho*. London: Calder, 1983.

Begam, Richard. *Samuel Beckett and the End of Modernity*. Stanford: Stanford University Press, 1996.

Benjamin, Walter. "Theses on the Philosophy of History." In *Illuminations*, ed. Hannah Arendt, trans. Harry Zohn. New York: Harcourt, Brace and World, 1955.

Benjamin, Walter. *Versuche über Brecht*. Frankfurt am Main: Suhrkamp, 1981.

Ben-Zvi, Linda. "Fritz Mauthner for *Company*." *Journal of Beckett Studies* 9 (1984): 65–88.

Ben-Zvi, Linda. *Samuel Beckett*. Boston: Twayne, 1986.

Ben-Zvi, Linda. "Samuel Beckett, Fritz Mauthner, and the Limits of Language." *PMLA* 95 (1980): 183–200.

Berkeley, George. *Philosophical Commentaries*. London: Nelson, 1944.

Berkeley, George. *The Works of George Berkeley DD*. Ed. Alexander Campbell Fraser. Oxford: Oxford University Press, 1871.

Berman, David. "The Irish Counter-Enlightenment." In *The Irish Mind: Exploring Intellectual Traditions*, ed. Richard Kearney. Dublin: Wolfhound Press, 1985.

Berry, Cicely. *The Actor and His Text*. London: Harrap, 1973.

Blanchot, Maurice. *The Space of Literature*. Trans. Ann Smock. Lincoln: University of Nebraska Press, 1982.

Blau, Herbert. *Sails of the Herring Fleet: Essays on Beckett*. Ann Arbor: University of Michigan Press, 2000.

Boswell, James. *Boswell's Life of Johnson*. 4 vols. Ed. G. B. Hill, rev. L. F. Powell. London: Oxford University Press, 1934.

Brater, Enoch. *Beyond Minimalism: Beckett's Late Style in the Theater*. New York: Oxford University Press, 1987.

Brater, Enoch. *The Drama in the Text: Beckett's Late Fiction*. New York: Oxford University Press, 1994.

Brater, Enoch. *The Essential Samuel Beckett*. London: Thames and Hudson, 2003.

Brater, Enoch. "The 'I' in Beckett's *Not I*." *Twentieth Century Literature* 20 (1974): 189–200.

Brater, Enoch. *Why Beckett*. London: Thames and Hudson, 1989.

Brecht, Bertolt. *Brecht on Theater: The Development of an Aesthetic*. Ed. and trans. John Willett. New York: Hill and Wang, 1964.

Brecht, Bertolt. *Collected Plays*. Ed. Ralph Manheim and John Willett. Vols. 1–2. London: Methuen, 1970, 1979.

Brecht, Bertolt. *Collected Poems*. London: Methuen, 1976.

Brecht, Bertolt. *The Good Person of Szechwan*. In *Collected Plays*, vol. 6, ed. Ralph Manheim and John Willett. New York: Vintage, 1976.

Brecht, Bertolt. *Diaries, 1920–1922*. London: Methuen, 1979.

Brecht, Bertolt. *The Measures Taken.* In *The Jewish Wife and Other Short Plays,* trans. Eric Bentley. New York: Grove Press, 1965.

Brecht, Bertolt. *Über die bildenden Künste.* Ed. J. Hermand. Frankfurt am Main: Suhrkamp, 1983.

Brecht, Bertolt. *Werke, Große kommentierte Berliner und Frankfurter Ausgabe.* Berlin: Aufbau-Verlag; Frankfurt am Main: Suhrkamp, 1988–.

Burke, Edmund. *A Philosophical Inquiry into the Origin of Our Ideas of the Sublime and the Beautiful* (1757). Ed. James T. Boulton. London: Routledge and Kegan Paul, 1958.

Butler, Judith. *Bodies That Matter: On the Discursive Limits of "Sex."* New York: Routledge, 1993.

Cage, John. *Silence: Lectures and Writings.* Middletown, Conn.: Wesleyan University Press, 1961.

Calder, John, ed. *Beckett at 60: A Festschrift.* London: Calder and Boyers, 1967.

Calder, John. "Editorial and Theater Diary." *Gambit: International Theater Review* 7 (1976): 3–10.

Carlson, Marvin. *The Haunted Stage: The Theatre as Memory Machine.* Ann Arbor: University of Michigan Press, 2001.

Case, Sue-Ellen. "Brecht and Women: Homosexuality and the Mother." *Brecht Yearbook* 12 (1983): 65–74.

Caselli, Daniela. *Beckett's Dantes: Intertextuality in the Fiction and Criticism.* Manchester: Manchester University Press, 2005.

Chabert, Pierre. "The Body in Beckett's Theatre." *Journal of Beckett Studies* 8 (1982): 23–28.

Cohn, Ruby. *A Beckett Canon.* Ann Arbor: University of Michigan Press, 2001.

Cohn, Ruby. *Just Play: Beckett's Theater.* Princeton: Princeton University Press, 1980.

Cohn, Ruby. *Samuel Beckett: The Comic Gamut.* New Brunswick, N.J.: Rutgers University Press, 1962.

Connor, Steven. "Over Samuel Beckett's Dead Body." In *Beckett in Dublin,* ed. S. E. Wilmer. Dublin: Lilliput Press, 1992.

Connor, Steven. *Samuel Beckett: Repetition, Theory, and Text.* Oxford: Blackwell, 1988.

Cronin, Anthony. *Samuel Beckett: The Last Modernist.* London: Flamingo, 1997.

Cunningham, Conor. *Genealogy of Nihilism.* London: Routledge, 2002.

Debord, Guy. *Society of the Spectacle.* Detroit: Red and Black, 1983.

Derrida, Jacques. *Writing and Difference.* Trans. Alan Bass. Chicago: University of Chicago Press, 1978.

Descartes, René. *Discourse on Method, and Meditations.* Ed. F. E. Sutcliffe. Harmondsworth, Middlesex: Penguin, 1968.

Dieckmann, Friedrich. "Brechts Utopia." In *Brecht 88. Anregungen zum Dialog über die Vernunft am Jahrtausendende,* ed. Wolfgang Heise. Berlin: Henschelverlag Kunst und Gesellschaft, 1987.

Duckworth, Colin. "Beckett's New *Godot.*" In *Beckett's Later Fiction and Drama,* ed. James Acheson and Kateryna Arthur. Basingstoke: Macmillan, 1987.

Eagleton, Terry. *Crazy John and the Bishop and Other Essays on Irish Culture.* Cork: Cork University Press in association with Field Day, 1998.

Eagleton, Terry. *Heathcliff and the Great Hunger: Studies in Irish Culture.* London: Verso, 1996.

Eagleton, Terry. *Holy Terror.* Oxford: Oxford University Press, 2005.

Eagleton, Terry. *The Meaning of Life.* Oxford: Oxford University Press, 2007.

Edwards, Michael. "Beckett's French." *Translation and Literature* 1 (1992): 68–83.

Esslin, Martin. *Mediations: Essays on Brecht, Beckett, and the Media.* Baton Rouge: Louisiana State University Press, 1980.

Fehsenfeld, Martha. "Beckett's Reshaping of *What Where* for Television." *Modern Drama* 29 (1986): 229–40.

Flynn, Carol Houlihan. *The Body in Swift and Defoe.* Cambridge: Cambridge University Press, 1990.

Foster, Cheryl. "Ideas and Imagination: Schopenhauer on the Proper Formulation of Art." In *The Cambridge Companion to Schopenhauer,* ed. Christopher Janaway. Cambridge: Cambridge University Press, 1999.

Foucault, Michel. *The Order of Things: An Archaeology of the Human Sciences.* New York: Vintage, 1973.

Garrett, Eileen J. *Many Voices: The Autobiography of a Medium.* New York: G. P. Putnam's Sons, 1968.

Gaskell, Philip. *From Writer to Reader: Studies in Editorial Method.* Oxford: Oxford University Press, 1978.

Gersch, Wolfgang. *Film bei Brecht.* Berlin: Henschelverlag, 1975.

Goehr, Lydia. "Schopenhauer and the Musicians." In *Schopenhauer, Philosophy, and the Arts,* ed. Dale Jacquette. Cambridge: Cambridge University Press, 1996.

Gontarski, S. E. "Blin on Beckett." In *On Beckett: Essays and Criticism,* ed. S. E. Gontarski. New York: Grove Press, 1986.

Gontarski, S. E. *The Intent of Undoing in Samuel Beckett's Dramatic Texts.* Bloomington: Indiana University Press, 1985.

Gontarski, S. E. "Texts and Pre-texts in Samuel Beckett's *Footfalls.*" *Papers of the Bibliographical Society of America* 77 (1983): 191–95.

Gontarski, S. E. "What Where II: Revision as Re-creation." *Review of Contemporary Fiction* 7 (1987):120–23.

Grimm, Reinhold. *Brecht und Nietzsche oder Geständnisse eines Dichters.* Frankfurt am Main: Suhrkamp, 1979.

Grimm, Reinhold. "Der katholische Einstein: Brechts Dramen- und Theatertheorie." In *Brechts Dramen, Neue Interpretationen,* ed. Walter Hinderer. Stuttgart: Reclam, 1984.

Harmon, Maurice, ed. *No Author Better Served: The Correspondence of Samuel Beckett and Alan Schneider.* Cambridge: Harvard University Press, 1998.

Harper, George Mills. *Yeats's Vision Papers.* Vol 1. Ed. Stephen L. Adams, Barbara Frieling, and Sandra L. Sprayberry. London: Macmillan, 1992.

Harper, George Mills, and John S. Kelly. "Preliminary Examination of the Script of E[lizabeth] R[adcliffe]." In *Yeats and the Occult,* ed. George Mills Harper. London: Macmillan 1975.

Harrington, John P. *The Irish Beckett.* Syracuse: Syracuse University Press, 1991.

Haug, W. F. *Philosophieren mit Brecht und Gramsci.* Berlin: Argument Verlag,1996.

Hecht, Werner. *Aufsätze über Brecht.* Berlin: Henschelverlag, 1970.

Hecht, Werner. *Brecht Chronik 1898–1956.* Frankfurt am Main: Suhrkamp, 1997.

Heise, Wolfgang, ed. *Brecht 88. Anregungen zum Dialog über die Vernunft am Jahrtausendende.* Berlin: Henschelverlag Kunst und Gesellschaft, 1987.

Hendry, Michael. "Improving the Alliteration: Ovid, *Metamorphoses* 6.376." *Mnemosyne* 49 (1996): 443–45.

Hérail, René James, and Edwin A. Lovatt. *Dictionary of Modern Colloquial French.* London: Routledge, 1987.

Hill, Leslie. *Beckett's Fiction: In Different Words.* Cambridge: Cambridge University Press, 1990.

Hinderer, Walter, ed. *Brechts Dramen, Neue Interpretationen.* Stuttgart: Reclam, 1984.

Jacobus, Mary. *The Poetics of Psychoanalysis: In the Wake of Melanie Klein.* Oxford: Oxford University Press, 2005.

Jameson, Frederic. *Brecht and Method.* London: Verso, 1998.

Janaway, Christopher, ed. *The Cambridge Companion to Schopenhauer.* Cambridge: Cambridge University Press, 1999.

Jacquette, Dale, ed. *Schopenhauer, Philosophy, and the Arts.* Cambridge: Cambridge University Press, 1996.

Johnson, Samuel. *Rasselas.* In *Eighteenth-Century English Literature,* ed. Geoffrey Tillotson et al. New York: Harcourt, Brace, 1969.

Junker, Mary. *Beckett: The Irish Dimension.* Dublin: Wolfhound Press, 1995.

Kalb, Jonathan. *Beckett in Performance.* Cambridge: Cambridge University Press, 1989.

Kearney, Richard, ed. *The Irish Mind: Exploring Intellectual Traditions.* Dublin: Wolfhound Press, 1985.

Kelly, Veronica, and Dorothea von Müke. *Body and Text in the Eighteenth Century.* Stanford: Stanford University Press, 1994.

King, William. *Sermon on Predestination* (1709). Ed. Andrew Carpenter. Dublin: Cadenus Press, 1976.

Knowlson, James. *Damned to Fame: The Life of Samuel Beckett.* London: Bloomsbury; New York: Simon and Schuster, 1996.

Knowlson, James. *Images of Beckett.* Cambridge: Cambridge University Press, 2003.

Knowlson, James, and Elizabeth Knowlson, eds. *Beckett Remembering, Remembering Beckett: Uncollected Interviews with Samuel Beckett and Memories of Those Who Knew Him.* London: Bloomsbury, 2006.

Koopmann, Helmut, and Theo Stammen, eds. *Bertolt Brecht—Aspekte seines Werkes, Spuren seiner Wirkung.* Munich: Ernst Vögel Verlag, 1983.

Krull, Edith. *Herbert Ihering.* Berlin: Henschelverlag, 1964.

Lake, Carlton, ed. *No Symbols Where None Intended: A Catalogue of Books, Manuscripts, and Other Material Relating to Samuel Beckett in the Collections of the Humanities Research Center.* Austin, Texas: Humanities Research Center, 1984.

Löwe, N. F. "Sam's Love for Sam: Samuel Beckett, Dr. Johnson and 'Human Wishes.'" *Samuel Beckett Today/Aujourd'hui* 8 (1999): 189–203.

Maddox, Brenda. *George's Ghosts: A New Life of W. B. Yeats.* London: Picador, 1999.

Mallarmé, Stéphane. *Correspondance.* Vol. 2. Ed. Henri Mondor and L. J. Austin. Paris: Gallimard, 1965.

Mallarmé, Stéphane. *Oeuvres complètes.* Ed. Bertrand Marchal. Paris: Gallimard, 2003.

Mallarmé, Stéphane. *Recueil de "Nursery Rhymes."* Ed. C. P. Barbier. Paris: Gallimard, 1964.

Mangan, James Clarence. *The Prose Writings of Jámes Clarence Mangan.* Ed. D. J. O'Donoghue. Dublin: O'Donoghue; London: A. H. Bullen, 1904.

Mason, Jeffrey, ed. *The Complete Letters of Sigmund Freud to Wilhelm Fließ, 1887–1904.* Cambridge: Harvard University Press, 1985.

Mauthner, Fritz. *Beiträge zu einer Kritik der Sprache.* 3rd ed. 3 vols. Hildesheim: Georg Olms Verlag, 1967.

Mayer, Hans. "Beckett und Brecht. Erfahrungen und Erinnerungen. Ein Vortrag." Berliner Ensemble, Drucksache 15, 1995.

Mayers, David. "Bion and Beckett Together." *British Journal of Psychotherapy* 17 (2000): 192–202.

Mays, J. C. C. "Irish Beckett, a Borderline Instance." In *Beckett in Dublin,* ed. S. E. Wilmer. Dublin: Lilliput Press, 1992.

McGann, Jerome J., ed. *Textual Criticism and Literary Interpretation.* Chicago: University of Chicago Press, 1985.

McMillan, Dougald, and Martha Fehsenfeld. *Beckett in the Theatre: The Author as Practical Playwright and Director.* London: Calder, 1990.

McMullan, Anna. *Theatre on Trial: Samuel Beckett's Later Drama.* London: Routledge, 1993.

McMullan, Anna. "Virtual Subjects: Performance, Technology and the Body in Beckett's Late Theatre." *Journal of Beckett Studies* 10 (2002): 165–72.

Mercier, Vivian. *Beckett/Beckett.* New York: Oxford University Press, 1977.

Millan, Gordon. *Mallarmé: A Throw of the Dice: The Life of Stéphane Mallarmé.* London: Secker and Warburg, 1994.

Mitchell, Breon. "Art in Microcosm: The Manuscript Stages of Beckett's *Come and Go.*" *Modern Drama* 19 (1976): 245–60.

Moorjani, Angela. "*En Attendant Godot* on Michel Polac's Entrée des auteurs." *Samuel Beckett Today/Aujourd'hui* 7 (1998), 47–56.

Müller, Heiner. "Der Dramatiker und die Geschichte seiner Zeit. Ein Gespräch zwischen Horst Laube und Heiner Müller." In *Theater Heute, Theatersonderheft,* 1975, 119–23.

Müller, Heiner. *Germania, Tod in Berlin.* Berlin: Rotbuch Verlag, 1977.

Nicholls, Moira. "The Influence of Eastern Thought on Schopenhauer's Doctrine of the Thing-in-Itself." In *The Cambridge Companion to Schopenhauer,* ed. Christopher Janaway. Cambridge: Cambridge University Press, 1999.

Nietzsche, Friedrich. *Also Sprach Zarathustra.* Stuttgart: Kröner Verlag, 1956.

Nietzsche, Friedrich. *The Birth of Tragedy.* Trans. Francis Golffing. New York: Doubleday, 1956.

Nietzsche, Friedrich. *Sämtliche Werke, Kritische Studienausgabe.* Munich: Deutscher Taschenbuch Verlag, 1988.

Nietzsche, Friedrich. *The Will to Power.* Trans. Walter Kaufmann and R. J. Hollingdale. London: Weidenfeld and Nicholson, 1968.

O'Brien, Eoin. *The Beckett Country.* Dublin: Black Cat Press; London: Faber and Faber, 1986.

O'Brien, Flann. *The Third Policeman.* London: MacGibbon and Kee 1967; reprinted London: Paladin, 1993.

Opie, Iona, and Peter Opie. *The Lore and Language of Schoolchildren.* Oxford: Oxford University Press, 1959.

Oppenheim, Lois. *Directing Beckett.* Ann Arbor: University of Michigan Press, 1994.

Osofisan, Femi. *The Oriki of a Grasshoper and Other Plays.* Washington, D.C.: Howard University Press, 1995.

Owen, Alex. *The Darkened Room: Women, Power, Spiritualism in Late Nineteenth Century England.* London: Virago Press, 1989.

Parks, Suzan-Lori. *The America Play.* New York: Dramatist's Play Service, 1995.

Pearson, Roger. *Unfolding Mallarmé: The Development of a Poetic Art.* Oxford: Oxford University Press, 1996.

Perkins, David, ed. *English Romantic Writers.* New York: Harcourt, Brace and World, 1967.

Petrie, George. *The Ancient Music of Ireland.* Dublin: Society for the Preservation and Publication of the Melodies of Ireland, 1855.

Phelan, Peggy. "Lessons in Blindness from Samuel Beckett." *PMLA* 119 (2004): 1279–88.

Phelan, Peggy. *Unmarked: The Politics of Performance.* London: Routledge, 1993.

Pietzcker, Carl. "Ich kommandiere mein Herz." In *Brechts Herzneurose—ein Schlüssel zu seinem Leben und Schreiben.* Würzburg: Königshausen und Neumann, 1988.

Pilling, John. *Beckett before Godot.* Cambridge: Cambridge University Press, 1997.

Piozzi, Hester Lynch (Thrale). *Anecdotes of Samuel Johnson.* Ed. S. C. Roberts. New York: Arno Press, 1980.

Pothast, Ulrich. *Die eigentlich metaphysische Tätigkeit. Über Schopenhauers Ästhetik und ihre Anwendung durch Samuel Beckett.* Frankfurt am Main: Suhrkamp, 1982.

Pseudo-Dionysus. *The Complete Works.* Trans. Colm Luibheid. New York: Paulist Press, 1987.

Quinn, Peter. "Closets Full of Bones." In *Irish Hunger: Personal Reflections on the Legacy of the Famine,* ed. Tom Hayden. Boulder, Colo.: Roberts Reinhardt, 1997.

Reichard, Hugo. "Boswell's Johnson, the Hero Made by a Committee." *PMLA* 95 (1980): 225–33.

Reid, Alec. *All I Can Manage, More Than I Could.* Dublin: Dolmen, 1968.

Reid, Alec. "Impact and Parable in Beckett: A First Encounter with *Not I*." *Hermathena* 141 (1986): 12–21.

Richards, Sandra. *Ancient Songs Set Ablaze: The Theatre of Femi Osofisan.* Washington, D.C.: Howard University Press, 1996.

Rilke, Rainer Maria. "Puppen: Zu den Wachspuppen von Lotte Pritzel." In *Werke: Kommentierte Ausgabe in 4 Bde,* ed. Manfred Engel und Ulrich Fülleborn, 4:685–92. Darmstadt: WBG, 1996.

Rilke, Rainer Maria. "Some Reflections on Dolls." In *Rodin and Other Prose Pieces,* trans. G. Craig Houston. London: Quartet, 1986.

Robinson, Helen Taylor. "'The Bespoke Universe': Shakespeare, Freud and Beckett, Tailors and Outfitters." *British Journal of Psychotherapy* 17 (2000): 181–91.

Scarry, Elaine. *The Body in Pain.* New York: Oxford University Press, 1985.

Scarry, Elaine. *Resisting Representation.* New York: Oxford University Press, 1994.

Schneider, Alan. *Entrances: An American Director's Journey.* New York: Viking, 1986.

Schopenhauer, Arthur. *Essays and Aphorisms.* Trans. R. J. Hollingdale. Harmondsworth: Penguin, 1970.

Schopenhauer, Arthur. *Manuscript Remains.* Trans. E. F. J. Payne. Oxford: Berg, 1989.

Schopenhauer, Arthur. *Parerga and Paralipomena.* Trans E. F. J. Payne. Oxford: Clarendon Press, 1974.

Schopenhauer, Arthur. *Sämtliche Werke.* Mannheim: Brockhaus, 1988.

Schopenhauer, Arthur: *Die Welt als Wille und Vorstellung.* In *Sämtliche Werke,* vol. 2. Trans. E. F. J. Payne as *The World as Will and Representation* (New York: Dover, 1966).

Schutte, Ofelia. *Beyond Nihilism: Nietzsche wihout Masks.* Chicago: University of Chicago Press, 1984.

Schwitters, Kurt. "She dolls with dollies" (1944). In *Poems, Performances Pieces Proses Play Poetics.* Eds. and trans. Jerome Rothenberg and Pierre Joris. Philadelphia: Temple University Press, 1993.

Sharkey, Rodney. "Irish? Au Contraire! The Search for Identity in the Fictions of Samuel Beckett." *Journal of Beckett Studies* 3 (1994): 1–18.

Shenker, Israel. "An Interview with Samuel Beckett." In *Samuel Beckett: The Critical Heritage,* ed. Lawrence Graver and Raymond Federman. London: Routledge, 1979.

Smith, Frederick. *Beckett's Eighteenth Century.* New York: Palgrave, 2002.

Stephen, Leslie. *Samuel Johnson.* New York: Harper and Brothers, 1878.

Stokes, John. "The Raven Herself Is Hoarse." *Times Literary Supplement,* February 2, 2007.

Swift, Jonathan. *A Tale of a Tub & Other Works.* Ed. Angus Ross and David Woolley. Oxford: Oxford University Press, 1986.

Tabori, George. *Unterammergau oder Die guten Deutschen.* Frankfurt am Main: Suhrkamp, 1981.

Tatlow, Antony. *Brechts Ost Asien.* Berlin: Parthas Verlag, 1998.

Tatlow, Antony. "Ghosts in the House of Theory." *Brecht Yearbook* 24 (1999): 1–13.

Tatlow, Antony. *The Mask of Evil.* Berne: Peter Lang, 1977.

Taylor, Jeremy. *The Rules and Exercises of Holy Living and of Holy Dying.* Rev. ed. Ed. Charles Page Eden. Hildesheim: Georg Olms Verlag, 1969.

Terry, Philip. "Waiting for God to Go: *How It Is* and *Inferno* VII–VIII." *Samuel Beckett Today/Aujourd'hui* 7 (1998): 349–60.

Toíbín, Colm. "My Darlings: On Beckett's Irish Actors." *London Review of Books,* April 5, 2007.

Trevor, William. *A Writer's Ireland: Landscape in Literature.* New York: Viking, 1984.

Unseld, Siegfried. "Bis zum Äußersten. Samuel Beckett zum 80. Geburtstag—1986." *Theater Heute,* February 1990.

Valentin, Karl. *Die Raubritter von München. Szenen und Dialoge.* Munich: Deutscher Taschenbuch Verlag, 1964.

Wain, John. *Samuel Johnson.* New York: Viking, 1974.

Waugh, Katherine, and Fergus Daly. "*Film* by Samuel Beckett." *Film West* 20 (1995), http://www.iol.ie/~galfilm/filmwest/20beckett.htm.

West, Trevor. *The Bold Collegians.* Dublin: Lilliput, 1991.

Whitelaw, Billie. *Billie Whitelaw . . . Who He?* New York: St. Martin's Press, 1995.

Wilmer, S. E., ed. *Beckett in Dublin.* Dublin: Lilliput, 1992.

Wiltshire, John. *Samuel Johnson in the Medical World.* Cambridge: Cambridge University Press, 1991.

Winnicott, D. W. *Playing and Reality.* 1971; Hove: Brunner-Routledge, 2001.

Woolf, Virginia. *On Being Ill.* Ashfield, Mass.: Paris Press, 2002.

Worton, Michael. "*Waiting for Godot* and *Endgame:* Theater as Text." In *The Cambridge Companion to Beckett,* ed. John Pilling. Cambridge: Cambridge University Press, 1994.

Wright, Elizabeth. *Postmodern Brecht: A Re-Presentation.* London: Routledge, 1989.

Yeats, William Butler. *Explorations.* London: Macmillan, 1962.

Yeats, William Butler. *The Poems.* Ed. Daniel Albright. London: Everyman's Library, 1992.

Zilliacus, Clas. *Beckett and Broadcasting: A Study of the Works of Samuel Beckett for and in Radio and Television.* Åbo, Finland: Åbo Akademi, 1976.

Zilliacus, Clas. "Three Times Godot: Beckett, Brecht, Bulatovic." *Comparative Drama* 4, no. 1 (1970): 3–17.

Contributors

Linda Ben-Zvi is Professor of Theatre Studies at Tel Aviv University and Professor Emerita in English and Theatre at Colorado State University. She was named a John N. Stern Distinguished Professor at Colorado and was a Lady Davis Professor at Hebrew University, Jerusalem. She was president of the International Samuel Beckett Society from 1988–90, and from 2006–8, and Chair since 1996 of the Beckett Working Group of the International Federation for Theatre Research. Her books include *Samuel Beckett* (1986), and the biography *Susan Glaspell: Her Life and Times* (2005), which won the George Freedley Special Jury Prize, Theatre Library Association, 2006. She has edited *Women in Beckett* (1992); *Theatre in Israel* (1996); *Susan Glaspell: Drawing on Beckett* (2003); Glaspell's *The Road to the Temple* (2005); *Brecht: Philosophy and Performance* (with Gad Kaynar) (2005); *Staging Calamity* (with Tracy C. Davis) (2007); *Beckett at 100* (with Angela Moorjani) (2007); and is presently editing *The Complete Plays of Susan Glaspell* (with J. Ellen Gainor).

Herbert Blau is Byron W. and Alice L. Lockwood Professor of the Humanities at the University of Washington. He has also had a parallel career in the theater, as cofounder and codirector of The Actor's Workshop of San Francisco, then codirector of the Repertory Theater of Lincoln Center in New York, and as artistic director of the experimental group KRAKEN, the groundwork for which was prepared at California Institute of the Arts, of which he was founding Provost, and Dean of the School of Theater and Dance. His most recent books are *The Dubious Spectacle: Extremities of Theater, 1976–2000* (2002); *Nothing in Itself: Complexions of Fashion* (1999); and *Sails of the Herring Fleet: Essays on Beckett* (2004). He is currently working on *As If: An Autobiography* and *Reality Principles: From the Absurd to the Virtual*.

Enoch Brater is the Kenneth T. Rowe Collegiate Professor of Dramatic Literature and Professor of English and Theater at the University of Michigan. His most recent publications are *Arthur Miller: A Playwright's Life and Works* (2005), *Arthur Miller's America: Theater and Culture in a Time of Change* (2005), and *Arthur Miller's Global Theater: How an American Playwright Is Performed on Stages around the World* (2007). His major contributions to Beckett studies include *Beyond Minimalism: Beckett's Late Style in the Theater* (1987); *The Drama in the Text: Beckett's Late Fiction* (1994); *Why Beckett* (1989); *The Essential Samuel Beckett* (2003); *The Theatrical Gamut: Notes for a Post-Beckettian Stage* (1995); *Around the Absurd: Essays on Modern and Postmodern Drama* (1990); *Approaches to Teaching Beckett's "Waiting for Godot"* (1991); and *Beckett at 80/Beckett in Context* (1986). His many other publications include *Feminine Focus: The New Women Playwrights* (1989) and the revised version of Phyllis Hartnoll's *The Theatre: A Concise History* (1998). Professor Brater is the immediate past President of the Samuel Beckett Society. He is currently working on a new book entitled *The Falsetto of Reason: Ten Ways of Thinking about Samuel Beckett*.

Terence Brown, who was born in China of Irish parents, was educated at Sullivan Upper School, Holywood, Co. Down, at Magee University College, Derry, and at Trinity College Dublin. He is Professor of Anglo-Irish Literature in Trinity College Dublin. He is also a Senior Fellow of the college, a member of the Royal Irish Academy and of Academia Europaea. He has published extensively on Irish literature and cultural history and has lectured on those subjects in many parts of the world. His study of MacNeice, *Louis MacNeice: Sceptical Vision,* was published in 1975. His *Ireland a Social and Cultural History, 1922–79* appeared in 1981 with a new expanded edition in 2004. His critical biography of W. B. Yeats was published in 1999 with a second edition in 2001.

Ruby Cohn is Professor Emerita of Comparative Drama at the University of California, Davis. She completed the first doctoral thesis on Samuel Beckett in the 1950s and has published or edited many books on Beckett and on contemporary theater, including *Samuel Beckett: The Comic Gamut* (1962), *Back to Beckett* (1973), *Just Play: Beckett's Theater* (1980), and *A Beckett Canon* (2001).

Terry Eagleton is John Taylor Professor of English Literature at the University of Manchester. He is author of some forty works of literary, cultural, and political theory, including *Literary Theory: An Introduction* (1983/1996), *The Ideology of the Aesthetic* (1990), *Heathcliff and the Great*

Hunger (1996), *Crazy John and the Bishop and Other Essays on Irish Culture* (1998), *Sweet Violence: The Idea of the Tragic* (2002), *After Theory* (2003), and *Holy Terror* (2005).

S. E. Gontarski is currently Sarah Herndon Professor of English at Florida State University, where he is Director of Graduate Studies and General Editor of the *Journal of Beckett Studies* and Journal of Beckett Studies Books. His most recent books are *The Grove Companion to Samuel Beckett* (2004) and *The Faber Companion to Samuel Beckett* (2006) (both written with C. J. Ackerley), and *Beckett after Beckett* (2006) (edited with Anthony Uhlmann). He was Visiting Professor of Theoretical Studies of Theatre at the 21st Century COE [Center of Excellence] Institute of Theatre Research at Waseda University, Tokyo, in the autumn of 2006.

Dennis Kennedy was the first occupant of the Samuel Beckett Chair of Drama in Trinity College Dublin, which he held from 1994 to 2006, and with Anna McMullan initiated the annual series of Beckett Lectures. Previously he taught at the University of Pittsburgh and has held distinguished visiting professorships at the Chinese Central Academy of Drama, The National University of Singapore, The University of Karachi, and various universities in Canada and the United States. His books include *Assisting at the Spectacle: Essays on Audiences, The Oxford Encyclopedia of Theatre and Performance, Looking at Shakespeare, Foreign Shakespeare,* and *Granville Barker and the Dream of Theatre.* He is a member of the Royal Irish Academy and Academia Europaea, and is also a playwright, dramaturg, and director.

Barry McGovern is a Dublin-born actor who has performed to international acclaim in many Beckett plays for stage and radio. He was a board member and actor in the Beckett Festival that the Dublin Gate Theatre launched in 1991 in partnership with Trinity College and Radio Telefís Eireann, and which toured to New York in 1996 and London in 1999. His award-winning one-man show *I'll Go On,* from the novels *Molloy, Malone Dies,* and the *Unnamable,* was originally presented by the Gate Theatre at the Dublin Theatre Festival in 1985 and has toured all over the world.

Anna McMullan, Chair of Drama Studies at Queen's University Belfast, is author of *Theatre on Trial: Samuel Beckett's Later Drama* (Routledge, 1993). She was postdoctoral Fellow in Beckett Studies at the Samuel Beckett Archive at University of Reading, from 1987 to 1989. She lectured on Irish theater and the theater of Samuel Beckett at the School of Drama at Trinity College from 1994 to 2005, and was a Fellow of Trinity College Dublin. She has lectured and published internationally on Beckett's theater, with essays in *Palgrave Advances in Beckett Studies,* ed. Lois Oppenheim (Palgrave, 2004), *Samuel Beckett: A Casebook,* ed. Jennifer Jeffers (Garland Press, 1998), and *A Companion to Twentieth Century Literature: Samuel Beckett,* ed. John Pilling (Cambridge University Press, 1994).

Joseph Roach, the Charles C. and Dorathea S. Dilley Professor of Theater at Yale University, is the author, most recently, of *It* (2007), a consumer's guide to iconic celebrity and ageless glamour, and coeditor with Janelle Reinelt of the second edition of *Critical Theory and Performance* (2007). He is also the author of *The Player's Passion: Studies in the Science of Acting* (1993), which won the Barnard Hewitt Award, and *Cities of the Dead* (1996), winner of the MLA's James Russell Lowell Prize. He is the recipient of a Distinguished Scholar Award from the Andrew W. Mellon Foundation and Principal Investigator of the World Performance Project at Yale.

Antony Tatlow, Honorary Professor in the Department of Drama, Trinity College Dublin, was Professor of Comparative Literature at Trinity College Dublin (1996–2005), Founding Head of the Department of Comparative Literature at the University of Hong Kong (1987–96), President of the International Brecht Society (1982–90), and has been Consultant to the Central Academy of Drama, Beijing from 1986, and a Member of Academia Europaea from 1999. He is the author of *Shakespeare, Brecht, and the Intercultural Sign* (2001), *Brechts Ost Asien: Ein Parallog* (1998), *Benwen Renleixue (Textual Anthropology: A Practice of Reading)* (1996), *Repression and Figuration—from Totem to Utopia* (1990), *The Mask of Evil: Brecht's Response to the Poetry, Theatre, and Thought of China and Japan* (1977), and *Brechts Chinesische Gedichte* (1973).

Marina Warner read French and Italian at Lady Margaret Hall, Oxford. Her award-winning studies of mythology and fairy tales include *Alone of All Her Sex: The Myth and the Cult of the Virgin Mary* (1976), *Joan of Arc: The Image of Female Heroism* (1982), *Monuments & Maidens: The Allegory of the Female Form* (1985), *From the Beast to the Blonde* (1994), and *No Go* *the Bogeyman: Scaring, Lulling and Making Mock* (1998). In 1994 she gave the BBC Reith Lectures on the theme of *Six Myths of Our Time*. Her recent books include *Fantastic Metamorphoses: Other Worlds* (2002); *Signs & Wonders* (2004); and *Phantasmagoria: Spirit Visions, Metaphors, and Media* (2006). Her fiction includes the novels *The Lost Father* (1988), *Indigo* (1992), and *The Leto Bundle* (2000). Lecturing in many parts of the world, she has taught independently for a long time, but in 2004 was appointed Professor of Literature, Film, and Theatre Studies at the University of Essex. She is a Chevalier de l'Ordre des arts et des Lettres, a Fellow of the British Academy, and holds an Hon. D. Litt. from the University of Oxford.

S. E. Wilmer is Associate Professor in Drama at Trinity College Dublin and edited *Beckett in Dublin* (1992). He is also the author of *Theatre, Society, and the Nation: Staging American Identities* (Cambridge University Press, 2002) and (with Pirkko Koski) *The Dynamic World of Finnish Theatre* (2006). Other publications include *Portraits of Courage: Plays by Finnish Women* (1997); (with Hans van Maanen) *Theatre Worlds in Motion: Structures, Politics, and Developments in the Countries of Western Europe* (1998); (with Helka Mäkinen and W. B. Worthen) *Theatre, History, and National Identities* (2001); *Writing and Rewriting National Theatre Histories* (2004); (with Pirkko Koski) *Stages of Chaos: The Drama of Post-war Finland* (2005); (with John Dillon) *Rebel Women: Staging Ancient Greek Drama Today* (2005); (with Pirkko Koski) *Humour and Humanity* (2006); and *National Theatres in a Changing Europe* (2008). He is also a playwright and has been a member of the executive committees of the American Society for Theatre Research and the International Federation for Theatre Research.

Index